MW00774655

GREAT

CARIBBEAN

FAMILY

VACATIONS

ALSO BY LAURA SUTHERLAND
(WITH VALERIE WOLF DEUTSCH)

INNOCENTS ABROAD:
TRAVELING WITH KIDS IN EUROPE

THE BEST BARGAIN FAMILY
VACATIONS IN THE U.S.A.

LAURA SUTHERLAND

GREAT

CARIBBEAN

FAMILY

VACATIONS

ST. MARTIN'S GRIFFIN/NEW YORK

All prices and information included in this book were accurate at press time. However, information changes over the course of time, and smart travelers will always make inquiring phone calls before they make firm plans.

As you travel through the islands with your children, let me know if you discover any new family-friendly destinations, or if any of the places listed in this book have not lived up to your expectations, so that future entries can be altered where warranted. Write to:

Laura Sutherland
Great Caribbean Family Vacations
c/o St. Martin's Press
175 Fifth Avenue
New York, NY 10010-7848

GREAT CARIBBEAN FAMILY VACATIONS. Copyright © 1995 by Laura Sutherland. All rights reserved. Printed in the United States of America. No part of this book may be used or reproduced in any manner whatsoever without written permission except in the case of brief quotations embodied in critical articles or reviews. For information, address St. Martin's Press, 175 Fifth Avenue, New York, N.Y. 10010.

Design by Pei Loi Koay

Library of Congress Cataloging-in-Publication Data

Sutherland, Laura.
    Great Caribbean family vacations / Laura Sutherland.
        p.   cm.
    ISBN 0-312-13502-5
    1. Caribbean Area—Guidebooks.   2. Family
recreation—Caribbean Area—Guidebooks.
    3. Children—Travel—Caribbean Area—
Guidebooks.
    F2165.S95   1995
    917.2904'52—dc20   95-31013
                                                          CIP

First St. Martin's Griffin Edition: November 1995
10 9 8 7 6 5 4 3 2 1

CONTENTS

ACKNOWLEDGMENTS

To my reliable, cheerful, and entertaining travel companions, Madeleine and Walker, whose spirits of adventure and funny observations add countless new dimensions to my own travel experiences.

To my wonderful husband, Lance Linares, who is always ready and willing to hop a plane, board a ship, scale a mountain, or do handwashing in the hotel sink.

Special thanks go to "Taking the Kids" travel columnist Eileen Ogintz; my agent, Vicky Bijur; and my editor, Anne Savarese. I am especially grateful to the many families who eagerly shared their favorite island getaways with me. The assistance and advice offered by the Caribbean Tourist Office and each of the island's tourist boards was extremely useful and greatly appreciated.

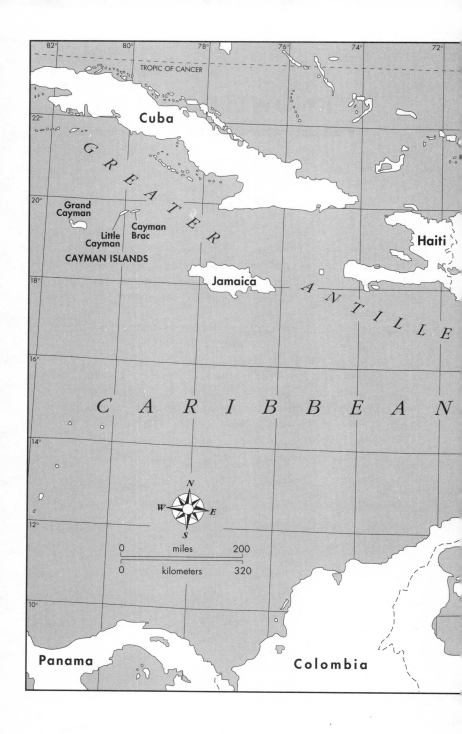

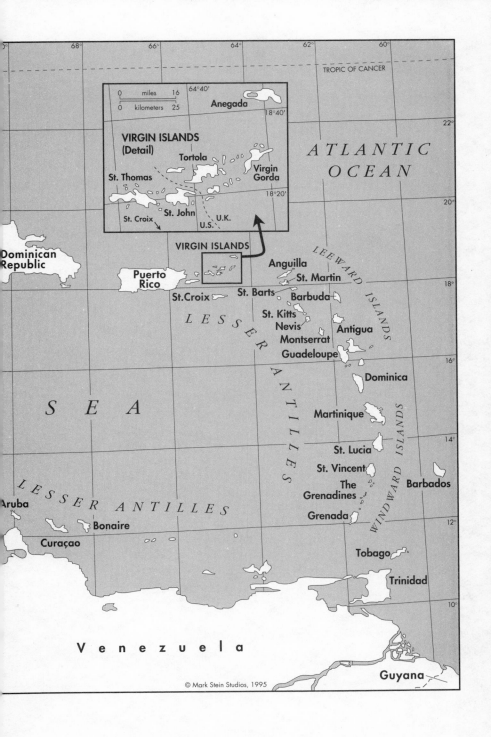

GREAT

CARIBBEAN

FAMILY

VACATIONS

1

PLANNING THE TRIP

WE HAD FINALLY GOTTEN AWAY from it all. Memories
of the lessons, the lunch boxes, the carpools, the clutter, and the
incessant ringing of the telephone had faded. We were a world
away at the edge of a tiny tropical island surrounded by a sapphire
blue sky and a warm and tranquil turquoise sea. Graceful seagrape
and palm trees fringed the powder-soft white sand. As I looked
across the beach at my dozing husband, I saw my son gleefully
patting sand over every inch of his body. Go ahead, rub it in
your hair, I thought, we're on vacation. I sipped my icy tropical
fruit drink and checked my watch. My daughter had been happily
playing in the waves for two straight hours and was still going
strong. I settled back into my beach chair, feeling like one of the
frigatebirds circling high overhead, keeping one eye on everything
but blissfully floating on air.

Later that day we gathered for dinner on the terrace and
watched the sun set over an island-dotted sea. My family's sweet
faces expressed the happiness and contentment we all felt. It was
going to be the perfect holiday.

There is simply no better family vacation spot than one with
sun, sea, and sand; and on the islands of the Caribbean it's beach
weather year-round. And what beaches—long stretches of white
sugar sand warmed by the balmy tropical sun and cooled by gentle
trade winds; strands of rich, velvety black volcanic sand; and
hidden coves with crescents of pink pulverized coral. At the
beach, children can run, swim, splash, and scream without re-
straint. The luxurious radiance of the Caribbean sun and the

invigorating aquamarine sea refresh and renew even the weariest of parents. World-class windsurfing, sailing, and scuba diving challenge any water sports enthusiast from novice to hotshot. Coral reefs close to shore teem with marine life, and the entire family can go nose to nose with the creatures of the undersea world simply by donning mask, fins, and snorkel.

The islands of the Caribbean Sea extend in a 2,800-mile arc from the western edge of Cuba to the coast of Venezuela. Some, such as Aruba, are desertlike islands—cactus-filled, flat, and sun-baked—while others like Dominica and St. Lucia are a tangle of lush tropical forests cascading down volcanic mountainsides. Bustling islands like St. Thomas have dozens of hotels, restaurants, and duty-free shops to browse, while quieter islands, such as Nevis or St. Vincent, have just a handful of resorts.

The island experience can be as varied as the hundreds of colorful tropical fish that navigate Caribbean waters. You can retreat to a tranquil private island where you won't see anyone else for a week, or you can fill your days with golf, tennis, and planned activities at full-service resorts. Meander from one gorgeous island beach to another aboard a private crewed sailboat, or enjoy a circuit of the islands from the comfort of an expansive cruise ship jam-packed with fun activities for all ages. High rollers can brush shoulders with jet-setters at glamorous and exclusive resorts. Laid-back types need never change out of their swimsuits at condos where guests can cook their own dinners. Visitors can delve into fascinating Caribbean cultures, or they can relax for days at an all-inclusive resort without ever leaving the property.

A surprising number of Caribbean hotels and resorts now offer children's programs, and more are adding them every month. Most are free of charge and offer a variety of entertaining and educational activities, allowing kids to drop in and out of the program depending on their interests and their family's daily plan. Children can meet and play with others their own age while parents read a book, play golf, try scuba diving, or just sit and soak up the sun in peace and quiet.

WHEN TO GO

The constant tradewind breezes that blow across the islands of the Eastern Caribbean keep summer's tropical temperatures bearable. In winter, the temperatures drop to their lowest, but rarely so low that you'll need to wear a sweater. Spring and fall are in between, but in any case the overall temperature rarely varies more than 10 Fahrenheit degrees between seasons.

High season (also called "The Season"), when prices and the number of tourists increase, is generally from December 15 through April 15. As the temperatures in the northern United States and Canada plummet, people head south to escape the snow and ice of home. Hotels and resorts charge 25 to 50 percent more during this time, and reservations, especially over holiday periods, become harder to obtain. Cruise ship prices also rise during high season. Prices are lower during the rest of the year, on some islands reaching their lowest level during the summer months. Many Europeans and the islanders themselves travel during the summer to take advantage of the reduced prices and to witness the season's spectacular tropical flower displays. A number of hotels have added family programs and specially priced family packages during this time. A few hotels and restaurants close during the late summer to renovate or recuperate.

Hurricane season (roughly August through October) is a slower time on the islands, since the Caribbean region ranks third worldwide in number of hurricanes per year. Some islands, however, such as Bonaire, Aruba, and Curaçao, are out of the hurricane belt. If you find yourself traveling or cruising during this time, remember that sophisticated weather reports will keep you informed of developing storms, and you can leave an island well before a hurricane threatens.

Carnival season for many islands is a pre-Lenten blowout in February; but St. Vincent, Anguilla, Antigua, the British Virgin Islands, Grenada, and St. John celebrate during the summer months, and Montserrat's carnival is in December. St. Thomas celebrates in April, the Cayman Islands in May, and the Dominican Republic in June. Trinidad's carnival rivals those of New

Orleans and Rio for its atmosphere, color, and excitement. Celebrations on the smaller islands are just as much fun because you can take an even closer look at the calypso competitions, queen shows (beauty contests with a talent and costume competition), parades of elaborate costumes, and jump-ups (street music that makes you jump up and dance). Children's carnivals are a regular feature on many islands, and often take place the week before the main event.

WHAT TO PACK

Traveling light in the tropics is a breeze. Shorts and T-shirts, sundresses, and swimsuits are about all you need. Each member of the family should bring one dress-up outfit, because some resorts and restaurants require more formal wear in the evening. Airplanes, airports, and restaurants are sometimes over-air-conditioned, so pack a lightweight sweater for each person. Choose easy-care natural fiber clothes that don't show dirt, and avoid nylon and synthetics, which are too hot in the humid tropics. Carry enough sunblock and insect repellent to get you through your first few days.

Before you leave home, itemize your suitcases' contents and their value in case your bags are lost along the way. Keep your name and address and a copy of your itinerary inside all bags you check to make them easy to locate. And pack a swimsuit in your carry-on bags for each member of the family, in case your luggage is delayed.

Let each child carry his or her own backpack; even a toddler can manage a small knapsack. It can be used on the plane to carry an extra set of clothes (a must, as many spills result from an airplane's close quarters), a beloved stuffed animal, and small toys and games. It can double as a beach bag, and can help carry home souvenirs. Best of all, it allows you to say, "Take whatever you want, as long as it fits in your pack."

Carry familiar favorite snacks for the plane trip and to get you through your first few days. Then pack some more to use on day trips and beach stops where more substantial fare is unavailable.

You'll eat them all, and the resulting empty space in your luggage can be filled with souvenirs.

TRAVEL WITH BABIES

Our motto for packing light gets tossed into the diaper pail for this age group, since you'll need as much gear on the road as you do at home. Practice using any new special equipment before you go. Find out if cribs, high chairs, laundry facilities, and carseats are available where you are going. Many parents like to bring their own portable cribs in case the safety standards on an island do not measure up to those in North America. Portable cribs can be handy on the beach to corral a wanderer and to let a tired baby nap.

Disposable diapers can be expensive and difficult to find on many islands. Plan to bring a complete supply unless you are absolutely sure you can easily find them at your destination. Pack a sun umbrella and wide-brimmed baby hat for use at the beach and in the stroller. Babies with sensitive skin may not be able to tolerate insect repellent; bring mosquito netting to protect them from uncomfortable bites. Cool cotton body suits help prevent the sun from burning a baby's delicate skin.

TODDLERS: THE YOUNG AND THE RESTLESS

Even if your child is toilet-trained, pack extra diapers; many young children revert to wetting in an unfamiliar situation. A plastic sheet will keep the bed dry in case of accidents, allowing Mom and Dad to sleep easier. If you have a very curious toddler, you may need to pack electrical outlet covers. Some islands have outlets that differ from ours, so bring a small roll of tape if you are not sure your outlet covers will fit. Life jackets or arm floats are a must for the pool and ocean.

SCHOOL-AGE KIDS

Since your child will spend most of his or her time in a swimsuit, pack two suits—one to wear, and one to dry—to avoid rashes from wearing damp suits. Check to see if your destination has child-size sporting equipment such as fins, snorkels, and masks. If not, purchase or borrow your own before you go. Kids who wear glasses can get custom-made masks with prescription lenses so they can enjoy the spectacular underwater sights. Wrap up a few surprises to bestow on this fidgety group for the plane ride or to keep them busy in a nice restaurant. A disposable underwater camera is a great gift for beginning snorkelers.

TEENS

Teens can pack for themselves with a measure of supervision. Give them their own suitcase, thereby limiting what they can take. As always, choose your battles carefully. One teenager we know packed her army boots, cutoff jeans, and black sweatshirt collection to take to Antigua, refusing to buy or take anything her parents deemed more appropriate. In exasperation, Mom and Dad went along with her packing list. After two days of misery in the tropics, the teen went shopping and settled for sandals and a sundress. Small portable radios are a great gift for this age group so they can tune in to the islands' calypso, reggae, soca, zouk, and steel band sounds.

INDISPENSABLE ITEMS

Sunscreen
Insect repellent
Hats for each member of the family
Sunglasses
Water shoes
Flashlight
First-aid kit
Plastic bags (for wet clothes and shell collections)

SOURCES OF INFORMATION

Request general information on the entire region from the Caribbean Tourism Organization:

In North America: 20 East 46th Street, New York, NY 10017; 212–682–0435, fax 212–697–4258.
In the Caribbean: Second Floor, Sir Frank Wolcott Building, Culloden Farm Complex, St. Michel, Barbados, West Indies; 809–427–5242, fax 809–429–3065.

If you want more island-specific information, see the addresses at the beginning of individual island chapters. If your children are stamp collectors, write to the tourist office on the island; the tiny island nations of the Caribbean have some of the most beautiful stamps in the world. Allow several weeks for a response, since mail service can be slow.

GETTING THERE

Unless you're cruising on a ship out of Miami, you'll need to take an airplane to get to the islands. American Airlines runs most flights from the United States to the Caribbean, out of its Miami and San Juan, Puerto Rico hubs. Delta operates from its Atlanta hub; and Continental, from the New York area through its Newark hub. Flights between the islands are handled by American Eagle, by small island-specific companies, or by LIAT airlines, which has been flying in the Caribbean for more than thirty years. Some islands have airports equipped to handle large jets; others do not, requiring that you change to a smaller commuter-type aircraft to fly in. You can request children's meals on all major airlines for no additional charge at the time you make your reservation or up to 24 hours before your flight.

ENTRY AND EXIT REQUIREMENTS AND CUSTOMS

American Citizens: All islands except the U.S. Virgin Islands and Puerto Rico require visitors to carry proof of citizenship. Passports, one for each member of the family (even infants), can be obtained through the Department of State Office of Passport Services at 1425 K Street, NW, Washington, DC 20522. The office's "Information Line" is 202–647–0518. Some islands allow you to use an original birth certificate or voter registration card, accompanied by an official photo ID. A driver's license alone is not always sufficient as the photo ID, but you should bring it along in case you plan to rent a car.

Canadian Citizens: Children under age sixteen may be included on a parent's passport, but they must have their own passport if they plan to travel alone. The passport office can give you information on where to obtain forms at 514–283–2152.

DEPARTURE TAX

Many Caribbean islands levy a departure tax (usually between $5 and $15) at the airport. Remember to save enough currency (try to have the exact change) to pay it before you go. Children under age twelve are exempt from the tax on certain islands.

When you return to the United States or Canada, you must declare everything you have purchased. American families traveling together can make a joint declaration and are allowed $600 worth of goods per person duty-free from most Caribbean countries as long as they've been gone for more than 48 hours and fewer than 30 days. For more information, contact the U.S. Customs Service at 202–927–6724. Canadians can bring in $300 worth of goods duty-free once a year if they've been out of the country for at least seven days. For more information, call the Revenue Canada Customs and Excise Department at 613–957–0275.

MONEY MATTERS

Local currencies are used throughout most of the Caribbean. U.S. dollars are the official currency in the U.S. Virgin Islands, British Virgin Islands, and Puerto Rico, but they are accepted on many other islands alongside the local currency. Traveler's checks and credit cards are readily accepted almost everywhere. ATMs are becoming increasingly common on the islands, but check with your bank to find out whether your network is used in this part of the world; not all are.

Find out about tipping customs before you get to your island destination. Some islands dictate the 15 to 20 percent tip that is typical of the United States, while on the other islands 10 percent is a standard tip. Tipping policies at different hotels and resorts vary as well. Some charge a service fee to cover tips for all staff; others expect guests to tip at the time of services rendered. Certain islands have a nightly room tax, and sometimes the room tax and service charges can add more than 20 percent to your bill. Always ask if service charges are included at a restaurant before you pay your bill, so you don't tip twice.

STAYING HEALTHY

In the Caribbean, a bad case of sunburn or a few mosquito bites are the most common problems you're likely to encounter. Many resorts have a doctor or nurse on staff, and local medical personnel often have been trained in the United States or Europe. Children or adults with chronic health problems should consider a Caribbean cruise. Virtually all of the larger cruise ships have medical staff and facilities on board, and some are outfitted for special medical needs.

Here are some common-sense guidelines for staying healthy in the Caribbean:

• Protect yourself from mosquito bites by conscientiously wearing insect repellent. Make sure your accommodations have window screens or air-conditioning.

• Bring a basic first-aid kit containing bandages, disinfectant, antibiotic ointment, medicine for diarrhea and stomach upsets, decongestant, aspirin or acetaminophen for adults and children, tweezers, and insect repellent.

• Bring prescription medicines in their original containers (to avoid problems with customs), and take enough to last your visit.

• Use bottled water for babies' formulas. Most islands have perfectly safe water, but even subtle changes in water can often upset a little one's delicate system. Boxed, unrefrigerated milk is common throughout the Caribbean and is safe to drink. It must be refrigerated once it's been opened.

• Avoid diarrhea: a change in diet or water or even the excitement of the trip can affect some children (and adults, too). Ask your pediatrician for diarrhea medication for younger children. Over-the-counter remedies such as Pepto-Bismol or Imodium can help relieve symptoms in older children. To counteract the effects of diarrhea, remember the BRAT Diet—Bananas, Rice, Applesauce, and Toast—and drink plenty of liquids.

• Swim with caution. Atlantic waters are generally much rougher than Caribbean waters. Ask about undertow and rip tides if you're unsure. Get water shoes for the family before you go, to avoid injury from sharp coral formations, broken shells, or sea urchin spines; and avoid jellyfish. Keep a vigilant watch on your little ones, as few beaches or pools are protected by lifeguards.

• Stay away from the highly poisonous manchineel tree that grows along the beach on some islands. It's small, with a short trunk, numerous branches, shiny green leaves, and tempting green applelike fruits. The sap from this tree was once used by the Arawak and Carib Indians as an arrow poison. Even touching the leaves or standing under the tree in a rainstorm can give you a severe rash. Most trees on or near hotels and resorts are posted with warning signs, and in more remote areas, the trunks may be painted red.

• No-see-ums, pesky little biting gnats found on beaches and in swampy areas, tend to gather on human ankles at dusk or after a heavy rain. They're so tiny you won't even know they're there until you feel an itchy tingle. A generous dose of insect repellent should be part of your late afternoon wardrobe at all times.

• The U.S. Public Health Service recommends that Americans receive diphtheria and tetanus shots prior to traveling in the Caribbean; and all children should be inoculated against measles, mumps, rubella, and polio, no matter where you live. In a few areas of the Caribbean (usually far away from tourist areas), dengue fever, malaria, and yellow fever have been reported; to find out about specific disease risks for your itinerary, call the Centers for Disease Control's International Health Requirements and Recommendations hotline at 404–332–4559.

THE TROPICAL SUN

Time melts away quickly under the hot tropical sun, and it's easy to forget how long you've been baking until your skin turns from rosy pink to painful scarlet. To escape sun trouble, avoid midday (10:00 A.M. to 2:00 P.M.) exposure for at least your first few days. Even if you never stray from under a beach umbrella, the sun's rays will bounce off the sand and water and can still burn you. Apply high-factor sunblock (SPF 30 or greater) religiously, liberally, and often—at least once every two hours. Wear protective clothing, sunglasses, and a hat, and drink plenty of water and fruit juices. The best preventive against sunburn is shade or covering up.

2

ISLAND
ACCOMMODATIONS
AND FOOD

ACCOMMODATIONS

ARE YOU LOOKING FOR AN ARISTOCRATIC retreat with gourmet dining or a package resort with limbo contests and all you can eat? A villa in the hills or a condo on the shore? Full-day kids program or full-time family togetherness? You'll find excellent tourist accommodations for every family's tastes, interests, ages, and budget on the islands of the Caribbean. The only challenge is deciding which experience to choose for your family.

Villas offer the atmosphere of a home away from home, where you can eat breakfast in your bathrobe and you don't have to worry if your children are disturbing other guests. Many larger villas are spacious enough for two families or small family reunions. Some have swimming pools and are staffed by cooks, maids, gardeners, even butlers.

Hotels and resorts have advantages you won't find in villas. Restaurants, water sports centers, dive shops, and transportation are only a few steps away from your room. Many hotels and resorts have Kids Clubs where you can drop off your children for an hour, an afternoon, or a full day. Always inquire about special price packages to get the lowest possible rate.

Condo and villa resorts try to combine the best features of both: they offer fully equipped villas or apartments with the services of a resort. You won't have the privacy of your own secluded villa, but you may be able to get room service at odd hours, excursions arranged for you, windsurfing lessons, and other children for yours to play with.

ALL-INCLUSIVE RESORTS

Inclusive resorts started out with some swinging singles and a few handfuls of beads as legal tender. As Club Med's singles turned into marrieds . . . with children, it began to add family programs to its resorts, and many other hotel operators followed. Today, you can find inclusive resorts on almost all of the Caribbean islands, some of which have been designed and built just for families.

At first glance an inclusive resort may appear to cost more than a vacation of separate but equal parts. But if you add up what you get, you'll find they do not cost more, and often cost much less. They're perfect for relaxing people whose blood pressure skyrockets every time they pull out their wallet on vacation. As one total-tallying traveler put it, "If we hadn't bought the full package, we would have been splitting entrées and drinking water instead of wine." Most inclusives have a price adjustment for children, and some offer free accommodations and meals for kids who stay in their parents' room.

"All-inclusive" means different things at different resorts. Always ask what is and what isn't included, and read the fine print carefully. Some resorts offer complimentary sports equipment but charge for motorized water sports such as waterskiing. Others charge for all sports but offer excursions in the price. Some cover meals but not drinks, and a few include tips and taxes in their price, while others do not. Some inclusives include absolutely everything under the sun.

CHILDREN'S PROGRAMS

"I hope I make some new friends at this one, too," my seven-year-old said as we prepared to step through the doors of yet another Kids Club. She had come to realize that children's programs were really mixers where kids got to know each other while building sand castles, hunting for shells, and playing board games. The success of each program depended on who the other children were, as well as on the quality of the program and the personality of the staff.

Nervous at first, she stepped through the door, not sure if she wanted to stay. But baskets of Legos, stacks of games, shelves of puzzles, and cups of colored markers beckoned, and both she and her brother decided they had better take a longer look. The easy introductions to others their own age through the children's centers helped my two kids solidify those new relationships later at the beach and pool.

Programs allowing drop-in visits rather than full- or half-day commitments work best. Drop-ins allow kids to pick and choose from a published schedule of activities, moving in and out of a program according to their interests. Since one of the pleasures of a family vacation is getting to spend unstructured, uninter-rupted time together, drop-in programs respect the family's need to have maximum flexibility and choice in scheduling.

The best children's programs have the following features:

- Daily activities that incorporate aspects of the island's unique culture, food, and natural environment.
- A separate children's room with high-quality toys, books, games, and art materials for all age levels served.
- Outdoor activities equal in time to indoor activities, and little use of television, VCR, and video games.
- Staff who have been trained in first aid and child development.
- A low staff-to-child ratio, and a well-designed plan to pull more staff in as the numbers of children increase.
- Flexibility: the ages and interests of young guests change daily, and the staff must know how to appeal to all types.

VILLA RENTALS

Staying in your own home gives you extra room, your own kitchen, and privacy when you want it. You can rent a place for just your family, or you can gather several families together and rent a big place, sharing the cooking and childcare. Most privately owned villas and condos rent in increments of one week or more, and a rental car is usually a necessity so you can pick up groceries and get out of the house. Villas on certain islands have permanent staff in attendance, while anything more than daily maid service can be hard to find on others. Generally speaking, the larger the villa, the larger the staff.

Before you rent a villa, be nosy. Find out if the rental agency has personally visited all of the villas it represents on the islands that interest you. Mention that you have children, since kids are not allowed in some properties. Ask about extras such as washer and dryer, dishwasher, linens, and safety features if you have toddlers or pre-school-age children. Ask to see a set of photographs and a floor plan, so you'll know the sleeping arrangement possibilities. Find out when the property was built and/or refurbished. Inquire about the types of furnishings—elegant villas with antiques and breakable collections are a nightmare for parents with toddlers—and find out if baby-sitting is available.

Get an island map before you commit to anything. On many islands, villas are not on the beach. Ask the tourist office about the best areas to find villas for rent, if you are not sure.

After you've made your decision, get information on the part of the island you'll be staying in, directions to the house, and a list of good local restaurants and supermarkets. Try to plan your arrival for the afternoon rather than the evening, so you can pick up supplies on your way to your villa.

A number of businesses handle villa rentals throughout the Caribbean:

Villa Leisure, with over 35 years in business, handles thousands of villas in the Caribbean. The staff personally inspects all properties and arranges car rentals and airport greeters. P.O. Box 30188, Palm Beach Gardens, FL 33420; 800–526–4244 or 407–624–9000.

At Home Abroad handles villas throughout the Caribbean, including quite a few on tony Mustique, the vacation home of Mick Jagger and Princess Margaret, among others. The staff personally inspect all its properties. 405 East 56th Street 6H, New York, NY 10022–2466; 212–421–9165, fax 212–752–1591.

Hideaways International is a travel club dedicated to villa and condo vacations. Members pay a fee and receive the *Hideaways Guide,* a directory published twice a year of vacation homes all over the world, with numerous listings in the Caribbean. Each listing has photographs and descriptions of locations, setting, accommodations, and rates. Members negotiate with the individual owners when they are ready to rent. 767 Islington Street, Portsmouth, NH 03801; 800–843–4433 or 603–430–4433, fax 603–430–4444.

Rent A Home International will send you villa and apartment listings in three places free of charge. Or, you can purchase a catalog for $15 that describes all of its properties in the Caribbean. 7200 34th Avenue NW, Seattle, WA 98117; 800–488–7368.

Villas International handles properties throughout the Caribbean and will send you listings for places that interest you. 605 Market Street, Suite 510, San Francisco, CA 94105; 800–221–2260.

SPECIAL FAMILY TOUR OPERATOR

Families who want a travel package with several other families should contact Rascals in Paradise, which specializes in this type of arrangement. 650 Fifth Street, Suite 505, San Francisco, CA 94107; 800-U-RASCAL or 415–978–9800, fax 415–442–0289.

SOURSOP AND CALLALOO: CARIBBEAN FOOD

Authentic Caribbean food is terrific, with a subtle blend of unusual flavors, often hot and pungent, always colorful and fresh. Delicious continental and nouvelle cuisine is available in resort areas and hotel restaurants. But don't worry: hamburgers and pizza are standard menu items on most islands. Of course you'll want to sample the local cuisine, but will your kids? There are a few delicious local dishes that may tempt them.

Many traditional Caribbean recipes come from the "make do" days when what grew locally—tropical fruits, root vegetables, pigeon peas, chicken, fish, goats, spices, and leaves—served as dietary staples. Some recipes are based on African fare, some came from Europe, and some were invented in the islands.

Fresh fish is available everywhere, prepared in a variety of ways. A local favorite is the "old wife," or triggerfish, which most children really like. The skin of this fish is so rough it was once used to scrub floors. Conch (pronounced *conk*), the animal that lives in the large shell with the shiny pink middle, is a mainstay of the local diet. You can find it prepared in chowder, salad, spicy garlic sauce, or dunked in batter and deep fried. Most children will try the fritters, usually accompanied by a key lime sauce. Johnnycakes are unleavened fried bread—plain but tasty.

Tropical fruits appeal to most children, who can't get enough of the flavorful bananas (tinier than Americans are used to seeing in supermarkets), juicy mangoes, papayas (often called pawpaws), and sweet pineapples. The same fruits are whirled into delicious tropical fruit slushes (like daiquiris without the rum), and can be found in every swim-up bar, restaurant, and sidewalk cafe throughout the islands.

Here are a few other Caribbean favorites:

Bullfoot soup is a thick stew of meat and vegetables flavored with local seasonings.

Callaloo is a big green leafy vegetable whose leaves taste like spinach, and is often made into a popular soup made with greens, ham, and crab.

Coconut water is the liquid found in large green coconuts. It's a refreshing treat.

Fried green bananas are sweet and delicious.

Fungi, pronounced *foon-jee*, is a staple made from cornmeal and okra, often served with fish.

Maubi is an extract from the bark of a tree. It is made into a drink that is nutritious and said to be good for high blood pressure.

Plantains are similar to bananas, though slightly less sweet, and are fried rather than eaten raw.

Pate turnovers, often sold at sidewalk stands, are pastries filled with spiced beef or salt fish.

Pepperpot soup is a rich savory stew containing beef, pork, vegetables, and spices.

Seamoss drink is locally considered an aphrodisiac, described with a wink as a "manly" drink.

Soursop, a green-skinned fruit with a sweet-and-sour citrus taste, is eaten raw or made into a drink that helps put babies to sleep.

3

FULL STEAM AHEAD: CARIBBEAN FAMILY CRUISES

THE CARIBBEAN IS THE WORLD'S NUMBER one cruise destination, attracting more than 2 million cruise vacationers every year. Its sunny climate and stunning beaches offer passengers an ideal opportunity to visit diverse islands on one easy vacation. Today's cruise ships are like self-contained floating resorts with decks of swimming pools, spas, gyms, game rooms, restaurants, nightclubs, and sunbathing areas. Unpack your bags once, and cruise from island to island as you sample the ships' action-packed entertainment and ample cuisine.

As more families take cruise vacations, more cruise lines develop programs and accommodations to appeal to all family types. Today's ships have family suites, connecting cabins, single cabins with three or four beds, and even refrigerators on request. A wealth of fun programs geared to children are offered, along with special play areas and supervised teen clubs where kids can safely have a good time. The lengthy roster of activities includes popular standbys such as arts and crafts, swimming, and games, and some enticing new ones like Rollerblading, batting cages, classes in children's radio and TV programming, pajama parties, parades, computer classes, language lessons, and a chance to publish a small newspaper.

There are cruise vacations to suit every budget, and special fare programs make many cruises especially family-friendly. Some charge half-price for a child in a room with his or her parents; others provide free fare for the kids. Some cruise lines offer discounts for single parents and for grandparents taking the grandchildren. Your cruise fare usually includes all meals, recreational activities, and entertainment. Shore excursions cost extra, and can be booked in advance or once you're on board. When selecting your cabins, remember that you'll have the same basic service and amenities as every other passenger on the ship, no matter which category of stateroom you choose. Your choice of cabin— size, location, and extras—will determine the price you pay.

The cruise lines discussed in this chapter all cover the Caribbean and offer some type of children's program as a regular part of their scheduled activities.

ROYAL CARIBBEAN CRUISES

Royal Caribbean offers three- to eleven-day cruises throughout the Caribbean and the Bahamas. All nine of its ships offer a special program for five- to seventeen-year-olds that includes onboard activities, a special kids' menu, and a teen disco. Five of the nine ships offer a supervised children's program year-round, while four have it during summer and vacation periods only. Some ships have their own children's playroom and children's books in their shipboard library.

The children's program is divided into three age groups with special activities planned for each: "Kids" (ages five to eight), "Tweens" (ages nine to twelve) and "Teens" (ages thirteen to seventeen). Youngsters receive a daily copy of the "Ship's Compass," a newsletter that describes dozens of choices available throughout the day and into the evening: stage-struck kids can practice for the talent show; sports lovers can sign up for triathlon team competitions or Ping-Pong, basketball, and golf putting tournaments; and creative types can design and make their own costumes to wear at the Masquerade Parade. The program times vary on each vessel but most are 9:00 A.M. to noon, 1:30 to 4:30 P.M., and 8:00 to 10:00 P.M.

Two-bedroom family suites are available on two of the largest ships; these suites include a sitting area and two bathrooms, perfect for bigger families who don't want to be in separate cabins.

Royal Caribbean Cruises, Ltd., 1050 Caribbean Way, Miami, FL 33132; 800–327–6700.

NORWEGIAN CRUISE LINE

At least one popular character from Universal Studios, such as Woody Woodpecker, Rocky the Flying Squirrel, or Bullwinkle the Moose, sails on all cruises that offer Norwegian Cruise Line's "Kids Crew" youth programs. Activities for Junior Sailors (ages three to five), First Mates (ages six to eight), Navigators (ages nine to twelve), and Teens (ages thirteen to seventeen) include sports competitions, dances, arts and crafts, and "Circus at Sea," a popular program in which children learn circus routines, juggling, and clown acts. A show is performed for adult passengers during the cruise. Children receive their own "Cruise News" newsletter detailing the day's events and can participate in as many of the activities as they like. Programs for three- to five-year-olds are available during the summer months and major holidays only, on sea days in the morning, and baby-sitting can be arranged on all ships.

Children under two travel free aboard all Norwegian Cruise Lines if they occupy the same cabin as the adult, with a maximum of two adults and two children per cabin. Baby-sitters are available on all ships from noon to 2:00 A.M. for a fee.

Norwegian Cruise Line, 95 Merrick Way, Coral Gables, FL 33134; 800–327–7030 or 305–445–0866.

PRINCESS CRUISES

Home of the original "Love Boat," the Princess Line's Caribbean cruises take place in the fall, winter, and early spring. Four of its vessels feature youth centers with supervised activities. The other ships have a children's program when fifteen or more kids are on board, with activities taking place throughout the ship since there is not a separate youth facility. Some ships have a special shallow swimming pool for children, with pool games and snorkeling lessons supervised by counselors.

Activities for kids start at 9:00 A.M. and run into the evening; they include board game tournaments, arts and crafts, bingo, ice cream and pizza parties, and storytelling. A different movie is shown each evening, and time is set aside for homework projects and educational information on the ports of call visited during the cruise.

Teens have their own area where they can participate in exercise classes, arts and crafts, and video games. They get a movie each night too, and a disco is open in the early evenings for dancing and socializing.

Children must be at least 24 months old to travel with Princess. The fare for children traveling as third and fourth berth passengers is about 50 percent of the minimum rate; otherwise they pay the standard double occupancy rate.

Princess Cruises, 10100 Santa Monica Boulevard, Los Angeles, CA 90067; 310–553–1770.

CARNIVAL CRUISE LINES

Carnival started its Junior Cruisers program of organized children's activities 15 years ago and has enhanced the program every year since. Today, the cruise line's "Camp Carnival" has supervised activities for four different age groups: "Toddlers," ages two to four, enjoy face and finger painting, splash pool fun, puppet making and shows, and ice cream parties; "Juniors," ages five to eight, create shell boxes and bear mobiles, and get movie time, talent shows, and pizza parties; "Intermediates," ages nine to thirteen, play bingo, charades, and Twister, and enjoy scavenger hunts, swimming under the stars, and publishing the "Fun Club" newsletter, distributed to passengers on the last day of the cruise; "Teens," ages fourteen to seventeen, have a disco party, lip sync and star search contest, and limbo, Hula Hoop, and Ping-Pong contests. All nine Carnival ships feature the Junior, Intermediate, and Teens programs, and all but two offer the Toddlers program year-round. Camp Carnival runs from 9:30 A.M., to 9:30 P.M., and nighttime baby-sitting in the form of a slumber party in the playroom costs extra.

Other special facilities for kids on all ships include playrooms, video arcades, pools with water slides, and children's wading pools. Most staterooms designed to accommodate families consist of one or two upper berths and twin beds that convert into a king. Cribs and rollaway beds can be accommodated in most rooms. Children's menus and high chairs are available.

Carnival Cruise Lines, Carnival Place, 3655 N.W. 87th Avenue, Miami, FL 33178; 800–438–6744 or 305–599–2600.

DOLPHIN CRUISE LINES

Dolphin's ships sail out of Miami or Aruba on three- to seven-night trips to the Bahamas and the eastern and western Caribbean. Its "Camp Jellystone" offers kids daily activities aboard every Dolphin Cruise plus a live-in Fred Flintstone, Yogi Bear, or Scooby Doo. The Hanna-Barbera theme is carried throughout the ship, and cartoon-crazy kids can get their pictures taken next the pool with Scooby, order Barney Rubble's favorite dishes, and try one of Yogi's tropical fruit concoctions.

Children are looked after by skilled counselors who blend a little education in with the fun, teaching children about ships, navigation, marine life, and the ports of call they'll be visiting. Noneducational activities include board games, balloon relays, plenty of ice cream and cookie parties, popcorn jewelry making, talent shows, and flying kites off the deck of the ship. Several different children's menus enable even the fussiest eaters to dine heartily in the ship's restaurants.

Cabins accommodate two to five people, and adjoining cabins are available.

Dolphin Cruise Lines, 901 South America Way, Miami, FL 33132–5122; 800–992–4299 or 305–358–5122.

PREMIER CRUISE LINES

Family programs are the hallmark of this cruise line, nicknamed The Big Red Boat after its bright cherry-red hulls. A seven-night vacation in which families divide their time between a cruise to the Bahamas and a visit to Disney World and other attractions in Orlando is one of Premier's most popular family packages. Many of the ship's activities are planned for the entire family, such as a 1950s dance party, Island Olympics (where families compete against each other), and multimedia education programs. When kids wake up at sea on The Big Red Boat they can breakfast with Bugs Bunny, Daffy Duck, Tasmanian Devil, or Tweety Bird. They also can be tucked in at night by their favorite costumed character (both for an extra fee).

Planned and staffed activities for children operate daily for five different age groups: First Mates (ages two to four), Kids Call (ages five to seven), Starcruisers (ages eight to ten), Navigators (ages eleven to thirteen), and Teen Cruisers (ages fourteen to seventeen).

After-hours baby-sitting in "Pluto's Playhouse" is available on all three of Premier's ships. The extended care begins when the official children's programs end at 10 P.M., and it ends when the program begins again at 9:00 A.M.

All kinds of package deals are available for families, from single-parent plans to family reunion packages and the special combined Walt Disney World visit and cruise.

Premier Cruise Lines, Ltd., 400 Challenger Road, Cape Canaveral, FL 32920; 800–726–5678.

4

TELL ME A STORY AND SING ME A SONG: BOOKS AND MUSIC

CHILDREN'S BOOK ILLUSTRATORS KNOW their readers love vibrant colors, and the Caribbean's banana yellows, hibiscus reds, flamboyant oranges, and bougainvillea purples backed by brilliant blue skies have inspired a slew of beautifully illustrated picture books. Many are popular titles that are easy to find at public libraries and bookstores. By learning in advance about the places they are going to visit, children develop an ear for the language and a greater appreciation of different cultures and island features. If their curiosity is piqued, you can dig deeper into a subject; or simply read for the sheer pleasure of cuddling up together with a good story.

Books of fiction and nonfiction for older readers take advantage of the exciting and somewhat nefarious history of the West Indies, with its seafaring explorers, pirates, treasure hunters, slave traders, and sugarcane barons. The area's natural history, both on land and undersea, can be studied in many excellent books on coral reefs, rain forests, and marine animals.

PICTURE BOOKS FOR VERY YOUNG CHILDREN

One White Sail: A Caribbean Counting Book by S. T. Garne, illustrated by Lisa Etre (New York: Green Tiger Press/Simon & Schuster, 1992). Lilting Caribbean verse and vibrant watercolors capture island scenes.

Baby-o by Nancy White Carlstrom, illustrated by Suçie Stevenson (Boston: Little, Brown, 1992). Each member of a family in the West Indies brings a different item—toys, mangoes, baskets, fish—to the local market aboard a jitney named for the baby, Baby-o.

One Smiling Grandma, a Caribbean Counting Book by Ann Marie Linden, illustrated by Lynne Russell (New York: Dial Books, 1992). This richly illustrated counting book is based on the author's memories of her childhood in Barbados.

PICTURE BOOKS
FOR ALL AGES

The Chalk Doll by Charlotte Pomerantz, illustrated by Frané Lessac (New York: J. B. Lippincott, 1989). This is the story of a little girl who urges her mother to tell again and again her favorite stories about growing up in Jamaica.

Under the Sunday Tree, paintings by Amos Ferguson, poems by Eloise Greenfield (New York: Harper & Row, 1988). Ferguson is a Bahamian primitive painter whose work, accompanied by Greenfield's poems, evokes scenes of daily life throughout the Caribbean.

Hue Boy by Rita Phillips Mitchell, illustrated by Caroline Binch (New York: Dial Books, 1993). Set in the Caribbean, this is a story with a universal theme about a little boy teased for his size who learns to stand tall.

Caribbean Alphabet by Frané Lessac (New York: Macmillan Caribbean, 1989). Lively pictures of three or four distinctly Caribbean objects accompany each letter of the alphabet. For example, T is for tourists, towels, turtles, and treasure.

Gregory Cool by Caroline Binch (New York: Dial Books, 1994). Gregory travels to visit his grandparents on the island of Tobago and has a tough time of it at first: the food is different, his room is sparsely furnished, and traditional American pastimes are nonexistent. Slowly he begins to gain an appreciation of the new place and of himself.

Feliz Nochebuena, Feliz Navidad: Christmas Feasts of the Hispanic Caribbean by Maricel Presilla, illustrated by Ismael Espinosa Ferrar (New York: Henry Holt, 1994). This book describes different family holiday feasts and festivities.

Not a Copper Penny in Me House: Poems from the Caribbean by Monica Gunning, illustrated by Frané Lessac (Honesdale, Pennsylvania: Boyds Mills Press, 1993). Charming poems, accompanied by vivid paintings, capture the humor and life-style of the islands.

Flamboyan by Arnold Adoff, illustrated by Karen Barbour (San Diego: Harcourt Brace Jovanovich, 1988). On a small green island in the blue Caribbean Sea, a girl is born with hair the color of the flame-red blossoms of the flamboyan tree.

The Little Island by Frané Lessac (New York: Macmillan Caribbean, 1984). Lessac's superb paintings illustrate the tale of a young boy who returns to visit his relatives on the lush green island of Montserrat. He brings a friend from home and together they experience the island's sights, sounds, and smells.

The Boy Who Sailed with Columbus by Michael Foreman (New York: Arcade Publishing, 1991). A twelve-year-old boy named Leif sails across uncharted seas to the New World as a ship's boy with Christopher Columbus. Shipwrecked, he is captured by natives and taken to live with a distant tribe, where he learns the ways and language of his new people. He must eventually choose between his new life and rejoining the Europeans who come back years later to settle the new land.

Island Baby by Holly Keller (New York: Greenwillow Books, 1992). Everyone knows where Pop and his bird hospital can be found on a Caribbean island. Young Simon helps care for the birds, but when it's time to release them, he has trouble saying good-bye, especially to his little favorite, Baby.

BOOKS FOR OLDER READERS

Ajeema and His Son by James Berry (New York: Willa Perlman Books/HarperCollins, 1991). Ajeema and his son Atu are snatched from their home in Africa in 1807 by slave traders and taken to Jamaica, where they never see each other again. The story is told in heart-rending personal parallel stories. The Jamaican author now lives in England.

Timothy of the Cay by Theodore Taylor (San Diego: Harcourt Brace, 1993). The lives of two people—one seventy years old, the other eleven—intersect on a Caribbean island for three months in 1942. The book flashes back to the life of the elder and his dreams to captain his own ship in the Caribbean Sea. His story leads to the point where the boy is discovered. The book is a prequel to *The Cay* (New York: Doubleday, 1987), also by Theodore Taylor.

Ship by David MacCaulay (Boston: Houghton Mifflin, 1993) begins with the present-day discovery and recovery of artifacts from a caravel that sank in the Caribbean almost 500 years ago. The narrative then shifts to the building of the ship in a Seville shipyard in 1504.

Wave in Her Pocket: Stories from Trinidad and *The Mermaid's Twin Sister: More Stories from Trinidad* by Lynn Joseph (Boston: Clarion Books, 1991 and 1994). "Tantie" tells Amber and her cousins favorite old tales of spirits and magical beings.

Treasure Island by Robert Louis Stevenson (1883; many editions available). This is the classic tale of a young boy's adventures involving pirates, buried treasure, and a dangerous ship journey to a destination inspired by Norman Island in the British Virgin Islands.

VIDEOS

My Little Island by Frané Lessac, a Reading Rainbow selection. Viewers hear the story and see pictures from Lessac's book, which Levar Burton reads to them from the airplane he is taking to visit the island of Montserrat. The camera follows him as he tours the island, stops at the market, hunts for "mountain chicken" (actually a large frog), and chats with the locals.

Treasure Island is a Disney classic with terrifying pirates, a brave young boy, an uninhabited island, and glittering pieces of eight.

M U S I C

Every island in the Caribbean seems to have developed its own special get-up-and-dance sound, taking bits and pieces from all the different cultures that settled on and around it. African and Latin rhythms, European folk and court music, and American blues, jazz, and rock get shaken up in spicy island stews that reveal different flavors in different places; there's reggae from Jamaica, calypso and soca from Trinidad, merengue in the Dominican Republic, zouk from the French islands of Martinique and Guadeloupe, and rumba from Cuba—the list goes on and on. Reggae has become the best-known over the last two decades, but all have made their way north to the United States and around the world. "Jump-ups" are popular throughout the islands and involve all kinds of catchy Caribbean music. They're simple: when you hear the music, jump up and begin to dance. Many jump-ups wind through the streets during holidays, festivals, and (of course) carnival time.

If you and your children like to listen to music, bring a small radio with you and explore the islands' many radio stations. In addition to hearing toe-tapping Caribbean popular music, you'll hear birthday and anniversary wishes, school updates, and all the news of a small island.

STEEL BAND MUSIC

A testimonial to human ingenuity, steel "pans" (as the drums are known) are made from large oil drums. The music originated in Trinidad, whose oil industry supplied the cast-off drums and whose poverty inspired the use of found objects for musical instruments. From these humble origins, steel band music has grown to be the mainstay of the tourist industry's evening entertainment.

The instruments are made by slicing off the head of an oil drum and 6 to 12 inches of its side. The top is heated and carefully hammered until a series of large indentations appear, each of which produces a different musical note when struck. Every pan is custom designed. Bass pans have only three or four notes; soprano pans, which provide the melody, have 26 to 32 notes.

Larger pans supply the harmony; and cymbals, drums, and other percussion instruments supply the beat. A contemporary steel drum orchestra on Trinidad usually has 20 or more pans, while those on other islands are usually smaller. Trinidad's steel band competition in February, "Panorama," brings the best steel band players from all over the Caribbean together for two weeks of fierce competition and public performances.

CALYPSO

The lyrics are paramount in calypso, with their biting political content, witty social commentary, and gossipy rhyming rants. Calypso is like a musical newspaper with an Afro-Spanish rhythm; if you want to find out what's been bothering the residents of a particular island, attend a calypso competition.

Calypso's origins are cloudy and debated, but the first calypsos probably were sung in the fields by African slaves. The songs were not laments on the harsh conditions of their lives, but rather plantation gossip and funny observations. The form survived underground for many years and, by the mid-twentieth century, began to get international recognition. Trinidad first dominated the calypso world because of its recording business, and calypso artists with names like Houdini, the Mighty Sparrow, Attila the Hun, the Tiger, the Roaring Lion, the Growler, and the Mighty Charmer spread the music over the globe. Today, the best calypso can be seen at carnival and festival time, when competitions showcase dueling calypso kings.

SOCA

Short for soul calypso, soca music is an updated and electrified form of calypso. Its shake-it-up party rhythms are part of every carnival, and its lyrics are often less political in tone.

ZOUK

Meaning "party" in Creole slang, *zouk* refers to a particular style of music with a driving powerful beat, high-tech production values, and sweet harmony vocals. It originated in Guadeloupe and Martinique, and is listened to all over the world.

REGGAE

In the 1950s, American urban blues and rhythm and blues were picked up over the radio by many Jamaicans. Riding the nationalistic spirit that came with Jamaica's independence from Great Britain, the R & B sound was reshaped by Jamaican musicians and ska and rock steady—the predecessors of reggae—were born. They were in turn transformed into reggae, whose loping bass and African-based backbeat have become recognizable around the world. Lyrically, reggae became the voice of the poor, eloquently decrying social predjudices and encouraging both spiritual and political awakening. Inventive recording techniques and catchy vocals derived from three- and four-part harmonies became a part of reggae's distinctive sound.

Bob Marley is still the best known and loved reggae artist in the world, and you'll see his face on T-shirts and hear his music emanating from record stores, cafes, and car windows throughout the islands. His music continues to sell in record numbers more than 15 years after his death. Reggae's influence on pop music can be heard in rap, hip-hop, and techno-pop music.

5

OCEAN SPORTS

THE CARIBBEAN SEA IS one of the world's best water playgrounds. Glimpses of spectacular tropical fish and coral colonies appear the minute you look through your mask whether you kick around in a set of fins near the surface or strap on an air tank and descend deep into the underwater world. The reliable tradewind breezes that keep the islands so comfortably cool make for superior sailing conditions, and the closeness of the islands allows sailors to meander from one sun-kissed beach to another. Windsurfers appear to skim effortlessly across the water's surface, pushed by the same steady trade winds. Waterskiing, kayaking, canoeing, and deep-sea fishing seem even better in the laid-back beauty of the islands.

SNORKELING

Everything you've ever heard about the exceptional underwater visibility in the Caribbean is true, and that's why families find it such a rewarding place to snorkel. Coral reefs teeming with life are a few flips of your fins from shore, and boats can take you to snorkeling spots livelier than any scene in *The Little Mermaid*.

Snorkeling is an excellent way to teach children to observe nature. The calming quiet under the sea helps them concentrate, and they can notice details that they might be too distracted to see on land. If you arrange for equipment from a water sports facility, ask if they have waterproof plant and animal identification cards. If not, the cards are usually easy to find in tourist shops throughout the islands. Children love being able to match a name and picture to a real fish or coral species. Buy each child an inexpensive one-use underwater camera. It's an excellent way to train their eyes, and a wonderful memento of their trip.

Test their mask, fins, and snorkel equipment first and practice in a pool or shallow water before attempting a reef. Children must learn how to breathe through the snorkel, how to clear it, how to defog their mask, and how to kick properly so they get maximum effort and avoid cramps. If mask fogging is a problem, you can buy a product to apply to a mask to keep it clear. Children can dive for coins or shells to learn how to clear their snorkel before heading out in the ocean. If you don't wear fins, wear water shoes to protect your feet from fire coral and sea urchins. A T-shirt can be helpful protection against the sun, and don't forget to apply sunscreen to the backs of your legs.

Younger children will tire less quickly if you take them out on a raft. Many families rent a boogie board with a "leash" that can be attached to a parent's arm. Children should always wear flotation devices unless they are very accomplished swimmers. You can rent a board with a viewing window in it for children who just can't seem to keep their masks on.

A few rules:

• Never snorkel alone, and never snorkel at dusk or at night.

• Snorkeling in rough seas is pointless and dangerous.

• Never touch coral; contact can damage an organism that takes many years to grow, and it in turn can injure you.

• Towing a dive flag is your best protection if you're in an area where there are boats.

• Avoid sea urchins, as their barbs can break off in your skin. If this happens, remove as much of the barb as possible, soak the area in vinegar or ammonia, and check with a doctor.

• Most important, take only photos and leave only bubbles behind.

LIFE DOWN UNDER:
FAMILY SCUBA DIVING

The number of families diving together has increased tenfold over the past decade. The pleasure of floating suspended in a crystal-clear world of breathtaking beauty offers an extraordinary experience parents and teenagers can share. Old or young, everyone is freed from the constraints of gravity and can glide from coral formation to sea sponge past graceful rays and sea horses.

Junior Diving Certification is available for youngsters of ages twelve and up, with a parent's approval. The juniors need to be good swimmers and must be accompanied by certified adults in all of their dives. One reason younger children cannot be certified is that classroom work teaches the physics of diving, a subject young teens can master but young children cannot. Unless divers fully understand why they cannot ascend as fast as they might like, they risk seriously injuring themselves. At age fifteen, teens can get a basic open-water certification. International standards with carefully thought-out guidelines govern the sport; consequently, the safety record of scuba diving parallels that of skiing and bicycle riding.

Becoming certified involves classroom sessions, pool practice, and four to six actual ocean dives. If you're not sure that you'll like diving, take a resort course once you've arrived at your Caribbean destination. Lasting between one and four hours, these courses usually culminate in a boat dive in shallow water. You can't count it toward your certification, but you'll get a feel for the sport that you can follow up on if you like.

People who know they want to learn the sport usually begin their full certification course at home, before they leave on vacation. That way they can get the classroom and pool work done and not waste time indoors while on holiday.

THE BASIC COURSE

Approximately 30 hours of classroom instruction is required. You learn about physical and physiological attributes of diving, pressure and how to correct for it, how deep you can go, how long you can stay under, safety stops, and what to do in case something should go wrong. Students are taught about the marine environment and are introduced to all the equipment they are likely to use. They practice with their diving gear in a pool or shallow ocean, rehearsing safety procedures under the watchful eye of an instructor until these become second nature.

The course concludes with open-water sessions, and many people save this part for their vacation. You can easily arrange to complete the course on just about any Caribbean island as long as you've taken instruction from an internationally certified dive outfit. Larger resorts have their own dive shops on the premises, while smaller ones are usually affiliated with a nearby dive shop. Once you've passed the full course (exams are required), you will be able to buy scuba gear and have air tanks filled. If you want to go further, there are advanced courses, specialty courses (such as cave diving), rescue courses, and special certification classes for instructors. People who want to spend most of their vacation diving go to special dive resorts that offer unlimited shore dives and several boat dives each day. Some of the dive resorts on Bonaire have family programs during the month of August.

The following organizations can put you in touch with facilities in your area that offer dive training. Their names are the ones to look for when you want to arrange dive trips on the islands, because they adhere to an international set of certification and safety standards. Never dive with anyone who can't show evidence of appropriate accreditation.

PADI (Professional Association of Diving Instructors). 1251 East Dyer Road #100, Santa Ana, CA 92705; 800–729–7234, 714–540–7234, fax 714–540–2609. Send for a free list of training facilities.

NAUI (National Association of Underwater Instructors). P.O. Box 14650, Montclair, CA 91763; 800–553–6284, 714–621–5801, fax 714–621–6405.

CMAS (Confederation Mondiale des Activités Subaquatics; translates into World Underwater Federation). This is a reputable name you are likely to see on the French-speaking islands.

WINDSURFING

Skimming the surface of the clear azure Caribbean Sea with just a small board between you and the sea and a sail between you and the blue sky is an exhilarating experience. The predictable waters and steady breezes make the Caribbean an ideal place to learn the sport.

If you are a good swimmer and are strong enough to hoist the lightweight sail without losing your balance, you are a candidate for windsurfing. The U.S. Sailing Association suggests that kids as young as six can learn to windsurf, but some instructors recommend starting children at about age ten. Small children are taught on scaled-down boards; if your kids plan to windsurf, be sure to ask if equipment in children's sizes is available. Children should always wear life vests while windsurfing, no matter how competent their swimming skills.

Windsurfing lessons are much the same throughout the Caribbean: the first half-hour is spent on land, practicing on a pedestal-mounted board or on a real board on the beach. You learn how to handle the mast and boom, feel how the sail reacts to wind, and begin to coordinate your footwork to the movements of the sail rig. After you've mastered the shoreside lessons, you head to waist-deep water, hop on the board, and try to stand up. Be prepared to fall at first. Once you've got the basics, though, you'll soar through the salt air with the greatest of ease. Always windsurf with someone around who can watch you and go for help if needed.

SAILING WITH CHILDREN

The Caribbean is one of the prime yachting spots in the world, with its constant trade winds, predictably sunny weather, and beautiful island anchorages. Experienced sailors usually rent a yacht to sail themselves, while novices can get a fully crewed boat complete with captain, cook, and mates to sail from one sun-swept beach to another.

Sailing is not just for the very rich anymore. Per-person charges aboard a yacht can equal that of a stay at a nice resort. Because crewed yachts cost more than bare boats and offer less privacy, many people are motivated to learn to sail on their vacations. You don't need to be athletic to learn; all you need is a good sense of balance.

Children of any age can go on sailing trips, but if you wait until your children are at least six, you won't have to keep your eye on them every minute. Children take to sailing quickly; the clever use of space and the sheer coziness of a boat appeal to them. Your family's yacht is your floating hotel, with scenery changing daily. Every time you anchor, you're in a new park and playground, and at night the entire family rocks to sleep to the sound of waves lapping against the boat.

Two of the most popular areas for sailing are the British Virgin Islands and the Grenadines, where beautiful anchorages are within an hour or two of one another.

CREWED YACHTS

If you're not experienced sailors, start with a crewed yacht and request crews who like to be placed with children. The captain and crew (including a cook) are at your service and will go wherever you want to go, within reason. One fee includes food, drinks, port fees, and fuel. Be sure to ask if there is special equipment aboard, such as safety harnesses and life jackets for children. Some boats are rigged for scuba diving, often with instructors.

Go through a broker if you plan to charter a crewed vessel. The broker will help you make a selection based on your particular needs, your budget, the size and ages of your family, and your preferred destinations. Two large charter yacht brokers that know most of the charter yacht companies in the Caribbean are Sailing Vacations (407–454–4646) and Caribbean Sailing Charters (800–824–1331).

BARE BOATING

Bare boating means chartering the boat "bare," or without food, fuel, captain, and mates. You plan, equip, sail, and explore on your own. Costs are about a third less than for crewed boats, and a further 20 percent less during the summer. Someone in your group must have skippering experience on a similar boat in comparable sailing conditions, and you'll be asked to fill out a sailing résumé. The charter company staff will review navigational charts, pointing out suggested routes, anchorages, places to avoid, and prevailing wind strengths and directions so you know what to expect.

The Moorings is the largest yacht-chartering company in the world, with six bases in the Caribbean: Tortola in the British Virgin Islands, St. Martin, Guadeloupe, Martinique, St. Lucia, and Grenada. It specializes in bare-boat vacations but also rents fully crewed yachts. It has three lines of yachts, which are distinguished according to the craft's age, amenities, and price.

The Moorings offers learn-to-sail adventures on a 27-foot sailboat, and land-and-sea combinations on Tortola (Treasure Isle Hotel), Grenada (Secret Harbor Resort), and St. Lucia (Marigot Bay Cottages). Land-and-sea packages combine land-based activities such as island tours, water sports, and skippered day sails with three nights in a private crewed yacht. 1935 U.S. Highway 19N, Clearwater, FL 34624; 800–535–7289.

Sun Yacht Charters is another large and highly regarded charter outfit, with bases on St. Martin, Antigua, and Tortola. Its boats are well-maintained and are all less than three years old. Both bare-boat and crewed charters are available, and you can opt to start your cruise on one island and end on another, instead of making a round trip. P.O. Box 737, Camden, ME 04843; 800–772–3500 or 207–236–9611, fax 207–236–3972.

Sunsail operates bare-boat and crewed yacht charters from Tortola, Virgin Gorda, St. Martin, Antigua, Martinique, St. Lucia, and Guadeloupe. Most of its boats are two years old; none is more than four years old. 115 E. Broward Boulevard, Fort Lauderdale, FL 33301; 800–327–2276, or, 305–524–7553, fax 305–524–6312.

SAFETY

Be sure that your charter outfit has flotation devices small enough to fit your children. The law requires that a flotation device, or life jacket, be on board for each passenger, and the law of common sense states that children should wear one at all times on deck. If your charter company does not carry sizes small enough for your children, purchase them before you go. Make sure that the life jacket fits snugly so your child cannot slip out of it. It should have leg straps and a collar to keep the child's head out of the water. Attach a whistle to each life jacket and instruct children to blow it if they fall overboard. Once older children become proficient swimmers they don't need to wear life jackets at all times. Sailing with toddlers and very young children necessitates the use of a safety harness, which is attached by a tether to the boat.

Pack light. Your kids will wear bathing suits from morning to night. (Bring two suits, one for wearing and one for drying.) If you plan to anchor and take the dinghy in to any nice restaurant, bring a set of dress clothes. Other than that, all you'll need are shorts, T-shirts, hats, and lots of sunscreen. Boats come with first-aid kits, and most have snorkel gear, but not necessarily in children's sizes.

6

ANGUILLA

SMALL, UNCROWDED, AND tranquil, Anguilla—one of the northernmost of the Leeward Islands—has several of the Caribbean's most elegant super-luxurious resorts, as well as casual and affordable beachfront retreats. Its 30 immaculate white sand beaches with hidden coves and grottoes are surrounded by a coral reef that transforms the translucent turquoise waters into a giant aquarium. Snorkelers can go eyeball to eyeball with fish, eels, and octopus just offshore. Over the years, the government has sunk nine surplus hulks in order to create habitats for marine life, making the waters popular with scuba divers, too.

The long and skinny eel-shaped island is just 3 miles across at its widest point and 213 feet high at its greatest elevation. The rocky limestone soil is unsuitable for agriculture, so sugar was never cultivated there. Instead, the island's economy has been based on fishing and boat building (and more recently, tourism), and many colorful and swift seacraft can be spotted in the harbors today. Not surprisingly, the national sport is boat racing. Races are a part of every public holiday and are usually accompanied by beachside barbecues, jump-ups, and betting. The sport reaches its high point during the first week of August, when Anguilla celebrates three holidays and stages its riotous multicolored carnival.

TOURIST INFORMATION

In the United States and Canada: Anguilla Tourist Information and Reservation Office, c/o Medhurst and Associates, Inc., 775 Park Avenue, Huntington, NY 11743; 800–553–4939.
On Anguilla: Department of Tourism, Social Security Building, The Valley, Anguilla, BWI; 809–497–2759, fax 809–497–3389.

KNOW BEFORE YOU GO

Arriving and Departing: Passports are preferred for American and Canadian citizens, but an original birth certificate with a photo ID can be used instead. Visitors must show an onward or return ticket. Anguilla's departure tax is $10 per person. Ferry boats leave for St. Martin/St. Maarten every 30 minutes, starting at 7:30 A.M.
Money: U.S. dollars are widely accepted, although the official currency is the Eastern Caribbean Dollar (EC$).
Language: A British possession for almost 350 years, Anguilla remains an English-speaking colony today.
Staying Healthy: The Princess Alexandra Hospital in Stoney Ground has a 24-hour emergency room. Beware of the manchineel tree and its poisonous green applelike fruit. Even touching the tree can cause blisters. Don't forget insect repellent to battle the mosquitoes and no-see-ums.

WHERE TO STAY

CAP JULUCA

Looking a little like something out of *Lawrence of Arabia*, with its North African architecture and furnishings from Moroccan souks, deluxe Cap Juluca spreads along a gleaming 1-mile strand of white sand at Maunday's Bay near the southwestern end of the island. Its white Moorish-style villas with domes, arches, and flowered courtyards are spacious and elegantly decorated. A romantic open-air restaurant sits at the water's edge. There's also a full range of water sports and tennis courts with lights for night play. Adults and children who want to perfect their croquet game can take a 30-minute "primer" for beginners and experienced players on the resort's immaculate regulation croquet court.

For Kids: Complimentary children's activities take place from mid-March through April, and in July and August. Kids of ages ten to fourteen get one-hour clinics in waterskiing, windsurfing, snorkeling, sailing, and swimming. Three- to nine-year-olds meet in the children's Club House next to the Junior Olympic–size pool from 10:00 A.M. to 8:30 P.M. and can drop in and out of activities as they wish. A daily schedule offers nature walks, arts and crafts, and beach activities in the morning, and pool swimming, tennis, story hour, and a movie in the afternoon. The program breaks for dinner and resumes at 7:00 P.M., when a movie is shown.

Accommodations: Eighteen villas house 58 private rooms, seven suites, and six complete villas, several of which have three to five bedrooms and their own private pool. All have marble bathrooms, huge tubs, private terraces, louvered doors and windows, and elegant Moroccan-style furnishings.

Children's rooms are half-price from June through October, and prices in general drop dramatically during the summer. Daily rates: summer, spring, and fall, rooms $275 to $450; one-bedroom suites $670 to $800; three- to five-bedroom villas $1,675 to $2,075; with pool $1,715 to $2,100. Winter: rooms $345 to $735; one-bedroom suites $755 to $1,725; villas $1,880 to $3,965. P.O. Box 240, Maunday's Bay, Anguilla, BWI; 800–323–0139 or 809–497–6666, fax 809–497–6617.

MALLIOUHANA HOTEL

Malliouhana is known for its sophistication, service, world-class French cuisine, and wine cellar, but will your kids care? They're more likely to notice the elaborate, supervised children's play area that was recently built along the beach at this elegant five-star resort. Its 53 luxurious guest rooms cover 25 acres of tropical grounds on a bluff overlooking soft white sand beaches and a secluded cove. A waterfall connects two freshwater pools, and the tennis courts, managed by Peter Burwash International, have lights and wind shields. The hotel also has two speedboats for waterskiing, windsurfing equipment, sailboats, snorkeling gear, a gym, and Jacuzzi. Dining is a large part of the Malliouhana experience, and the superb cuisine is French with a Caribbean twist.

For Kids: The adventure playground has equipment for both toddlers and older children, a wading pool and spray fountain, and a covered games area. It's supervised daily from 8:30 A.M. to 5:00 P.M. by a childcare counselor and assistant; structured activities are based on the number and ages of the children present. There is a half-court basketball court, Nintendo, Ping-Pong, tire swings, a sandbox, carousel, and seesaw. The program is complimentary for two- to twelve-year-olds.

Accommodations: The double rooms, junior suites, and one- or two-bedroom suites are spacious with exquisite furnishings, covered patios, and marble bathrooms. Many rooms have connecting doors. Seven villas, located on the beach, on the bluff, or in the gardens, can be rented as individual rooms or as an entire villa.

Daily rates, double occupancy: winter, $500 to $1,250; fall and spring, $325 to $850; summer, $250 to $650. Daily charge for extra bed per child is $25 in summer, $50 in winter. Rates include watersports; food is not included. No credit cards. P.O. Box 173, Meads Bay, Anguilla, BWI; 800–835–0796 or 809–497–6111, fax 809–497–6011.

THE MARINERS

Tucked between one of the island's prettiest white sand beaches and a gentle green hillside is this cottage hotel, which has special rates for families. Its water sports shop offers chartered fishing trips and sunset cruises in addition to more standard snorkeling, windsurfing, and sailing. There's also a swimming pool, two Jacuzzis, and tennis courts. The breezy beachside restaurant has a barbecue buffet on Thursday night and a traditional West Indian buffet on Sunday, both with live music.

Accommodations: Twenty cottages are set up as "triplets": Studios are in the middle and have small kitchenettes, with a bedroom and bath on either side. You can rent all or part of a cottage, depending on how much space you need.

Daily rates, double occupancy, for cliffside units: December 15 to March 31, rooms $215, suites $350, cottages $535; rest of year, rooms $125, suites $195, cottages $260. Children ages six to twelve, $25 per child per night. Rates for beachfront units are slightly higher. All-inclusive packages are available. P.O. Box 139, Sandy Ground, Anguilla, BWI; 800–848–7938 or 809–497–2671, fax 809–497–2901.

ARAWAK BEACH RESORT

Budding archaeologists might enjoy a stay at a property built on part of an ancient Amerindian Arawak village site, within walking distance of a petroglyph-decorated sacred cavern. Its restaurant serves original Arawak recipes, and a small museum on the premises displays pottery, furnishings, baskets, and other artifacts. The resort's pool is pleasant and the beach is so-so, but it's just a five-minute canoe trip from Gorgeous Scilly Cay, a small island with an excellent beach, good snorkeling, and a lively lunchtime restaurant. Canoes are available from the resort at no extra charge. **Accommodations:** Fourteen units are housed in octagonal villas inspired by the shape of the huts used by the Arawaks. Two beachfront suites are available for families, both with kitchenettes and covered terraces.

Daily rates, double occupancy: April 16 to December 15, $140 to $190; December 16 to April 15, $210 to $300. Extra beds, $25 each per night. P.O. Box 433, The Valley, Anguilla, BWI; 809–497–4888, fax 809–497–4898.

PARADISE COVE

An Olympic-size swimming pool, kiddy pool, children's playground, croquet court, and a homey atmosphere make these 14 fully furnished one- and two-bedroom suite apartments attractive to families. The tropically landscaped property is a short bike ride or drive away from beautiful Cove Beach on the island's southern shore, and the resort staff will arrange car rentals and bike rentals before you arrive. Its main pool bar and small cafe serves breakfast and lunch.

Accommodations: Two-bedroom suites have twin beds in one bedroom and a queen-size bed in the other. All have air conditioning, ceiling fans, cable TV, and fully equipped kitchens with microwave ovens. Private cooks can be arranged.

Daily rates: April 16 to October 31, $155 to $230; November 1 to December 18, $225 to $335; December 15 to April 15, $310 to $425. P.O. Box 135, The Cove, Anguilla, BWI; 800–728–0784 or 809–497–6959, fax 809–497–2149.

SEAHORSE APARTMENTS

Seahorse's five one-bedroom cottages right on the beach at quiet Rendezvous Bay on the island's southern coast are one of Anguilla's best buys. Children under twelve are not accepted in season (December 15 to April 14), but families visit regularly during the rest of the year. The small beach has very calm waters, and excellent snorkeling is found just offshore. All guests are welcome to use the barbecue area and picnic tables near the water's edge. You'll want a car for mobility, and rentals can be arranged in advance.

Accommodations: Spacious and spotless one-bedroom cottages have full kitchens, full baths, and housekeeping service six days a week. Bedrooms have king-size beds, and one or two rollaway beds can be added for children (advance notice required). All cottages have large porches with table and chairs.

Rates, double occupancy: April 15 to December 14, $490 per week or $75 per day; December 15 to April 14, $790 per week or $115 per day. Extra person $20 per day, regardless of age (unless it's a baby and you bring a portable crib). P.O. Box 17, Anguilla, BWI; 809–497–6751, fax 809–497–6752.

VILLA RENTALS

Inns of Anguilla is an association of small guest houses and inns with weekly rates; 809–497–3180, fax 809–497–5381. In North America, 516–491–3207.

Anguilla Connection specializes in villa rentals. The staff meets you at the airport, gets you started with a bag of groceries, and is a phone call away if you have any problems; 800–648–1405 or 809–497–4403, fax 809–407–4402.

PREMS—Property Real Estate Management Services Company—also handles villa rentals; 809–497–2598, fax 809–497–3309.

WHERE TO EAT

There are a couple of casual family-friendly eateries on Anguilla where you can make an afternoon of lunch:

Uncle Ernie's on Shoal Bay is an unpretentious bar and restaurant with barbecued chicken, barbecued spare ribs, and local snapper specialties. The kids can play on the beach while you linger over some of the best chicken you've ever tasted. A local band entertains on Sunday. Open daily, 10:00 A.M. to 8:00 P.M.

Gorgeous Scilly Cay has an amusing name and is a favorite of many kids. Take the free boat ride to the private island in Island Harbour Sound for lunch. After you've finished your meal, lounge on the beach, take a swim, and snorkel the nearby coral reefs. Open 11:00 A.M. to 5:00 P.M. closed Mondays. Live music on Wednesdays, steel bands on Fridays, and reggae on Sundays.

7

ANTIGUA

THREE HUNDRED SIXTY-FIVE sandy coves and beaches surround the island; that's one for each day of the year. Some are nearly deserted, while many others are hemmed in by resorts of all sizes. Coral reefs protect much of the shoreline, offering calm water and exceptional snorkeling no matter where you flip your fins. Antigua is a good place to perfect your tan, as it receives the least rainfall of all islands in the eastern Caribbean.

Columbus "discovered" this island on his second voyage to the West Indies in 1493, but several Amerindian groups had settled there first. History buffs will want to visit English Harbour, where Captain Horatio Nelson took command of the British naval dockyard in 1784 in anticipation of invasions by the French and other European powers who played king-of-the-hill over various Caribbean islands. Antigua remained a British territory until 1981, when it received its independence in union with neighboring sister island Barbuda.

Summer carnival takes place in August with ten days of parades, wild costumes, and calypso and steel band competitions. Race week in late April consists of seven days of ocean racing and parties. Kids will enjoy Dockyard Day, which features a tug-of-war competition between sailing crews, a greased pole race, and a spinnaker flying contest. A yacht show in November showcases some of the world's most elegant yachts. Many local artists produce crafts in Antigua. Look for the WarriBoard, a game originally played with seeds, which originated in Africa.

TOURIST INFORMATION

In the United States: 610 Fifth Avenue, Suite 311, New York, NY 10020; 212–541–4117.

In Canada: 60 St. Clair Avenue East, Toronto, Ontario M4T 1N5; 416–961–3083.

In Antigua: Department of Tourism, Thames Street and Long Street, St. Johns, Antigua, WI; 809–462–0480.

KNOW BEFORE YOU GO

Arriving and Departing: You'll need a current U.S. passport or a birth certificate to enter Antigua. The airport departure fee is $10 per person.

Money: Antiguans use the Eastern Caribbean dollar (EC$), but U.S. dollars are accepted throughout the island.

Language: Antigua is an English-speaking island.

Staying Healthy: Holberton Hospital on Queen Elizabeth Highway (809–462–0251) has a 24-hour emergency room. Some beaches have manchineel trees, whose leaves and applelike fruits are poisonous even to the touch. Most such trees have warning signs posted.

Local Food: The Antigua black pineapple is a smaller, sweeter version of the more familiar Hawaiian variety. Pepperpot is a rich, thick stew containing beef, pork, vegetables, and spices that is normally served with fungee, a round dumpling made from cornmeal and okra. Ducana is a pudding made from grated sweet potato and coconut, mixed with sugar and spices and boiled in a banana leaf. Green figs are small green bananas that must be cooked before being eaten. Black pudding, a spiced blood sausage featuring highly seasoned pig intestines and rice, sounds much worse than it tastes.

WHERE TO STAY

ST. JAMES CLUB

Long cream-colored sand beaches wrap around this resort's private peninsula, which separates Mamora Bay from the Caribbean. On the calm bay side, you'll find the water sports center, beach cabanas, and sunbathing decks. The other side of the resort faces the Caribbean Sea, and its water is much rougher and more challenging for swimmers. The gated property is safe enough for older kids to roam wherever they wish—to the playground, the croquet court, the Ping-Pong table, or the game room. The club also has two pools, three restaurants, a European-style casino, and a good tennis program. Horseback rides along the beach and through the countryside start from stables on the property.

For Kids: A separate playroom houses the children's program, open daily from 1:00 to 4:00 p.m. Supervised activities vary depending on the age and interests of the children, but these often involve arts and crafts, cooking, and games. The video game room is next door.

Accommodations: Families usually stay in The Village, where the separate two-story villas have two bedrooms, roomy kitchens with dishwashers, decks with barbecues, and two full bathrooms. Spacious dining areas and comfortable living rooms have cable TV, and tropical-print rattan furnishings.

Club suites, closer to the main resort, have two rooms: one a bedroom with a queen-size bed, the other a sitting room that can accommodate several rollaway beds. You can even stay on a private yacht.

Daily rates, double occupancy: spring, summer, and fall, villas $510, suites $410; winter, villas $920, suites $770. Family Fun package, daily rates per person based on a minimum of four guests for four nights: spring, summer, and fall, villas $110; winter, $150; includes water sports and afternoon tea. If you don't have a car, you'll be stuck buying your groceries at the resort's well-stocked but exorbitantly priced market. P.O. Box 63, Mamora Bay, Antigua, WI; 800–274–0008 or 809–460–5000.

REX HALCYON COVE BEACH

This full-fledged resort with many different water sports plus nightly entertainment has its own ice cream parlor and a restaurant perched on stilts above the water; the latter serves lunch and dinner. It's located on Dickenson Bay on Antigua's northwest coast, about ten minutes from St. John's and 20 minutes from the airport. Most of the action takes place around the pool and the busy soft sand beach. Water sports such as Sunfish sailing, windsurfing, beach volleyball, snorkeling, and daytime tennis are included in the rates. Waterskiing, water sports lessons, nighttime tennis, and scuba cost extra.

For Kids: Supervised activities operate weekdays from 9:00 A.M. to 4:00 P.M. for four- to twelve-year-olds, with a midday break for lunch. The program changes according to the ages of the kids present, but you can anticipate field trips, swimming, sports, games, and arts and crafts.

Accommodations: The resort has a variety of room styles and sizes. Time-share units have a kitchenette, living room with fold-out couch, and bedroom. Most of the hotel rooms can accommodate two adults and two children, and connecting doors are available. A mini-market is nearby.

Children under age two stay and eat free; children ages two to twelve stay free and receive a 50 percent discount on meals. Daily rates, double occupancy: November 1 to April 22, $180 to $360, depending on the size, location, and amenities of the room; rest of the year, $150 to $300. Add $40 per night between December 24 and January 3. P.O. Box 251, Dickenson Bay, St. Johns, Antigua, WI; 800–255–5859 or 809–462–0256, fax 809–462–0271.

CLUB ANTIGUA

This massive all-inclusive resort, with 472 rooms on 40 acres of landscaped gardens, lets parents have two children under sixteen stay in their room at no extra charge. That means kids stay free, eat free, and play free. The resort is popular with tour groups, and its off-season rates make it even more affordable. Its large free-form pool and half-mile stretch of white sand beach are the center of resort activities, but bicycling, tennis, volleyball, Ping-

Pong, a jogging track, and evening entertainment such as casino, disco, and shows keep the fun rolling. Sunfish sailing, waterskiing, windsurfing, snorkeling, and pedal boats are included in the rates. **For Kids:** A supervised children's club for four-to twelve-year-olds runs Monday to Saturday with table tennis, volleyball, cartoons, and videos.

Accommodations: Rooms are rather plain but most have ocean views. Family suites sleep up to four in one large room. Standard rooms can take one child.

Daily rates, double occupancy, including all food, drinks, and water sports: December 15 to mid-April, $276 to $364; mid-April to mid-December, $220 to $320. P.O. Box 744, St. Johns, Antigua, WI; 800–777–1250 or 809–462–0062, fax 809–462–1827.

FALMOUTH HARBOR BEACH APARTMENTS

Twelve fully equipped apartments are situated right on the beach at Falmouth Bay on the southern coast of the island; 16 more perch on the hillside above the protected cove, just a short walk from the lively scene of English Harbour and its restaurants, shops, and historical sights. Its beach is right on busy Falmouth Bay harbor, with lots of boating activity to observe, and quieter Pigeon Beach is a ten-minute walk away. Snorkel gear and Sunfish are included in the very reasonable rate.

Accommodations: All units have three single beds, two of which can be made into a king. Rollaways and cribs are available. Units are on the small side but sparkling clean with outdoor decks or patios featuring table and chairs and lounge chairs. Some rooms have interior connecting doors. Daily housekeeping service, which includes dishwashing, is included in the rate.

Daily rates, double occupancy: December 15 to April 15, $100; rest of year, $70. Children under sixteen sharing apartment with parents, $15 per child per night. P.O. Box 713, St. Johns, Antigua, WI; 800–223–5695 or 809–460–1027, fax 809–463–1534

THE COPPER AND LUMBER STORE HOTEL

Situated within the walls of historic Nelson's Dockyard at English Harbour, the Copper and Lumber Store was the island's center for purchasing construction materials during the eighteenth century. The ground floor served as a supply store, and the upper floors were used as quarters for sailors whose ships had been hauled in for repairs. Today those quarters have been replaced by the elegant rooms of a Georgian hotel filled with period furnishing. It's within the historic area of Nelson's Dockyard, with shops, galleries, restaurants, and historic exhibits. A ferry runs frequently to the hotel's small beach across the harbor; you also can arrange for your own dinghy. Several sailing programs, including KITS (Kids in the Sea), are run from the hotel, as are dive programs and packages. Many guests combine their stay with a charter sailing expedition, which can be arranged by hotel staff.

Accommodations: Fourteen guest rooms with fully equipped kitchens are up one flight of stairs, surrounding a garden courtyard. Some can accommodate five people, and all comfortably house four. Contemporary suites are best for families because they contain simple furnishings instead of the fancy period pieces of the Georgian suites. A system of ceiling fans and good screened ventilation cools the units. The bottom floor of the building houses a breakfast room, pub, and more formal restaurant. Barbecues are held in season. Several grocery stores are within easy walking distance.

Kids under twelve stay free, and extra beds and cribs are available at no extra charge. Daily rates, double occupancy: mid-December through April, contemporary suites, $215; rest of year, $85. Third and fourth person, $30 per person per night. Fancier Georgian suites, double occupancy, $325 per night in season, $175 off-season. Nelson's Dockyard, Antigua, WI; 800–633–7411 or 809–460–1058, fax 809–460–1529.

WHAT TO SEE AND DO

In St. John's, the **Museum of Antigua and Barbuda** is a hands-on museum with a life-size Arawak house, models of a sugar plantation and a wattle-and-daub house, and more. Early Indian items have been collected from 120 prehistoric sites. Church and Market Streets; 809–463–1060.

Visit **St. John's Market** on a Saturday to see the colorful and noisy scene crammed with fruit and vegetable stands, fish and spice vendors, and buyers haggling for a good deal.

The British fleet in the West Indies called **Nelson's Dockyard** its headquarters and home from 1704 to 1889. The fleet's most famous commander, Admiral Horatio Nelson, arrived in 1784 to protect it from the French, but the fleet saw little action during his tenure there. After the British Navy abandoned the dockyard in 1889, it slowly decayed until a preservation group restored it to its former glory. The "new" Nelson's Dockyard opened in 1961 with replicas of colonial naval buildings standing as the originals did in the 1780s. The Admiral's House has been made into a museum with elaborate ship models, maps, prints, and a model of English Harbour. Stop for a drink or lunch at Admiral's Inn, built of ballast bricks jettisoned from sailing ships, where the yachting crowd gathers. The **Dow's Hill Interpretation Centre** uses a multimedia presentation to trace the history of Antigua and Barbuda from prehistoric times to the present. Time your visit to the dockyard on days that cruise ship visitors are not present. Open 8:00 A.M. to 6:00 P.M.

Just north of Nelson's Dockyard, the ruins of **Shirley Heights** include fortifications, barracks, and powder magazines that now serve as great lookout points. Plan to visit on a Sunday afternoon for a tasty barbecue meal and reggae and steel band entertainment (make reservations at Shirley Heights Lookout). The steel band plays from 3:00 to 6:00 P.M., and the reggae band from 6:00 to 9:00 P.M. If you can't be there on Sunday, you can still enjoy fresh fish or hamburgers any day of the week from 9:00 A.M. to 10:00 P.M.; 809–460–1785.

Bicycles can be rented by the day or by the week at Sun Cycles, which provides free delivery and pickup from any hotel on the island. Five-speeds cost $15 the first day, $10 per day after that, with one day free if you rent by the week. Eighteen-speed bikes cost $18 for the first day, $13 after that, and $85 for a week; 809–461–0324.

Cricket is a popular spectator sport, and you can see formal regional and international matches called test matches played at the recreational grounds in St. John's or see a "knockabout" played casually on the beach, street corner, or playground.

Jolly Rogers Pirate Cruise gives kids a chance to sail on a pirate ship complete with cannons, red sails, and pirate insignia. On day trips, the ship anchors in a quiet cove where passengers can swim, snorkel, walk the plank, and play on the beach.

Windsurfing is excellent for beginners along Antigua's west coast, while advanced windsurfers tend to prefer the much more challenging east coast surf. Lesson at all levels are available at Jolly Beach Hotel's Wind Surfing Sailing School (one of the best in the world) and at Patrick Scales Water Sports at Lord Nelson Beach Hotel.

Tours of Antigua's sister island Barbuda, 26 miles to the north, can be undertaken in one day. Barbuda's frigatebird sanctuary in Codrington Lagoon is accessible by small boat, through mangrove bushes that stretch for miles. The mangroves provide nesting grounds for more than 5,000 magnificent frigatebirds, known locally as man o' wars, which build their nests just a few feet above the water.

8

ARUBA

*T*HE *B*EACH *B*OYS *CROONED* about Aruba back in the 1960s, long before Aruba's 7-mile beach strand sprouted its string of resorts, casinos, restaurants, and boutiques. They sang about the startling turquoise water, bright white sand, and constant sunshine . . . all still there and continuing to attract young lovers, sun worshippers, and fun-loving families.

This flat, dry, deserty island buffeted by trade winds is prime windsurfing territory for beginners and experts alike. Beginners can start in quiet and shallow beach waters, while crack windsurfers whip through the air across the high waves of Boca Grandi on the southeast coast. In June, tournament windsurfers compete for the annual Hi-Winds Pro-Am World Cup.

Pack your strongest pair of jeans so you can sample the official sport of sand dune sliding; the fast and gritty slopes can sandpaper thin shorts right off your backside. Zooming across the sand and fields in a sailcart is another unusual sport to try.

Aruba is the A of the ABC islands (with Bonaire and Curaçao) off the coast of Venezuela. It was once part of the Netherland Antilles, but became an independent entity within the Netherlands in 1986. Its February carnival includes a children's carnival in Oranjestad, usually held a week before the main carnival parade. Quite a few of the large island's resorts offer children's activity programs and specially priced packages for families.

TOURIST INFORMATION

In the United States: Aruba Tourism Authority, 1000 Harbor Boulevard, Weehawken, NJ 07087; 800-TO-ARUBA or 201–330–0800, fax 201–330–8757.
In Canada: 86 Blower Street West, Suite 204, Toronto, Ontario M5S IM5; 800–268–3042 (Ontario and Quebec) or 416–975–1950, fax 416–975–1947.
On Aruba: Aruba Tourism Authority, L. G. Smith Boulevard 172, Eagle, Aruba; 297–8–21029, fax 297–8–34702.

KNOW BEFORE YOU GO

Arriving and Departing: U.S. and Canadian citizens need proof of identity such as a passport or a birth certificate or voter's registration card with some type of official photograph such as a drivers license. An airport departure tax of $12.50 is charged when you leave.
Money: The Aruba florin (A.FL) is the official currency.
Language: Dutch is the official language, but Papiamento—which evolved from Spanish, Dutch, Portuguese, and a sprinkling of Indian, English, and French influences—is the native language of Aruba. English is often spoken by people in the tourist industries.
Staying Healthy: Dr. Horatio Oduber Hospital has a 24-hour emergency room on L. G. Smith Boulevard; 297–8–24300.

WHERE TO STAY

HYATT REGENCY ARUBA RESORT AND CASINO

When some children hear the name *Hyatt*, they think "awesome swimming pool," and this resort doesn't disappoint; its sprawling three-level pool complex has cascading waterfalls, a two-story spiraling waterslide, and a 5,000-square-foot lagoon stocked with tropical fish and wildlife. Other features include a full array of water sports, perfect white powder sand beach, tennis, health spa, a 54-foot catamaran, and a beach volleyball court. Meanwhile, the elegant decor, four excellent restaurants, and superb service satisfy parents, too.

For Kids: Three- to twelve-year-olds can attend Camp Hyatt, which operates daily during the Christmas holidays, spring break, Easter week, July, August, and Thanksgiving, and on weekends throughout the rest of the year. Activities take place in a separate room where trained supervisors offer Papiamento language lessons, dancing classes, nature walks, movies, sand castle building, waterslide time, arts and crafts, tennis clinics, and wildlife tours. It's a full day program from 9:00 A.M. to 3:00 P.M. with a fee of $30 per child. On weekends, it also runs evenings from 6:00 to 10:00 P.M. The program for teens (thirteen to seventeen) includes "Hip Trip" excursions, sports clinics, barbecues, dances, and sunset sails.

Accommodations: Rooms have air-conditioning, mini-bars, ceiling fans, oversized bathrooms, and digital safes. All rooms are the same size; the view determines the difference in price. The top floor is reserved for Regency Club suites, which are more spacious, and quite elegantly furnished.

Parents can reserve a second room for children at half price year-round, depending on availability; and kids under eighteen stay free in their parents' room. Daily rates, double occupancy: December 20 to April 15, $340 to $400; June 1 to September 30, $155 to $260; rest of year, $210 to $305. L. G. Smith Boulevard 85, Palm Beach, Aruba; 800–233–1234 or 297–8–61234, fax 297–8–61682.

LA CABANA ALL SUITE RESORT AND CASINO

Every one-, two-, or three-bedroom suite has a kitchenette in this enormous all-suite hotel on Eagle Beach on Aruba's upper west coast. Two free-form swimming pools, a children's pool, a waterslide, a playground, and the Club Cabana Nana Children's program are aimed specifically at youngsters, but there's plenty for visitors of every age to do. Guests can enjoy every conceivable water sport, squash and racquetball courts, basketball, shuffleboard, aerobics classes, and tennis clinics. This small city of a resort also boasts a 600-seat theater, the Caribbean's largest casino, a mini-market, pharmacy, boutiques, health spa, and beauty salon.

For Kids: Club Cabana Nana keeps children five to twelve on the go from 10:30 A.M. until 3:30 P.M. every day except Wednesday, when the program shifts to the evening (5:30 to 8:30 P.M.) for movies and a pizza party. Days are filled with miniature golf, bowling, beach games, sports, and creative activities. The Club Cabana Nana package is priced at $80 per child weekly and includes daily lunch from the children's menu. Teenagers thirteen to seventeen are entertained with a beach disco party, bowling, tennis, windsurfing and snorkeling lessons, pizza night, table games, pool volleyball, and more. Separate fees are charged for some of these activities.

Accommodations: Versatile one-, two-, and three-bedroom suites in two sizes have master bedrooms, pull-out queen-size sofas, and fully equipped kitchenettes with extras like microwave ovens and blenders. All suites come with air-conditioning and ceiling fans; laundry facilities are located on each floor.

Kids under twelve stay free when accompanied by two adults. Additional person over twelve in room, $15 to $20 per night. Daily rates, double occupancy: mid-December to mid-April, studio $200 to $230, one-bedroom suite $240 to $275, two- and three-bedroom suites $425 to $755; spring and fall, studio $95 to $115, one-bedroom suite $125 to $150, two- and three-bedroom suites, $210 to $395. Inclusive rates available. J. E. Irausquin Boulevard 250, Oranjestad, Aruba; 800–835–7193 or 297–8–79000, fax 297–8–77208.

AMERICANA ARUBA BEACH RESORT AND CASINO

A clover-leaf pool in a grottolike setting in the middle of this 419-room resort on the upper west coast features waterfalls and two whirlpools. The place hums with activity throughout the day and evening, and children are kept busy in their own Adventure Club every day of the week. Inclusive rates cover a catamaran cruise, snorkel equipment, rafts, Sunfish and paddle boats, all meals and beverages, special ice creams, and gratuities. Scuba,

windsurfing, waterskiing, and banana boat rentals cost extra. American and Canadian tour groups come to enjoy beautiful Palm Beach, the Las Vegas-style shows, and the nonstop entertainment.
For Kids: The Americana Aruba Adventure Club operates seven days a week from 9:45 A.M. to 5:00 P.M. It's free of charge for children ages four to thirteen. A special activities room has toys, table games, books, and arts and crafts materials. Off-site excursions for an extra fee include bowling, miniature golf, and museum trips. Counselors will often accept younger children if they're toilet-trained.
Accommodations: Rooms have two doubles or one king-size bed; one-bedroom suites have a parlor with a queen-size sofa bed and a king-size bed in the bedroom. A second bedroom can be added to create a two-bedroom suite.
Daily rates: December 15 to April 15, $210 and up per person; rest of year, $160 and up per person. Children two to twelve $50 each, under two free. L. G. Smith Boulevard 83, Palm Beach, Aruba; 800–203–4475, 203–866–6606, or 297–8–64500, fax 297–8–63191.

COSTA LINDA BEACH RESORT ARUBA

Large families of six or eight can stay in spacious comfort at Costa Linda's all-suite resort of 155 rooms on Eagle Beach. A casual kids' program, gorgeous beach, and free-form tropical swimming pools exhaust even the most energetic child. There's also a playground, game room, tennis courts, fitness center, whirlpool, and nightly entertainment.
For Kids: Five- to twelve-year-olds can attend the program weekdays from 10:30 A.M. to 3:30 P.M. and weekends until 4:00 or 5:00 P.M. Activities range from face and T-shirt painting and carnival mask-making to beach games and sports.
Accommodations: All accommodations face the ocean, are air-conditioned, and have fold-out couches in the living room. Washers and dryers are located on every floor. Three-bedroom suites have a sun deck with a table and chairs, Jacuzzi, and barbecue; two-bedroom suites have balconies with a table and chairs. Baby cribs, playpens, and high chairs are available free of charge.
Two-bedroom units accommodate up to six people, and three-

bedroom units accommodate up to eight. Daily rates: winter, two-bedroom $440, three-bedroom $920; summer, two-bedroom $275, three-bedroom $595. The resort offers many special promotions throughout the year; be sure to inquire. J.E. Irausquin Blvd 59, Oranjestad, Aruba; 800–992–2015 or 297–8–38000, fax 297–8–36040.

RADISSON ARUBA CARIBBEAN RESORT AND CASINO

Such celebrities as Eddie Fisher and Liz Taylor used to stay here when this was the island's first high-rise resort, originally called La Grande Dame. Radisson refurbished the property, which now has an Olympic-size pool, exotic tropical gardens, an ice cream parlor, four restaurants, a fitness center, four lighted tennis courts, and all kinds of complimentary water sports including windsurfing, snorkeling, and waterskiing. A lively social activity program for adults and kids features a folkloric festival on Monday and carnival show and barbecue on Wednesday.

Accommodations: Air-conditioned rooms feature a terrace with an ocean or garden view; all have two double beds or one king-size bed. Connecting rooms are available upon request.

Children seventeen and under stay free in their parents' room. Daily rates, double occupancy: December 15 to April 15, $205 to $325; spring and fall, $155 to $195; summer, $99 to $175. No personal checks. J. E. Irausquin Boulevard 81, Palm Beach, Aruba; 800–333–3333 or 297–8–66555, fax 297–8–63260.

BUSHIRI BOUNTY BEACH RESORT

This beachfront property is part of the Aruba Hospitality Trades Training Center, and the cheerful and fresh-faced young staff who apprentice here are always eager to please. Inclusive rates cover all meals, drinks, water sports, tips, taxes, and nightly entertainment. Adults keep busy with weekly tournaments, sightseeing tours, pool volleyball, snorkeling instruction, Papiamento language lessons, dance classes, and theme parties. Kids have their own planned fun. A poolside barbecue offers hot dogs, hamburgers, and ribs throughout the day and evening, should you need a between-meal snack.

For Kids: Camp Bounty, for four- to twelve-year-olds, operates from 9:00 A.M. to 5:00 P.M. but can be adjusted to include ages two to four and twelve to fifteen as well. Indoor and outdoor games and activities such as "beach Olympics," charades, shell and scavenger hunts, arts and crafts, theme parties, movies, and cooking lessons are regular features. Baby-sitting can be arranged for a fee after 6:00 P.M. with advance notice.

Accommodations: Simple standard rooms have two double beds; deluxe rooms have two queen-size beds or one queen and one pull-out sofa. All rooms are air-conditioned.

Children under two stay free in their parents' room; cost for each child of ages two to eleven in parents' room is $50 to $60 per day. Daily rates, per person: $100 to $145, depending on time of year and size of room. The maximum number of occupants in any room is four, excluding infants in cribs. Extra beds and cribs for children available at no extra charge. Rates include airport transfers, taxes, and gratuities. Baby-sitting after six P.M., $7 per child per hour. L. G. Smith Boulevard 35, Aruba; 800–462–6868, or 203–266–0100, or 297–8–25216.

ARUBA SONESTA BEACH HOTEL, SUITES, AND CASINO

A short water-taxi ride takes guests to Sonesta's exclusive 40-acre tropical garden island with six beaches, water sports, tennis, a fitness center, and restaurants. Sonesta has two hotels that use the island, and both are in capital city Oranjestad in the Seaport Village Complex along the waterfront overlooking the city. Aruba Sonesta Resort and Casino is a traditional hotel with standard rooms; Aruba Sonesta Suites is best for families, featuring one-bedroom suites with kitchenettes and two enormous free-form pools. Sonesta Island is the headquarters for the water sports program, where guests can scuba dive, snorkel, and windsurf. Deep-sea fishing, sailing cruises, parasailing, and waterskiing can be arranged for an extra fee.

For Kids: Kids who participate in the "Just Us Kids" program for five- to twelve-year-olds take daily field trips to caves, nature trails, and natural bridges of Aruba; then they swim and play games the rest of the day. The program is offered to guests at no charge and operates from the Sonesta Suites hotel. Children can participate in whatever activities they wish. The daily program runs year-round from 10:00 A.M. to 4:30 P.M. and from 6:00 to 10:00 P.M. Evenings offer bingo, movie night, miniature golf, and arts and crafts.

Accommodations: Three-night family packages include accommodations for two adults and two children, full breakfast buffet, water sports, and all taxes and service charges: $689 to $828. Daily rates for one-bedroom suites start at $275 in season and $185 off-season. Children under eleven stay free in parents' room. L. G. Smith Boulevard 82, Oranjestad, Aruba; 800-SONESTA or 297–8–36000, fax 297–8–34389.

TAMARIJN ARUBA BEACH RESORT

Guests can borrow neon-bright bicycles to explore the surrounding neighborhood, but the action-packed program at this beachfront all-inclusive resort keeps most people on the property. There's every kind of theme night imaginable, from carnival to toga parties, plus goofy races, sunset cruises, beach volleyball, and unlimited food and drink. Kids can spoil their dinner with self-service popcorn, pizza, and TCBY frozen yogurt day or night, or they can dine at any of five restaurants. More action can be found around the swimming pool, a fitness area, and full water sports center.

For Kids: Two activities—one in the morning and one in the afternoon—are offered every day except Saturday. Three- to seven-year-olds might play hide-and-seek, watch a video, have a treasure hunt, or paint. Eight- to twelve-year-olds play bocce ball and soccer, make pizza, or hunt for shells. Most morning activities begin at 10:00 A.M., and the afternoon offerings usually start at 2:00 P.M.

Accommodations: Two-story buildings house air-conditioned standard hotel rooms with TV, terrace or patio, and one king-size or two double beds. All rooms are only a few steps from the white sand beach, and all have ocean views.

Daily rates, seven-night minimum. April 1 to September 31,

$144 per person; Christmas holiday period, $250 per person; rest of year, $156 to $200 per person. Children under two stay free in parents' room; ages two to twelve, $50 per child. For stays of less than seven nights, add $25 per person per stay. J. E. Irausquin Boulevard 41, Oranjestad, Aruba; 800–554–2008 or 297–8–24150, fax 297–8–34002.

WHAT TO SEE AND DO

Enjoy the pleasures of scuba diving without getting wet on an **Atlantis Submarine** tour. A catamaran transports you to the battery-powered, environmentally friendly sub. Once you're inside and have positioned yourself in front of your porthole window, the submarine descends and cruises past elaborate coral formations, lacy sea fans, and multicolored tropical fish. A crew member identifies the various sea plants and animals and is available to answer any questions. Discounts are available for families of four and up and for children ages four to sixteen. Departs from the Seaport Village Marina. Information, 297–8–37077, fax 297–8–26944; reservations, 297–8–36090, fax 297–8–37277.

Aruba also is known for its exceptional **windsurfing**. Those glorious trade winds create some of the most consistent and challenging windsurfing found anywhere. Beginners start in shallow, calmer waters, while expert windsurfers sail the high waves of Boca Grandi. Aruba's reputation among windsurfers has spread, and the island now hosts the annual Aruba Hi-Winds Pro Am World Cup in June, drawing top competitors from around the world.

Imagine a go-cart body with a windsurfer sail and you've got a **breeze-powered sailcart** that speeds across the fields. Aruba Sailcart supplies the carts, helmets, gloves, and instruction. Bushiri 23; 297–8–35133.

Boca Prins, about two-thirds of the way down the the north coast, is the location for the best **dune sliding.** Dress in jeans or heavy pants and strong shoes.

9

BARBADOS

THE COURTEOUS AND GOOD-NATURED residents of Barbados, known as Bajans, are among the best-liked in the Caribbean. Ask any recent visitors, and along with their vivid descriptions of white sandy beaches and balmy turquoise waters, you'll hear praises for the Bajans' warmth and their gracious hospitality. Good manners are expected in return, and it's a pleasure to see how quickly visiting children incorporate "good morning," "good evening," "please," and "thank you" into their daily routine.

Off the beaten track and the most easterly of all the Caribbean islands, Barbados went unseen by Columbus on his four expeditions to the West Indies. The British were the first Europeans to settle the island, in the 1600s. Unlike most other Caribbean islands, Barbados remained protected from invasion by other European colonizers, thanks to the trade winds that blow east to west, making it difficult to sail to Barbados from the other islands. Although Barbados achieved independence in 1966, many British customs, such as afternoon tea and a passion for cricket, have taken firm root here.

The rugged and windy east coast of Barbados softens the breeze of the trade winds, making the protected west coast relatively calm and sunny. As you might expect, the bulk of the tourist development is along the western and southern edges of the island, where you can find everything from extremely elegant hotels and lavish villas to simple cottages and rather ordinary condos. The hills and valleys in the interior are thick with sugarcane. Bridgetown, the capital city, houses about half of Barbados's population and sits at its southwest corner.

TOURIST INFORMATION

In the United States: Barbados Board of Tourism, 800 Second Avenue, New York, NY 10017; 212–986–6516 or 3440 Wilshire Boulevard, Suite 1215, Los Angeles, CA 90010; 213–380–2199.
In Canada: 5160 Yonge Street, Suite 1800, New York, Ontario M2N 6L9; 416–512–6569 or 615 Dorchester, Suite 960, Montreal, P.Q. H3B 1P5; 514–861–0085.
In Barbados: Barbados Board of Tourism, Harbour Road, Bridgetown, Barabdos, WI; 809–427–2623.

KNOW BEFORE YOU GO

Arriving and Departing: U.S. and Canadian citizens need a valid passport or an original birth certificate and photo ID (a voter's registration card is not sufficient), and a return ticket. Departure tax costs $10 per person.
Money: Barbados has its own currency, the Barbados dollar (BD$), which equals about 50¢ in U.S. currency, but U.S. and Canadian dollars are widely accepted.
Language: English is spoken throughout Barbados.
Staying Healthy: Avoid the manchineel tree, whose small green fruits, leaves, and sap are highly poisonous. Even standing under a manchineel tree during a rain can cause blisters.
Local Food: The flying fish is the national dish of Barbados, and you can find this delicate moist fish broiled, baked, deep-fried, stuffed, or stewed. Cou-cou is a mixture of cornmeal and okra with a spicy red Creole sauce. Pepperpot stew is a mix of oxtail, beef, and other meats, simmered overnight and flavored with cassareep, an ancient seasoning. Buljol is a cold salad of codfish, tomatoes, sweet peppers, onions, and celery, marinated and served raw.

WHERE TO STAY

SANDY LANE

The legendary Sandy Lane on the island's west coast has added a "Tree House Club" for children of ages two to seven to its list of amenities. The luxurious and refined resort is situated on 380 acres of a former sugarcane plantation and overlooks a half-mile crescent of sandy beach. It has a 3,000-square-foot free-form pool, an 18-hole golf course, a full water sports center, five tennis courts for day and night play, bikes for rent, and weekly entertainment. Children over the age of seven can enjoy supervised water sports, tennis and golf clinics, organized meals, and "coketail" parties before dinner. The resort's gourmet cuisine, world-class service, and sheer elegance have long drawn sophisticated guests. Now their sophisticated offspring can enjoy one of the Caribbean's most celebrated resorts.

For Kids: Located in the hotel gardens, the Tree House Club has indoor and outdoor play areas and a schedule that includes arts and crafts, sports, games, stories, nature walks, beach time, and movies. Activities change daily. Parents can participate in the activities with their kids or drop the children off anytime between 10:00 A.M. and 8:00 P.M. The program is complimentary and includes dinner but not lunch, which costs $10.

Accommodations: Choose from 30 elegant suites, most of which overlook the ocean, or from 90 double rooms. All have air-conditioning, room safes, mini-bars, and private patios or balconies. Two ocean-front restaurants serve fine cuisine, and a poolside snack bar offers more casual meals.

Rates include breakfast and dinner daily, airport transfers, and unlimited golf and tennis. Daily rates, double occupancy: mid-April to mid-December, $485 to $600 per person; mid-December to January 5, $820 to $1,200 per person; rest of year, $720 to $1,000 per person. St. James, Barbados, WI; 800–223–6800 or 809–432–1311, fax 809–432–2954.

GLITTER BAY

Originally the home of shipping magnate Sir Edward Cunard, Glitter Bay's sparkling Mediterranean-style buildings are set amid acres of exquisite gardens and perfectly manicured lawns. Two outdoor swimming pools are connected by a gently cascading waterfall and wooden footbridge. The smaller pool is shallow for children. Guests at Glitter Bay and its sister property, the Royal Pavilion, use the Robert Trent Jones golf course next door, and have signing privileges at the deluxe restaurants on both properties. The full complement of water sports—waterskiing, windsurfing, snorkeling, and catamaran sailing—are available to all guests. Horseback riding, scuba diving, fishing, and motor boating can be arranged for a fee. Two hard-surface tennis courts are lit for night play. There is an air-conditioned fitness and massage center and aerobics and body sculpting classes. A children's program operates during two months of the summer and over the Christmas and Easter holidays.

For Kids: Daily activities include some type of arts or crafts, such as leaf printing or making holiday decorations; sports such as ball games, relay races, or obstacle courses; beach time, sand castle building, treasure hunts, singing and dancing, story time, video shows, and free play. The program operates from 10:00 A.M. until 4:00 P.M., with a break for lunch from noon to 1:00 P.M. A special children's menu is available at breakfast, lunch, and dinner.

Accommodations: Glitter Bay's 83 guest rooms include double and twin bedded rooms, one- and two-bedroom suites, and two- and three-bedroom penthouses. Children sharing a room with their parents must stay in suites (which have fully equipped kitchens) or penthouses. All have air-conditioning, ceiling fans, mini bars, and private balconies. Cribs, high chairs, rollaway beds, and baby-sitting services can be arranged.

A full breakfast is included in the room rate during the summer (April 22 to December 15), and children under twelve in their parents' one-bedroom suite stay free during this time. The rate for a child under twelve in the parents' one-bedroom suite is $55 per night in winter, $35 in spring; children under age two stay free year-round. Meal plans are available. Daily rates, double occupancy: summer (April 24 to December 16), one-bedroom suite $250, two-bedroom suite $465, two- or three-bedroom penthouse $510 to $710. Winter (December 17 to March 31), one-bedroom suite $485, two-bedroom suite $880, two- or three-bedroom penthouse $930 to $1,320 (all higher over Christmas holidays); spring (April 1 to April 23), one-bedroom suite $365, two-bedroom suite $665, two- or three-bedroom penthouse $710 to $995. Porters, St. James, Barbados, WI; 800–283–8666 or 809–422–5555; fax 809–422–3940.

ALMOND BEACH VILLAGE

Shushing the kids for the benefit of other guests is a thing of the past at Almond Beach Village, where families have their own separate "village" complete with comfortable accommodations, a family restaurant, a children's center, playgrounds, and a family pool, all at one end of the 30-acre property. Couples and honeymooners (and families, too, if they want) stay in other secluded low-rise buildings in a villagelike atmosphere. Nine freshwater swimming pools, five tennis courts, all kinds of water sports (Sunfish sailing, waterskiing, aqua cycles, banana boats, windsurfing, kayaking, and catamaran sails) are available to all guests. A nursery takes care of infants under the age of two, while two- to thirteen-year-olds enjoy their own activities. The property stretches along a 1-mile strand of beach, and one price includes absolutely everything.

For Kids: Children can drop in daily between 9:00 A.M. and 5:00 P.M. and are divided into three age groups: two to four, five to nine, and ten to thirteen years. The large kids' room has video games, board games, toys, and computers with educational software. Kids are treated to nature walks, story time, pool and beach games, water sports, instruction in steel pan music, calypso and reggae dance, basketry, and boat rides.

Accommodations: One-bedroom suites have a living area with a fold-out couch, and a spacious bedroom. Laundry facilities are available. All rooms have balcony or patio, air-conditioning, coffee machine, and safe. The resort has a family restaurant, three other restaurants, and four bars.

Rates include meals, afternoon tea, drinks, water sports, room service for lunch and dinner, kids' program, field trips, nightly entertainment, island tours, airport transfers, and all gratuities and service charges. First child under twelve stays free in parents' suites, all other children under twelve, $50 per child per night. Daily rates, double occupancy: junior and one-bedroom suites $280 to $630 depending on season, size, and view. St. Peter, Barbados, WI; 800–4–ALMOND or 809–422–4900, fax 809–422–0617.

VILLA AND CONDO RENTALS

Villas and Apartments Abroad handles villa rentals throughout the island. 420 Madison Avenue, New York, NY 10017; 212–759–1025 or 800–433–3020, fax 212–755–8316.

Barbados Board of Tourism lists rental properties. 809–427–2623.

WHAT TO SEE AND DO

Snorkelers can follow marked underwater snorkeling trails around 7-mile-long Dottin's Reef at **Folkstone Underwater Park**, off the west coast north of Holetown. The reef is teeming with colorful fish, sea anemones, human-size sea fans, soft corals, and sea lilies. Glass-bottom boats are available for visitors who don't want to get their feet wet. Folkstone Park has a playground and picnicking area and a small restaurant. A small marine museum open Monday through Friday 10:00 A.M. to 5:00 P.M., Saturday and Sunday 10:00 A.M. to 6:00 P.M., contains exhibits showing the life of the sea.

Underground streams have carved out spectacular limestone caverns over the centuries at **Harrison's Cave**. A small electric tram carries you through lighted subterranean passages and chambers that glow with actively growing crystalline stalagmites and stalactites. Near the lowest point of the cave, visitors encounter a dramatic 40-foot waterfall that crashes into a deep blue-green pool. Tours are given every hour from 9:00 A.M. to 4:00 P.M.

Night tours of the cavern are combined with a dinner served on top of the cave, cleverly staged so you appear to be dining deep inside the caverns; 809–438–6640.

Tiny sea anemones that look like delicate flowers as they open and close their tentacles have given **Animal Flower Cave** near North Point its name. The sea cave, which has been eroded by wave action and drips with stalactites and stalagmites, is open to visitors for a small fee. You can tour the cave and see the tiny creatures, also known locally as seaworms, and then pause for a cold glass of lemonade at the quirky refreshment stand/cafe run by Winston and Manuel Ward when you're done. Ask to see their pet sheep and its 7-Up-drinking talent-show trick; 809–439–8797.

Footpaths through a lush glade of mahogany trees at the **Barbados Wildlife Reserve** travel past groups of West African green monkey families playing, feeding their babies, and foraging for food. Other resident animals include raccoons, box tortoises, caimans, peacocks, deer, wallabies, and otters. Squawking parrots converse in the aviary. Open daily, 10:00 A.M. to 5:00 P.M. On Highway 1 between Speightstown and Belleplaine in northern Barbados. 809–422–8826.

Sam Lord's Castle was built by the infamous and treacherous buccaneer who made his reputation (and much of his fortune) by lighting lanterns to trick ships' captains into thinking they had reached a safe harbor. After the ships foundered on the rocks and reefs, he would plunder them and carry off their treasures. Legend has it that some of his loot is still buried on the castle grounds. The castle is now the Marriott resort, but visitors can view the old building and see its magnificent mahogany columns, plaster ceiling, and furniture Sam Lord imported and used. Keep an eye out for the ghosts that are said to haunt the castle. Long Bay; 809–423–7350.

Atlantis Submarine descends as deep as 150 feet to explore shipwrecks, coral reefs, and the creatures that inhabit them. The battery-run environmentally friendly sub gives a scuba diver's-eye view of the magnificent underwater world of Barbados. Hour-long tours are offered for persons of ages four and up, with special discounts for children; 809–436–8929 or 809–436–8932.

If you like **horseback riding**, Valley Hill Stables in Christchurch (809–423–6180) at the southern end of the island will pick you up at your hotel and transport you to the horses. In southeast Barbados, Ye Old Congo Road Stables in St. Philip (809–423–8293) specializes in rides through sugarcane plantations; and Brighton Stables (809–425–9381) on the west coast offers sunrise and sunset rides along beaches and through palm groves.

Cricket season is June through late December, but test matches are played from January through May. Check the local paper for details when you arrive.

The rough east coast is famous for its **surfing** waves, and travelers have come here for years to surf the Soup Bowl near Bathsheba. Each November, an international surfing competition is held on this part of the island.

Kids get a chuckle out of walking the plank and jumping into the clear turquoise water beneath the **Jolly Rogers Pirate Party Ship**. On trips, the ship anchors off a beautiful beach where lunch is served, and kids can play on the sand or swing off a rope on the ship. A small skit is presented, sometimes using guests as members of the cast; 809–436–6424.

10

BONAIRE

DURING THE ISLAND-WIDE "Family Month" in August, Bonaire resorts, restaurants, and tour operators offer enticing family price packages and programs, but families come to Bonaire year-round to enjoy unparalleled diving and snorkeling in one of the world's most unspoiled and protected coral reef systems. The island is out of the hurricane belt, which means that the reefs have never been destroyed by storms, nor are they clouded by freshwater runoff, since only about 12 inches of rain falls annually. Water visibility of 100 to 150 feet is common.

Credit for the far-sighted preservation of this pristine underwater paradise goes to the government and people of Bonaire who created the Bonaire Marine Park. The park includes the entire island's coastline down to a depth of 200 feet, and strict rules govern its use.

The lush and spectacular underwater landscape, bursting with crowds of coral and throngs of fish, is in direct contrast to the flat and dry conditions above the water. The entire desertlike northern section of the island has been set aside as 13,500-acre Washington-Slagbaai National Park and is either home or waystation to 190 different species of birds. Snorkeling and birdwatching are superb here. Unique ground-bound Bonaireian animal species include the blue lizard and the anolis tree lizard with its distinctive yellow dewlap. At the southern end of the island, adjacent to salt ponds still in operation is a sanctuary for the island's largest pink flamingo nesting ground.

Bonaire is the "B" in the ABC islands (Aruba and Curaçao

are the other two) that lie just off the coast of Venezuela. Carnival is a lively affair held from late February to early March, but the island's biggest celebration is the International Sailing Regatta in October, when the island delights in boat racing, steel band music, dancing, and feasting.

TOURIST INFORMATION

In the United States: Bonaire Government Tourist Office, 444 Madison Avenue, Suite 2403, New York, NY 10022; 800-U-Bonaire or 212–832–0779, fax 212–838–3407.
In Canada: 512 Duplex Avenue, Toronto, Ontario, M4R 2E3; 800–267–7600 or 416–484–4864, fax 416–485–8256.
On Bonaire: Kaya Simon Bolivar 12, Kralendijk, Bonaire; 599–7–8322 or 599–7–8639.

KNOW BEFORE YOU GO

Arriving and Departing: U.S. and Canadian citizens need a passport, a notarized birth certificate, or a voter registration card plus a return or ongoing ticket. Departure tax is $6 for visitors going to Curaçao, $10 for all other destinations.
Money: The official currency is the Netherlands Antilles florin or guilder (NAfl or Afl), but U.S. dollars are accepted everywhere. A government tax of $4.50 per night is levied on all room rates.
Language: Bonaire's official language is Dutch, but most residents speak Papiamento, a mix of Spanish, Portuguese, Dutch, English, African, and French. *Bon bini* isn't candy; it's the way to say "welcome" in Papiamento. English is spoken by most people who work in the tourist industry.
Staying Healthy: The main hospital is in Kralendijk. Mosquitoes come out in force in fall and early winter, so coat yourself with bug repellent throughout the day. The eastern side of Bonaire is subject to violent trade winds, rough surf, and dangerous undertows. Beware of snorkeling or diving in this area.

FAMILY MONTH

Billing itself as the ideal family retreat, Bonaire has established August as Family Month, when hotels, resorts, dive operators, and restaurants offer special deals for parents and kids. Children receive a special welcoming kit at check-in that contains a Bonaire coloring book, NAUI snorkeling book, marine life mini-puzzle, and coupon book.

Special activities are held weekly, including a "Sports Day" at Lac Bay with local children, eco-walks in Washington-Slagbaai National Park, windsurfing, and snorkeling lessons. In the evenings, magicians, folkloric dance, movies, and games entertain the whole family.

Oscarina Yacht Charters takes families on a special Treasure Hunt Cruise. Kids are picked up at the waterfront of their hotels for a tradewind sail to uninhabited Klein Bonaire—a 1,500-acre island due west of Kralendijk. Guided by a special treasure map, the kids' search for treasure begins, followed by a swim or snorkel and a pizza party.

WHERE TO STAY

In this scuba-centered island, most hotels offer dive packages with unlimited use of tanks, unlimited shore diving, boat trips, meals, and more.

CAPTAIN DON'S HABITAT

Captain Don Stewart has developed a local reputation as a raconteur, a diver extraordinaire, and the driving force behind efforts to preserve Bonaire's reefs and marine life. His resort is best known as a five-star diving training facility, but he also has welcomed families for many years. In August, Captain Don hosts two all-inclusive family weeks. Parents can scuba dive as much as they like, while kids of ages five to thirteen head out on special supervised snorkeling trips, excursions, island tours, treasure hunts, and boat trips. People come to Captain Don's to dive, and they get what they come for, with unlimited round-the-clock shore dives and two boat dives a day with most packages, and unlimited boat dives with upgraded packages. Dive guides present slide shows on marine creatures Sunday and Monday nights throughout the year, and Captain Don himself shows up once or twice a week to entertain his guests with stories of life in the deep.

Accommodations: All units are air-conditioned, with private baths. Two-bedroom cottages and villa deluxe suites sleep four and have kitchens, living rooms, and patios. Standard hotel rooms face the ocean. All units can accommodate an extra person.

Family week packages for two adults and up to two children with both parents diving cost $2,687 to $3,500 (less if only one parent dives). Rates include one week's accommodations, unlimited diving for parents, the children's activities program, unlimited boat trips, daily buffet breakfast, airport transfers, lunch for the kids, entertainment, beach parties, and trips. P.O. Box 88, Bonaire; 800–327–6709 or 599–7–8290, fax 599–7–8240.

SAND DOLLAR BEACH CLUB

This resort's spacious time-share apartments and a five-star dive center and photo shop attract serious divers and their families. Scuba instruction for all levels of diving includes coursework for junior certification (ages twelve and up). The Sand Dollar Club for children offers supervised activities for a few hours each week during the year, and more during the month of August. The resort sits on a low bluff overlooking the Caribbean, and there's an Olympic-size swimming pool and a tiny beach right in front. Serious beachcombers head to Sunset Beach a short walk away. Snorkelers can jump off the dive platform, swim a few strokes and come to Bari Reef just offshore, where views of orange elephant-ear sponges and purple tube sponges provide a backdrop for schools of carnival-costumed fish.

For Kids: All kids under fifteen are handed a Sand Penny Club book when they arrive, filled with coupons for snacks, surprises, and various discounts on lessons and sailing trips. The supervised activities take place on the terrace around the pool on Wednesdays and Fridays from 1:00 to 3:00 P.M. and usually feature an arts and crafts project. In August the program has expanded hours, and Rascals in Paradise operates a program from here (see page 16).

Accommodations: Luxurious and comfortable studios and one-, two-, and three-bedroom condominiums (84 units in all) have air-conditioning, private patios or balconies, and complete kitchens. Living-room couches turn into beds, and each unit's contemporary tropical decor varies a bit according to the individual owner's taste. Studios can accommodate two adults and two children, as can one-bedroom units. Two-bedroom units sleep four adults and two kids, and three-bedroom units house up to six adults and two kids. The club has an ice-cream parlor and beachside restaurant open for breakfast, lunch, and dinner.

Children twelve and under stay free in parents' room (maximum two children). Daily rates, double occupancy: December 15 to April 15, $160 to $350; rest of year, $150 to $300, depending on size. Meal plans and scuba equipment rentals are available. P.O. Box 262, Bonaire; 800–328–2288, or 599–7–8738, fax 599–7–8760.

SUNSET BEACH HOTEL

This popular 85-unit hotel is located on a 600-foot strand of white sand beach with shallow water for swimming. Rooms are in two-story buildings overlooking tree-filled gardens. The on-site dive shop offers trips in three boats, and a water sports center rents windsurfing equipment, Sunfish, snorkeling gear, and boogie boards. Indoor and outdoor games, two lighted tennis courts, and a miniature golf course keep the kids busy when they're not in the water.

Accommodations: Air-conditioned rooms have two double beds or one king-size bed, a small refrigerator, coffeemaker, safe, TV, and phone.

Daily rates, double occupancy: December 18 to April 15, $110 to $175, depending on size of room; April 16 to December 17, $75 to $140. Extra rollaway beds available at no charge. P.O. Box 333, Bonaire; 800–354–8142 or 599–7–8291, fax 599–7–8118.

DIVI FLAMINGO BEACH RESORT AND CASINO

With more beach to offer than other hotels, this resort attracts its fair share of families. Parents who dive take advantage of the five-star dive shop, and the entire family can splash around in a special safe area roped off for swimming on the beach overlooking Calabas Reef. The property, originally called the Zeebad, opened in 1952 as Bonaire's first hotel, but it's been redone many times since. Informal, friendly, and lively, the active beachfront is the scene for beach games and contests for kids and adults. The resort also has freshwater pools, a tennis court, and two open-air dining rooms.

Accommodations: Hotel rooms and studio apartments are available, all of them air-conditioned. The studios have kitchenettes and are newer.

Children under sixteen stay free in parents' room (maximum two children). A special inclusive family package is offered in August; call for prices. Daily rates, double occupancy: December 15 to April 15, $125 to $215; rest of year, $84 to $125 per night. Dive and meal packages available. J. A. Abraham Boulevard, Kralendijk, Bonaire; 800–367–3484 or 599–5–8285, fax 599–7–8283.

WHAT TO SEE AND DO

Bonaire Marine Park was created when the World Wildlife Fund, in cooperation with the Bonaire government, supplied seed money to ensure that the island's magnificent coral reefs would remain undeveloped and in pristine condition for future generations. Virtually the entire coastline and the small offshore island of Klein Bonaire are protected down to 200 feet below sea level. Visitors may not take anything from this area, and permanent moorings minimize anchor damage. Divers pay an admission charge of $10, which entitles them to unlimited diving for one calendar year. Fees are used to maintain the park, and can be paid at all scuba facilities or at the Marine Park headquarters in the Old Fort at Kralendijk. Pick up a copy of the guidebook, *The*

Guide to Bonaire Marine Park, which lists 44 dive sites that have been marked by moorings and identifies their degrees of difficulty. 599–7–8444.

To visit Bonaire's unusual **Salt Flats**, head south out of Kralendijk along the southern scenic route past one of the world's most powerful radio transmitters, the 810,000-watt Trans World Radio. Continue south along the shore full of sea birds until you reach mountains of white sea salt, where AKZO Antilles International Salt Company maintains its salt-gathering operation. The distillation process starts with sea water that flows into a rectangular pond. The sun and winds evaporate most of the water, and the remainder is pumped into a second pond where more water evaporates; this process continues until the water is completely evaporated. Pink flamingos can be seen feeding in the briny, multi-colored ponds.

Salt production was once Bonaire's most important source of revenue, since the island didn't have enough fertile soil or fresh water to support a sugar crop. Slaves imported to the island to work the salt pans lived in horribly cramped **slave huts**, which have been reconstructed in Rode Pan. The men who worked the salt pans walked seven hours each Friday afternoon to visit their families on another part of the island. On Sundays they returned to their labor camp.

Washington-Slagbaai National Park is a 13,500-acre tract of tropical desert terrain at the northern end of Bonaire which can be explored with a four-wheel drive vehicle or on foot (bring lots of sunscreen and water). Pick up an Excursion Guide at the entrance to the park to learn about the park's geography, history, geology, and plant and animal life. Keep a sharp look out for iguanas, donkeys, and goats. Salina Mathijs, a salt flat on the eastern side of the national park, is another good spot for viewing flamingos. The park is open daily from 8:00 A.M. to 5:00 P.M.

Pink flamingoes also feed and nest at **Goto Meer,** a beautiful saltwater lagoon with an island in the middle, in the northern part of Bonaire. The flamingoes' main nesting season is between January and June. Bonaire is home to 15,000 of the spindly-legged creatures.

Lac Bay on Bonaire's windward (eastern) side is the ultimate

windsurfing location due to its steady onshore winds and protected cove. Windsurfing Bonaire rents boards and offers lessons for beginning to advanced windsurfers. The staff makes pickups twice a day at all hotels on the island; 800–748–8733, fax 599–7–5363.

11

BRITISH VIRGIN ISLANDS

DOZENS OF HIDDEN ISLANDS and secret coves once lured pirates to the British Virgin Islands (BVI) to stage raids on galleons carrying Mexican and Peruvian gold and silver. Legend has it that some of the nefarious seadogs hid their stolen treasure in concealed caves and never returned to retrieve it. Tales of pirate treasure hidden on Norman Island, just south of Tortola, inspired Robert Louis Stevenson's classic tale, *Treasure Island*. Another uninhabited BVI, Dead Chest Island, inspired the song, "Fifteen Men on the Deadman's Chest (Yo, Ho, Ho, and a Bottle of Rum)," after the infamous Long John Silver punished 15 of his crew by leaving them on this tiny island without food or water for a week. Other well-known pirates and privateers who made the BVI their headquarters were Blackbeard Teach, Bluebeard, Captain Kidd, and Sir Francis Drake.

To this day, the islands' calm waters, steady breezes, and beautiful island anchorages make them a first-class sailing destination. You can charter a yacht for a day, a week, or a month, and spend lazy hours on a different private island beach every day.

The British Virgin Islands are a major center for crewed charter boats and host the largest concentration of bare boats (boats rented without crew to experienced sailors) in the world. See page 36 for more information on bare-boat charters.

The clarity of the water and the protection the islands themselves provide from winds and currents combine to offer exceptional snorkeling and diving. Most popular with pint-size snorkelers are the four caves at Norman Island where schools of tropical fish swim by close enough to touch, and legends of hidden treasure motivate the most reluctant swimmer to take a deeper look.

Hundreds of wrecks coated in coral lie offshore. The most famous of these, the *RMS Rhone*, sank in 1867 and sits in 75 feet of water, but her rudder juts up to within 15 feet of the surface, allowing snorkelers to enjoy the view. The *Rhone* is the center-piece of Rhone National Marine Park, which includes underwater coral caves, Blonde Rock (a submerged rock pinnacle), and Dead Chest Island, a nesting site for sea birds.

Resorts in the British Virgin Islands tend to be small and personal, since no building can be higher than the tallest palm tree. Virgin Gorda and Tortola, the two largest islands, handle the core of the tourist trade, but neither is very crowded.

TOURIST OFFICES

In North America: British Virgin Island Tourist Board, 370 Lexington Avenue, New York, NY 10017; 800–835–8530 or 212–696–0400. Or 1804 Union Street, San Francisco, CA 94123; 800–835–8530 or 415–775–0344.

In the British Virgin Islands: Social Security Building, Water-front Street, Road Town, Tortola, BVI; 809–494–3134 or Virgin Gorda Yacht Harbour, 809–495–5181.

KNOW BEFORE YOU GO

Arriving and Departing: You'll need a passport, voter registration card, or birth certificate with photo ID to enter the islands. Departure tax is $8 per person if leaving by air and $5 if leaving by sea.

Money: The U.S. dollar is the official currency.

Language: English is spoken throughout the British Virgin Islands.

Staying Healthy: Peebles Hospital in Road Town, Tortola, handles emergencies; 809–494–3497.

TORTOLA

Steep green hills traverse along the narrow length of this slow-paced, easygoing island. If you plan to rent a car, you'll need a four-wheel drive to maneuver the roads' hairpin turns and steep grades. At Tortola's southern edge, jagged mountain peaks soar 1,700 feet; and on its northern shore, you'll find sugar-fine white sand and tropical groves. The island is 12 miles long and 3 miles wide, so you're never far from a beautiful beach or breathaking view.

WHERE TO STAY

FORT RECOVERY

Ten charming little bungalows are steps away from their own white sand beach on the calm Caribbean side of the island. Built around the remains of a seventeenth-century fort, the clean and fully equipped cottages create their own friendly small community. Boat trips, car rentals, and island tour arrangements can be made from the front desk. It's best to have a car to pick up groceries and explore some of the island's other magnificent beaches.
Accommodations: Villas accommodate two to eight people and feature air-conditioning, full kitchens, and daily housekeeping service. Rates include a continental breakfast, and a restaurant serves other meals when you tire of cooking. A supermarket is a ten-minute walk away.

Daily rates: one-bedroom villa for two people (accommodates up to four), $160 in high season, $108 in low season; two-bedroom villa for four people, $260 in high season, $190 in low season. Additional people in villas, $25 per person per night; cribs, $10 per night. P.O. Box 239, Road Town, Tortola, BVI; 800–367–8455 or 809–495–4467, fax 809–495–4036.

LONG BAY BEACH RESORT

Families wanting to headquarter in spacious surroundings can have all the comforts of home (plus daily housekeeping service—

the staff even washes the dishes) in Long Bay's two- and three-bedroom private villas set on a hill above a long, sparkling white beach. These beautifully decorated units feature large outside terraces with barbecues and completely outfitted kitchens. Other simpler and smaller accommodations are tucked into the hills or sit on stilts at the water's edge. The ruins of an old sugar mill house a casual restaurant next to the pool, just steps from the powdery beach, and a second restaurant serves sophisticated candle-lit dinners. On-site car rental allows guests to rent for a day or two at a time.

Accommodations: Simple hillside rooms overlook the ocean; studios farther up the hill are larger, and beach-front cabanas at the water's edge have their own hammocks. All units have refrigerators, toaster ovens, coffee machines, air-conditioning, and safes. Two- to five-bedroom villas have complete kitchens, living and dining areas, patios with grills, and ocean views; the largest have pools.

Children under twelve stay free in parents' room; two children sharing a separate room are charged the single rate. Each additional adult is $30 in any accommodation. The Family Escape package includes rooms, airport transfers, eight dinners, daily breakfast, rental car for three days, sailing trip, and other extras: rates start at $2,099 for seven nights. Daily rates: two-bedroom villas, $250 to $425; five-bedroom villas, $600 to $1,180, depending on time of year. Three- and four-bedroom villas also available. P.O. Box 433, Road Town, Tortola, BVI; 800–729–9599 or 809–495–4252.

RHYMER'S BEACH HOTEL

Remember the places you stayed on the cheap as a college student, with small and tired rooms but great locations? If raising kids has reduced your vacation budget to that of your college days, Rhymer's is a real bargain. It's situated on the west coast of Tortola, right on white sand Cane Bay Beach backed by towering green hills. All units have tiny kitchenettes and air-conditioning, and its market on the ground floor has a wide selection of fresh produce, dairy products, and groceries at decent prices. Rhymer's is also known for its lively beachfront bar and restaurant. A police station sits directly behind the hotel across the street, so the college students who do stay here can't get too wild.

Accommodations: Very basic rooms have queen-size beds, and a single bed can be added easily. Rooms can connect through the balcony—a good option if you have several older kids. Don't expect much in the way of service; housekeepers clean and supply fresh linens daily. A laundromat is on the premises.

Daily rates, double occupancy: December 15 to April 15, $85; rest of year, an unbelievable $50. Additional per person in room, $10 per night. P.O. Box 570, Cane Garden Bay, Tortola, BVI; 809–495–4639 or 809–495–4215.

HERITAGE VILLAS VACATION APARTMENTS

Heritage's plain one- and two-bedroom apartments are perched on a cliff overlooking a scalloped line of some of Tortola's most beautiful white sand beaches, along the Island's north coast. You'll need a car to get to the beaches, but if you are looking for a low-priced, clean place where you can cook and sleep, this is a good option.

Accommodations: Six one-bedroom and three two-bedroom apartments are a little tired and very simply furnished but have small kitchens, and living and dining areas. All have breathtaking views.

Daily rates, double occupancy: December 15 to April 15, $115 to $170 ($800 to $1,300 per week); rest of year, $70 to $110 ($485 to $750 per week). P.O. Box 2019, Carrot Bay, Tortola, BVI; 809–494–5842.

VIRGIN GORDA

WHERE TO STAY

BITTER END YACHT CLUB

Long popular with the yacht crowd, this one-of-a-kind inclusive resort with a strong emphasis on sailing offers many interesting daily options in addition to swimming, sunning, and snorkeling.

Guests have unlimited use of the club's 65 sailboats, as well as small motorboats, windsurfing equipment, kayaks, and dinghies. Captained boat trips are offered to the famous Baths (see page 87), to nearby small islands, and to exceptional snorkeling sites. The Bitter End's location at the northernmost "bitter end" of Virgin Gorda is accessible only by boat, and a small ferry takes you to its dock. The 25-acre resort faces the naturally protected, lagoonlike North Sound, and offers near-perfect sailing conditions: steady trade winds and calm seas. Beginning sailors find the gentle breezes and peaceful waters perfect for safe learning. Your kids can participate in a special three-hour daily sailing class from May to September, or the entire family can take a complimentary short course any time of year. If you're bitten by the bug, the resort's worldclass sailing school will teach you to master the seas.

The water sports center is the hub of the place, but there's also action at the large pool (with a bar and grill) and at each of the three different beaches roped off for swimming, complete with rafts and diving boards. Fins are furnished, but bring your own mask and snorkel.

Accommodations: Two types of rooms are available. Beachfront rooms are rustic, cooled by ceiling fans and window-screen ventilation. All have small refrigerators, decks with hammocks and lounge chairs, ventwood closets and partitions, and no phone or TV. Beachfront units are duplexes; a single family can reserve both sides, which connect through the deck.

Commodore rooms are much more elegant, with air-conditioning, phones, TVs, and VCRs by request. They have two queens or a king-size bed, refrigerator, coffee maker, fans, and an open screened garden shower. These rooms also have connecting doors through the decks.

Eight liveaboard charter yachts are provisioned, and can accommodate up to six people.

There are no room keys: safety deposit boxes are available in the office, and a security guard patrols the property at night. No cribs, high chairs, or baby supplies are provided.

Daily rates do not include excursions, but a number of packages include three meals a day, unlimited sailing, the sports program, and all excursions. Daily rates, double occupancy: winter, $430 to $570; summer, $330 to $470. Extra child age six to sixteen in parents' room, $100 per day. Seven-night Admiral's Summer Family Package for two adults and two to four children: pay for one room and the second room is free. Thanksgiving week is family week, and kids ages six to sixteen stay for half price. The week-long Admiral's Package costs seven times the daily rate but includes all excursions plus meals, airport transfers, and water sports. P.O. Box 46, Virgin Gorda, BVI; 800–872–2392 or 809–494–2746, fax 809–494–3557.

BIRAS CREEK RESORT

Each guest is assigned a fat-tire bicycle at check-in for his or her personal use on the paths at Biras Creek's 150 acres. Since the country estate–like resort is accessible only by boat and is entirely self-contained, it's a safe place to let your children explore on their own while you relax in the sun. Accommodations are very private, with one-story villas housing two separate suites, perfect for a family of four or more. Supervised lessons are available for children who want to learn to windsurf, sail, snorkel, waterski, or play tennis. The resort has a lovely swimming pool, and nature trails for hiking and jogging crisscross the property. The full array of complimentary water sports are available, and meals are included in the rates. Everything here is done well. Children must be at least six years old.

Accommodations: Suites have sitting rooms, separate bedrooms, patios, and ceiling fans. Grand suites have air-conditioned bedrooms and oversized living rooms with terraces. A two-bedroom private villa with its own kitchen is available for families seeking the ultimate in privacy. All suites overlook the ocean or gardens.

Summer Family Vacation package, available mid-June through October, features a second suite free, a half-day outing to the Baths, and other extras.

Daily rates, double occupancy including breakfast and dinner: garden suite, winter $395, summer $340; ocean suite, winter $495, summer $425; grand suite, winter $595, summer $550; and villa, winter $695, summer $625. Extra person in room $60 per day.

Lunch is $15 per person per day. P.O. Box 54, Virgin Gorda, BVI; 800–223–1108 or 809–494–3555, fax 809–494–3557.

LITTLE DIX BAY

"Casual elegance" is the phrase often used to describe the beauty and service at Little Dix Bay, in the northwest corner of Virgin Gorda. Set on a half-mile crescent-shaped bay and protected by a coral reef, this resort offers hilltop rooms with views of the sea beyond or seaside rooms where the beach is a few steps from the door. Children of all ages are welcome to while away the hours swimming, snorkeling, collecting shells, and enjoying special lessons tailored just for them. Toys and books are available to young visitors, and the restaurant has a special children's menu. A complimentary water taxi ferries guests to other island beaches. Sunfish, sailboats, kayaks, waterskiing, snorkel gear, and tennis are complimentary; sailing excursions, hoserback riding, scuba diving, fishing, and boat charters are available for an extra charge.
For Kids: A children's program operates daily year-round. Children of all ages may participate, as long as they are toilet-trained. Activities include nature walks, games, swimming, and videos.
Accommodations: Rooms differ in location more than in interior amenities. Regular rooms have garden or ocean views, slightly larger deluxe rooms have ocean views, and premium rooms are on the beach; one-bedroom beachfront suites are also available.

From May 1 to September 30, a second bedroom for children accompanying their parents is half price, year-round kids up to sixteen years are free in their parents' room, but only three people to a bedroom. P.O. Box 70, Virgin Gorda, BVI; 800–928–3000 or 809–495–5555, fax 809–495–5661.

GUAVABERRY SPRING BAY VACATION HOMES

Reasonable prices, fully equipped kitchens, and a great location within walking distance of a good swimming beach and Virgin Gorda's famous Baths make these vacation homes an excellent value for families who want a self-catering holiday. Sixteen modern, fully equipped one- and two-bedroom homes are elevated to provide views of Sir Francis Drake Channel, especially attractive at dusk when glorious sunset colors play over the water. A small, well-stocked "mini-mart" operates on the honor system, and the office is open daily to help guests arrange dinner reservations, car rentals, day sail charters, and snorkel trips.

Accommodations: One- and two-bedroom houses are completely equipped with full-size refrigerators and stoves, linens, and beach towels. Each house has a barbecue and daily housekeeping service. Two-bedroom houses have two baths and can accommodate five people; one-bedrooms house three people. The owners also manage privately owned deluxe homes in the vicinity, some with their own pools and tennis courts.

One-bedroom houses, $90 in summer, $135 in winter; extra person, $15 per day in summer, $20 per day in winter. Two-bedroom houses, $140 in summer, $200 in winter; fifth person, $15 per day in summer, $20 per day in winter. P.O. Box 20, Virgin Gorda, BVI; 809–495–5227, fax 809–495–5283.

WHAT TO SEE AND DO

Named for the huge granite boulders that form a natural sculpture display, **the Baths** offer superb snorkeling in calm weather. Walk the beach trail through the giant boulders and weave in and out of tide pools, across skinny wooden bridges, and through narrow crevices. Even when they are crowded with day-trippers, the Baths are still worth a visit. A complex with a restaurant, swimming pool, and gift shops at the top of the path offers refreshing snacks and souvenirs.

PETER ISLAND

WHERE TO STAY

PETER ISLAND RESORT AND YACHT HARBOR

If luxury and seclusion are what your family is looking for, this elegant 1,800-acre private island resort has every comfort you could possibly desire. Sun and swim on Deadman's Bay Beach, one of the world's most picturesque palm-fringed crescents of sand, or choose from the island's four other secluded beaches; Reef's Bay Beach is known for its excellent shelling. Explore the private island on mountain bikes or beach cruisers, or on foot along hiking and jogging trails. Active families can windsurf, snorkel, and sail, while those wanting undisturbed privacy can arrange to be dropped off alone with a picnic lunch on White Bay Beach. Dive BVI offers scuba lessons and all levels of dives, and Peter Island has more than 80 dive sites. Full and half-day snorkeling, day sails, and world-class sport fishing expeditions are available. The resort's freshwater pool overlooks the ocean, and a number of restaurants, casual cafes, and bars keep guests well fed. An airy clubhouse has a library with books, board games, and movies in the evenings. Children must be at least eight years old.

Accommodations: All guest rooms overlook the beach or ocean, and have fans and air-conditioning, separate sitting areas, verandahs, and patios. Three villas offer spacious family accommodations that include a living room, two bedrooms, kitchen facilities, and two bathrooms. One four-bedroom villa has its own private saltwater pool, two housekeepers, and a gardener. Tortola is a 20-minute boat ride from Peter Island.

Children stay free in their parents' room during Peter Island's summer resort packages. Mailing address: P.O. Box 211, Road Town, Tortola, BVI; 800–346–4451 or 809–494–2561, fax 809–494–2313 or 616–776–6456.

12

CAYMAN ISLANDS

SCUBA ENTHUSIASTS FROM ALL over the globe rank the Cayman Islands as one of the world's top dive destinations, but if your children are too young to strap on a tank of compressed air, the diverse and abundant sea life and crystalline waters are just as rewarding to explore with mask and snorkel. Dozens of spectacular underwater sites offer views of colorful fish, elaborate coral formations, sea turtles, hidden caves, and shipwrecks. The island government has created marine park systems on all three islands—Grand Cayman, Cayman Brac, and Little Cayman—to protect these undersea treasures.

Stingray City in North Sound off Grand Cayman is the Cayman's most famous dive site, and certainly one your children should not miss, where Atlantic stingrays frolic with snorkelers and divers in 12 feet of water. About 30 of the huge pancake-flat rays cavort with divers at any one time, hoping for a handout and a gentle rub on the stomach.

Gorgeous beaches entice sun worshippers just as the hidden caves and coves once lured pirates like Blackbeard and Sir Henry Morgan, who darted out to plunder Spanish galleons carrying gold from Mexico and South America. Sea turtles were once so abundant here that Columbus named the islands Las Tortugas (The Turtles) when he spotted them in 1503, but the name was later changed to Cayman. Sailors and fishermen brought the turtles to the edge of extinction, but these creatures are now protected.

Tourism and banking drive the Caymanian economy, with

Grand Cayman, the largest and most populated island, carrying most of the activity. Full-service resorts with children's programs and spacious beach-front condominiums line the edges of Grand Cayman's sparkling Seven Mile Beach on the island's western shore; and many families headquarter here to enjoy the sun, sand, and convenient services. Those wanting quiet and seclusion head to other parts of Grand Cayman or to Little Cayman and Cayman Brac.

TOURIST INFORMATION

In the U.S.: *Houston*: 2 Memorial City Plaza, 820 Gessner, Suite 170, Houston, TX 77024; 713–461–1317. *Illinois*: 9525 Bryn Mawr Avenue, Suite 160, Rosemont, IL 60018; 708–678–6446. *Los Angeles*: 3440 Wilshire Boulevard, Suite 1202, Los Angeles, CA 90010; 213–738–1969. *Miami*: Cayman Islands Department of Tourism: 6100 Waterford Building, 6100 Blue Lagoon Drive, Suite 150, Miami, FL 33126–2085; 305–266–2300. *New York*: 420 Lexington Avenue, Suite 2733, New York, NY 10170; 212–682–5582.
In Canada: Cayman Islands Department of Tourism: 234 Eglinton Avenue E, Suite 306, Toronto M4P 1K5; 416–485–1550.
On Grand Cayman: Department of Tourism, N. Church St., George Town; 809–949–0623. Island-wide tourist hotline, 809–949–8989.

KNOW BEFORE YOU GO

Arriving and Departing: Americans and Canadians need proof of citizenship—either a passport or a birth certificate or voter registration card plus photo ID—and a return ticket. Visitors pay a departure tax of $10.00.
Money: The Caymanian dollar is worth about $1.25 in U.S. dollars, which are widely accepted.
Language: The Cayman Islands have an English-speaking population.

Staying Healthy: A government hospital in George Town is staffed by doctors who trained in the United States, Canada, and Britain (809–949–8600). An air ambulance service to Miami makes the trip in about an hour. No-see-ums, the tiny flying bugs that love to bite people after a rain or at dusk come out in force in the Caymans; remember to apply insect repellent as a regular part of your routine.

GRAND CAYMAN

WHERE TO STAY

The long powdery ribbon of sand along the west coast known as Seven Mile Beach (although it's really 5½ miles long) has most of the island's hotels and condominium complexes. It's a very safe and clean stretch of beach.

HYATT REGENCY GRAND CAYMAN

Elegant sky-blue Colonial-style low-rise buildings overlook a private waterway and an 18-hole golf course designed by Jack Nicklaus at this premiere Caymanian resort. Three pools, including one with a swim-up bar, maintain the Hyatt trademark of water fun. The hotel has tennis courts, every imaginable water sport (including sunset cruises and parasailing), three restaurants, and nightly entertainment. Bedrooms are elegant and spacious, with marble baths and French doors.

For Kids: Camp Hyatt for three- to twelve-year-olds operates on weekends, during holiday periods, and throughout the summer. The program includes swimming, windsurfing lessons, sand castle building, movies, games, and arts and crafts. Rock Hyatt, for thirteen- to seventeen-year-olds, includes Jeep tours and snorkeling trips, volleyball and tennis clinics, movies, video games, sunset sails, and barbecues. Guests must sign up for these programs in advance and pay a fee of $35 per child per day.

Accommodations: Rooms, suites, and villas are available; all 236 units are air-conditioned and have mini-bars, safes, and hair dryers. One- and two-bedroom villas are situated along the golf course and have fully furnished kitchens and washers and dryers. Special Regency Club rooms offer a higher level of personal service, continental breakfast, and upgraded amenities.

Children eighteen and under stay free in parents' room (maximum two children). A second room for children traveling with their parents is half-price, subject to availability. Daily rates: double rooms, spring and fall, $225 to $425; June to September, $180 to $370; winter, $295 to $500. Villas (one to four bedrooms): winter, $470 to $1,000; spring and fall, $335 to $875; summer, $300 to $650. P.O. Box 1588, Grand Cayman, BWI; 800–421–4213 or 809–949–1234, fax 809–949–8528.

RADISSON RESORT GRAND CAYMAN

Another of Grand Cayman's most complete resort hotels, the Radisson sits on its own section of Seven Mile Beach. There's a good snorkeling reef 50 yards offshore, every kind of water sport, a dive shop, a gym, a whirlpool, a swimming pool, and several very good restaurants. Five floors of rooms have sitting areas and balconies or terraces with chairs for lounging. The resort's complimentary tennis courts are three blocks away. Small refrigerators can be rented for $10 per day to keep your crew supplied with refreshments.

Accommodations: The Radisson's 315 rooms are identical throughout the resort; their location determines the price. All have one king-size or two double beds, air-conditioning, and connecting doors if you wish.

Children under seventeen stay free in parents' room. Daily rates, double occupancy: December 15 to April 15, $245 to $360; April 16 to December 14, $165 to $250. P.O. Box 30371, Seven Mile Beach, West Bay Road, Grand Cayman, BWI; 800–333–3333 or 809–949–0088, fax 809–949–0288.

INDIES SUITES

One- and two-bedroom suites in this attractive all-suite hotel are airy and ample in size. The property is across the street from

Seven Mile Beach, where guests are provided with beach towels and lounge chairs. A swimming pool surrounded by lush tropical gardens stretches along the middle of the U-shaped hotel. A dive shop on the property arranges dive and snorkeling trips. Ground-floor units have dive lockers, and upper floors have balconies for hanging wet dive equipment. Washers and dryers are on premises. **Accommodations:** All but two of the 40 units are one-bedroom suites, with a sofa bed in the living room and either one king-size or two double beds in the bedroom. Spacious kitchenettes have burners, a microwave oven, a coffee maker, and a refrigerator.

Children of ages eleven and under stay free; additional persons of ages twelve and up, $10 per person per night. Daily rates, double occupancy: December 15 to April 15, one-bedroom unit $240; April 15 to December 14, $160. P.O. Box 2070, Grand Cayman, BWI; 800–654–3130 or 809–947–5025, fax 809–947–5024.

HOLIDAY INN GRAND CAYMAN

Situated on its own 600 feet of soft white sand, the "Inn on the Beach," as it calls itself, has one of the prettiest sections of Seven Mile Beach. Its free-form freshwater pool has a thatch-roofed refreshment stand in the middle. Bob Soto's Dive Shop on the premises offers resort courses and wall and reef dives. A water sports center supplies everything from jet skis and snorkel equipment to glass-bottom boat rides. Comics perform five nights a week in the Coconuts Comedy Club, and there is musical entertainment by the pool. A children's menu and bonded baby-sitters are available.

Accommodations: The 213 rooms are furnished in typical Holiday Inn style with two doubles or a king-size bed, and a small table and chairs by the window. Many rooms have connecting doors. Rooms are priced by location: parking lot view, garden view, poolside, and ocean front.

Children of ages nineteen and under stay free in room with one or both parents. Daily rates, double occupancy: December 15 to April 15, $208 to $298; April 16 to December 14, $158 to $228. P.O. Box 904, Grand Cayman, BWI; 800–421–9999 or 809–947–4444, fax 809–947–4213.

TREASURE ISLAND RESORT

A five-minute swim offshore takes you to Treasure Island's breathtaking coral reef, which stretches along the beach for about 300 yards. Its own underwater snorkel trail has crystal-clear visibility in 15 to 30 feet of water.

The 280-room resort has two swimming pools. Waterfalls spill into the undulating free-form pool, which has its own tropically landscaped island in the middle. Older kids can belly up to the swim-up bar in the second pool for a Shirley Temple or strawberry smoothie while tiny tots splash in their own separate wading pool. A dive shop, water sports center, and two tennis courts are on the premises. Be sure to ask about the summer and winter sale rate, which is available for a limited number of rooms year-round.

Accommodations: Three different categories of rooms differ only in their location. All have one king-size or two double beds, air-conditioning, ceiling fans, balconies or patios, and mini-bars. Connecting doors are available.

Children of ages seventeen and under stay free in their parents' room. Be sure to ask about the sale rate ($115 in summer, $175 in winter); only a limited number of rooms are available at that price. Daily rates, double occupancy: December 15 to April 15, $220 to $275; April 16 to December 14, $155 to $190. P.O. Box 1817, Seven Mile Beach, Grand Cayman, BWI; 800–327–8777 or 809–949–7777, fax 809–949–8489.

CAYMAN ISLANDER

Just across the road from Seven Mile Beach, this unpretentious hotel is an excellent value for the budget-conscious vacationer. It has a small playground with swings and a playhouse near the pleasant swimming pool. Boardwalks lead out into a lake on the property, where you can view turtles and fish, and cabanas and hammocks are placed alongside it for picnicking and relaxing. A small cafe serves breakfast only, but other restaurants and shops are a short walk away. A dive shop and rental car agency are on the property.

Accommodations: Sixty-seven simple rooms have two double beds, air-conditioning, and TV; the three efficiencies have microwave ovens, sinks, and refrigerators.

Children under twelve stay free in their parents' room. Extra person age twelve or older, $10 per night. Daily rates, double occupancy: December 15 to April 15, rooms $89, efficiencies $109; April 16 to December 14, rooms $75, efficiencies $95. P.O. Box 30081, Seven Mile Beach, Grand Cayman, BWI; 800–962–2028 or 809–949–0990, fax 809–949–7896.

CONDO RENTALS

The Cayman Islands Department of Tourism (see page 90) has a list of condos and apartments available for rent.

WHAT TO SEE AND DO

Grand Cayman's capital city, **George Town**, situated near the southwest corner of the island, is action central for tourism, trade, and government. It's packed with duty-free goods, shoppers, and cruise boat passengers many days of the week. The small **National Museum** showcases the natural and cultural history of the islands; old coins, shipbuilding tools, books, rope-making techniques, and special attractions just for kids are among the items on display. Harbour Drive. Open Monday through Saturday, 9:30 A.M. to 4:30 P.M.; 809–949–8368.

The **Treasure Museum**'s name alone is enough to motivate action-oriented kids to slow down for a closer look. Owned by a professional treasure hunting firm, the museum displays the fruits of the firm's labor, including a hefty seven-pound gold bar and all kinds of shipwreck booty. Dioramas show how Cayman Islanders became boat builders and turtle farmers, while Blackbeard the animated pirate spins salty tales of the pirates and buccaneers who plundered the region. West Bay Road. Open Monday through Saturday, 9:00 A.M. to 5:00 P.M.; 809–947–5033.

Tiny sea turtle hatchlings, adolescents, and full-grown breeding adults are on display in enormous circulating water tanks at the

Cayman Turtle Farm in northwestern Grand Cayman. Each year, a number of hatchlings and yearlings are released to repopulate the region's waters; others not so lucky are sold for food, and the turtle meat dishes you taste on the islands most likely have come from here. A cafe has snacks (including turtle soup), and a gift shop sells all kinds of turtle-theme memorabilia; remember, however, that it is against the law to bring anything made of turtle back into the United States. West Bay Road. Open daily, 9:00 A.M. to 5:00 P.M.; 809–949–3893.

Parents who take their kids to the tiny village of **Hell** near the northwest corner of Grand Cayman can get a postcard and postmark or T-shirt to prove it to their friends back home. The fascinating spiky, stark rock formations around Hell inspired the town's name.

Atlantis Submarine takes passengers deep down in air-conditioned comfort along the **Cayman Wall** to view the island's spectacular coral reefs, sponges, and brilliantly colored tropical fish. Guides identify sea life as it passes by the porthole windows. Kids need to be at least four years old to take the trip. Reduced rates are available for families; 809–949–7700.

Bodden Town, midway along Grand Cayman's south shore, is known for its cemetery, which is reputed to contain pirate remains. Some say that pirate bones rest in the odd A-frame structures in the graveyard; other say that those are the remains of early pioneers.

The Cayman's underwater gardens are among the Caribbean's most spectacular, and **scuba diving** certification for the adventurous (ages twelve and up) is a worthwhile investment of time and money. It's best to take the classroom and/or pool sections of the course in your hometown (see chapter 5), leaving the assisted open-water dive for the glorious green-blue Caribbean.

Snorkeling opportunities abound; consider purchasing your own equipment before you go, as it can be hard to find smaller children's sizes in many resorts. Custom masks with prescription lenses can be obtained at a surprisingly reasonable price.

All dive operations on Cayman are well-run.

CAYMAN BRAC

Diving and fishing are the big attractions on Cayman Brac, named for the 140-foot bluff (or *brac*, in Gaelic) dotted with ancient pirate caves that dominates the island. Two hotels—the Brac Reef Beach Resort and DIVI Tiara Beach Resort—and the luxury beachfront condominiums at Brac Caribbean Beach Resort are the only tourist accommodations on the island.

WHERE TO STAY

BRAC CARIBBEAN BEACH RESORT

Living rooms and master bedrooms overlook the sea in these comfortable two-bedroom condominiums on a reef-protected white sand beach. The kitchen is stocked upon your arrival with snacks, sodas, and breakfast foods—everything you need to get started—and you can get the pantry filled for the week on request. **Accommodations:** All units are air-conditioned and have shady verandahs or balconies and French doors. Both the master bedroom and guest bedroom have private bathrooms. Children ages eleven and under stay free of charge. Daily rates, double occupancy: high season, $165; off-season; $150. P.O. Box 4, Stake Bay, Cayman Brac, BWI; 800–327–8777 or 809–948–2265, fax 809–948–2206.

13

CURAÇAO

ROWS OF PASTEL-COLORED GABLED houses dominate the view in Willemstad, capital city of Curaçao, where homeowners were once forbidden by law to paint their homes white. Government officials deemed white to be too blinding in the tropical sun, and thus the city's penchant for pastels was born.

Willemstad is one of the most photogenic cities in the Caribbean, and its architecture and historical heritage make it one of the island's big draws. A trolley takes passengers throughout the old part of the city. Other attractions are dependably sunny weather and superb snorkeling and scuba, especially in Curaçao Underwater Marine Park, which encompasses almost a third of the island's southern diving waters. Constant year-round winds and suitable wave conditions have put Curaçao on the World Cup Windsurfing Tour in mid-June.

The island's austere countryside reflects its dry climate, and Dutch windmills are still used for irrigation. Historic plantation houses bordered by cactus and wind-sculpted divi-divi trees have the same quaint Dutch style as buildings in the capital city. Several of these manors now house restaurants; one is a restored museum; and one offers a weekly folkloric show.

Mikve Israel, the oldest synagogue in continuous use in the western hemisphere, was built in Curaçao in 1732. Jewish settlement of the island begin in 1651 when twelve families from Amsterdam arrived and were followed by Jews escaping religious persecution in Portugal, Spain, and Brazil.

Curaçao is the largest of the ABC islands (Aruba and Bonaire are the A and the B) and the largest of the five-and-a-half islands constituting the Netherlands Antilles (Saba, St. Eustatius, and the Dutch half of St. Maarten are the windward cousins of the ABC islands, separated from them by some 500 miles of open Caribbean Sea). Just 35 miles north of Venezuela, its population is a lively mix of Latin, European, and African roots. Tourism is a relatively new industry, and visitors are warmly welcomed.

Curaçao's carnival begins in January.

TOURIST INFORMATION

In the United States and Canada: Curaçao Tourist Board, 475 Park Avenue South, Suite 2000, New York, NY 10016; 800–3–CURACAO or 212–683–7660, fax 212–683–9337; or 330 Biscayne Boulevard, Suite 808, Miami, FL 33132; 800–445–8266 or 305–374–5811, fax 305–374–6741.
In Curaçao: At Pietermaii No. 19 in Willemstad; 599–9–616000.

KNOW BEFORE YOU GO

Arrivals and Departures: U.S. and Canadian citizens need passports or a birth certificate accompanied by a photo ID. All visitors must have a return or continuing ticket. Airport departure tax, per person, is $10 for international flights and $6 for interisland flights.
Money: The official currency is the guilder or florin, but the U.S. dollar is accepted everywhere.
Staying Healthy: St. Elisabeth's Hospital is the place to go for emergencies; 599–9–624900. Beware of the poisonous manchineel tree, which grows along the beach in certain areas.
Language: Dutch is the official language, but many inhabitants speak Papiamento, a mixture of Dutch, Portuguese, Spanish, and English. The language developed during the eighteenth century as the means of communication among slaves and landowners. Today, children learn English and Spanish in school, and anyone connected with tourism speaks English.

WHERE TO STAY

PRINCESS BEACH RESORT AND CASINO

Boasting a premiere water sports center with windsurfing instruction (the Curaçao High Wind Center) on the premises, windsurfing plays a central role in this resort's many water sports. But don't worry if you don't know a mistral from a mainsail; the beach is one of the finest on the island, right in front of the protected Marine Water Park. There are two pools, plus a special children's pool and gorgeous tropical gardens. The Seaquarium is within walking distance.

For Kids: Children of ages two to twelve can participate in the complimentary daily program any time between 9:00 A.M. and 5:00 P.M. in a special toy-stocked room. Youngsters play indoor and outdoor games, enjoy the children's playground, and work on arts and crafts projects. A changing schedule of activities is published daily.

Accommodations: The resort has 341 large and comfortable rooms and suites with one king-size or two queen-size beds; rollaways can be added. Suites have fold-out couches in living areas.

Children ages nineteen and under stay free in parents' room. Daily rates, double occupancy: winter, rooms $140 and up, one-bedroom suites $300 and up; summer, rooms $95 and up, one-bedroom suites $230 and up. Martin Luther King Boulevard 8, Curaçao; 800–327–3286 or 599–9–614944, fax 599–9–614131.

KADUSHI CLIFFS

Twelve luxurious two-bedroom condominiums are on a hill above a beautiful crescent of beach sheltered by rocky cliffs. Fantastic snorkeling is just offshore. Private "villas," as they call them, are decorated in tropical motifs, and can accommodate up to six people. Each villa has a patio with a gas grill, a Jacuzzi in the master bedroom, and dishwasher and microwave in the modern kitchen. A central reception area has a swimming pool and open-air restaurant that offers magnificent sunset views. All water sports can be arranged, and there is a Laundromat, bicycles, and walking/jogging trail.

Accommodations: Villas have two bedrooms, modern kitchen, living room with pull-out couch, safe, TVs, patios and terraces. Baby cribs and baby-sitting are available.

Each villa $300 per night for up to four people. P.O. Box 3673, Curaçao; 800-KADUSHI or 599–9–640015; fax 599–9–640282.

SONESTA BEACH HOTEL AND CASINO CURAÇAO

A stunning beachfront location, five-star rating, and large free-form swimming pool make this sun-drenched resort a favorite getaway for families. Special "Family Fun" packages let kids ages twelve and under stay free and eat breakfast and lunch on the house. Windsurfing, waterskiing, scuba diving, and snorkeling can be arranged from the water sports desk. Little ones can splash in their own shallow wading pool. Two tennis courts are lit for night play.

For Kids: Operating Wednesday through Sunday from 10:00 A.M. to 4:30 P.M., the "Just Us Kids" program is for five- to twelve-year-olds. Kids leave the program to eat lunch with their parents, and can return to participate in treasure hunts, sand sculpture, arts and crafts, and movie shows. A special pizza-and-movie party Saturday night from 6:30 to 9:00 P.M. costs $5 per child.

Accommodations: The 202 rooms and suites have a terrace or balcony, air-conditioning, and a mini-bar. Guest rooms have two queen-size, two doubles, or one king-size bed; and many have connecting doors. Suites have bedrooms and living rooms with fold-out couches.

Family Fun packages (include room for two adults and a maximum of two children ages twelve and under, with free children's meals and activities) for three nights and four days start at $559 per room during the off-season and $745 per room in season. P.O. Box 6003, Piscadera Bay, Curaçao; 800-SONESTA or 599–9–398800, fax 599–9–627502.

WHAT TO SEE AND DO

At the **Curaçao Sea Aquarium,** learn to identify the sea creatures that live around the island before you go snorkeling. Indoor tanks exhibit 400 varieties of fish and vegetation, and outdoor tanks contain sea turtles, sharks, and sea lions. A "semi-submarine" stationary underwater observatory takes 46 people at a time below water level to view an underwater garden where fish, lobsters, stingrays, sharks, and sea turtles cavort in the crystalline water. Divers and snorkelers can swim outside the sub, explore a shipwreck, and visit the "Shark Encounter" where humans are protected behind a sheet of Plexiglas set into a fenced area under water. Special feeding holes allow swimmers to feed the sharks who gather for a handout; be sure to bring your underwater camera. The Sea Aquarium's beach is an enjoyable place to sun and swim. Open daily, 10:00 A.M. to 10:00 P.M.; 599–9–616666.

The *Seaworld Explorer* boards from the dock of the Sea Aquarium. Passengers descend into the hull of the boat and sit five feet below the surface of the water, looking out through clear glass windows. The hour-long narrated tour goes past coral reefs, shipwrecks, and hundreds of tropical fish; 599–9–604892.

You could find a version of **Coney Island,** a fair with a merry-go-round, pirate boat, and Ferris wheel, just about anywhere in North America. But if you happen to be on Curaçao during one of the two weekends per month that this one is open, your kids will certainly get a kick out of its West Indian flair. Jazz and Salsa concerts are held here too. Next to the water distillation plant; check with the tourist office for days and times of operation.

The **Hato Caves,** near the airport, are actually old coral reefs that emerged out of the water when the island's landmass uplifted and the sea level dropped, forming Curaçao. Hourly tours lead visitors through chambers studded with hundreds of stalactites and stalagmites and gleaming crystals. Guides tell stories about the different crystalline formations, giving them names such as the "pirate," "donkey," "iguana," or "turtle." Look closely to see the fossil coral formations and different species that made up the former reef. Outside, children can see iguanas, and a wooded path leads to Indian carvings etched into the rocks. Open Tuesday through Sunday 10:00 A.M. to 5:00 P.M.; 599–9–680379.

Curaçao Underwater Marine Park, a 12½-mile unspoiled coral reef, is protected by National Park status. Snorkel the marked 875-foot underwater trail of coral beds, sheer undersea walls, and shallow, well-preserved shipwrecks. Normal underwater visibility is 60 to 80 feet, and can be even better on especially clear days. The park begins near the Princess Beach Hotel in Willemstad along the southern shore and stretches to the eastern tip of the island; 599–9–618131.

The deep bay of **Vaersenbaai** in the center of the island's southern side has little sand and a rocky entry, but teens will enjoy jumping off the pier and swimming out to a floating platform, while little ones can splash in the wading pool and romp in the small playgrounds. Parents can sip drinks on the shaded terrace overlooking the water.

14

DOMINICA

DOMINICA'S BEAUTY LIES in its untamed soaring mountain peaks, primordial rain forests, and tumbling streams, as opposed to sun-drenched beaches or glamorous nightlife. Luxury-seeking vacationers can pick other places for their island Shangri-las, but eco-travelers often find that Dominica has just what they want.

The island government bills Dominica as the "Nature Island of the Caribbean," and its reputation as a premier hiking and diving destination is beginning to spread. There are hot and cold springs, waterfalls at every turn, emerald-green pools, boiling lakes, and rain forests resounding with the calls of exotic birds. Bird watchers are rewarded with sightings of bananaquits, imperial parrots, rufous-throated solitaires, pearly-eyed thrashers, and various hummingbirds, swifts, and flycatchers; over 135 avian species call Dominica their home or migratory way station. Divers claim that the island has the healthiest and most unspoiled reefs in the Caribbean.

Most hotels and virtually all of the island's residents live on the Caribbean (western) side of the island, the site of Dominica's capital city, Roseau. Very little of the mountainous interior is inhabited or even accessible, and 28 percent of the island is in some way protected, either as a national park or as a forest reserve. Descendants of the fierce Carib Indians, who gave the Caribbean its name, maintain here their only remaining community in the entire region. If you plan to explore the island on foot, bring sturdy hiking boots, and employ an experienced guide.

Dominica's carnival is a riotous ten-day pre-Lenten festival that includes jump-ups, parades of floats and fabulous costumes, and music competitions.

TOURIST INFORMATION

In the United States and Canada: The Caribbean Tourism Organization, 20 East 46th Street, New York, NY 10017; 212–682–0435.
On Dominica: Dominica Division of Tourism, Old Market Plaza, P.O. Box 73, Roseau, Dominica, WI; 809–448–2186 or 809–448–2351, fax 809–448–5840.

KNOW BEFORE YOU GO

Arriving and Departing: U.S. and Canadian citizens need either a passport or a birth certificate or voter registration card with a photo ID and a continuing or return ticket. Visitors pay a departure tax of $8 per person.
Money: Dominica's official currency is the Eastern Caribbean dollar (EC$), but U.S. dollars are accepted everywhere.
Language: Dominica's official language is English, but many residents also speak a French-Creole patois.
Staying Healthy: Princess Margaret Hospital, Federation Drive, in Goodwill, handles the island's health problems; 809–448–2231. Mosquitoes thrive like the plants of the rain forest on Dominica. Be sure to bring insect repellent.

WHERE TO STAY

PAPILLOTE WILDERNESS RETREAT AND NATURE SANCTUARY

Operating an inn situated in the middle of a small rain forest northeast of Roseau, Papillote's hosts Anne and Cuthbert Jon-

Baptiste take a personal interest in the well-being of their visitors. Guests can cool off in the river beneath a secluded waterfall or soak in a natural hot mineral bath. Peacocks and other friendly pets stroll through the inn's beautiful gardens, which are filled with begonias, hibiscus, bromeliads, and ferns. The open-air verandah restaurant serves natural and gourmet vegetarian cuisine. Fish are freshly caught, the bread is home-baked, and salads feature exotic fruits and vegetables from the garden. This is a good place to headquarter to explore Morne Trois Pitons National Park.

Accommodations: Ten rustic rooms or two cottages are available. Cottages are best suited for families because they have two bedrooms, two baths, and a small kitchenette and can sleep six people.

Daily rates remain the same year-round: basic room $50, suite $60, with kitchenette $70, cottage $120. P.O. Box 2287, Roseau, Dominica, WI; 809–448–2287, fax 809–448–2285.

PICARD BEACH COTTAGE RESORT

Scattered throughout this former coconut plantation in the Portsmouth area on the northwest coast are eight small wooden cottages that can sleep up to four people each. The golden sand beach is right outside the door, and guests may use the pool at the Portsmouth Beach Hotel next door. Each unit has locally made furniture, louvered windows, ceiling fans, a small porch, a bedroom, a sitting/dining room, a private bath, and a kitchen. A restaurant serves breakfast, lunch, and dinner when you tire of cooking. Snorkeling, windsurfing, sailing, and other water sports are available.

Daily rates, double occupancy: beachfront cottages, $80 low season, $140 high season; garden view, $70 low season, $120 high season. P.O. Box 34, Roseau, Dominica, WI, 800–424–5500 or 809–445–5131, fax 809–445–5599.

CASTLE COMFORT LODGE

This establishment on the water south of Roseau is a favorite of divers. Its owners, Derek and Ginette Perryman, operate the first-rate Dive Dominica from the premises. Three custom boats—two for divers and one for snorkelers—explore the reefs, shelves, subaquatic hot springs, and drops-offs around Dominica. The dive packages are a good value, and the Perrymans will arrange hiking guides and excursions for their guests. Ten simple air-conditioned guest rooms are small but comfortable, and a child can stay comfortably with parents in most rooms. Creole cuisine is the restaurant's specialty.

Packages include seven nights' accommodations, all meals, five boat dives, unlimited shore dives, airport transfers, taxes, and tips: $799 per person, nondivers $521. P.O. Box 2253, Roseau, Dominica, WI; 809–448–2188, fax 809–448–6088.

WHAT TO SEE AND DO

Popular **Trafalgar Falls** is just outside Morne Trois Pitons National Park, northeast of Roseau, and a short walk from Papillote Wilderness retreat (see page 105). This dramatic cascade of water tumbles 140 feet into an emerald-green pool framed by curling vines, and it runs both hot and cold. Half of the waterfall flows freezing cold and the other half, heated by volcanic action, approximates a warm shower at 104°F. As you might guess, the temperature of the pool changes depending on where you swim.

All kinds of hiking trails wind through the 16,000-acre **Morne Trois Pitons National Park**, dominated by Morne Trois Pitons whose three peaks are often capped by swirling clouds and mists. Some trails are clearly marked while others vanish into thick fern forests and disappear into pools of mud. It's a good idea to hire a guide for all but the best marked, most frequented paths.

An easy 30-minute walk that young children enjoy leads to sparkling **Emerald Pool** and the waterfall that feeds it. Overlooks along the trail offer panoramic views of the Atlantic coast and the thick, forested interior. The pretty pool into which the falls tumble lies in a forest grotto. It's the most accessible of the National Park's wonders, and one of the few you won't need a guide to reach.

Serious hikers explore **Boiling Lake** and **the Valley of Desola-**

tion, but this trek should only be attempted by older kids who are experienced and in top condition. You'll need to be in pretty good shape yourself, since the 6-mile climb takes a full day, but you'll be rewarded with sights of the world's second largest boiling lake (don't dip your toes) and vistas of everything from stark volcano-scarred landscapes to primordial rain forest jungles exploding with life.

Residents of the **Carib Indian Reservation** on the east coast live like any other West Indians in six small villages scattered throughout the territory. They have preserved and handed down their traditional skills in carving wood, weaving baskets, and building canoes. You can see (and buy) examples of their straw mats and their baskets made of dyed larouma reeds in the small shops lining the road.

Three hundred streams crisscross Dominica's mountainsides, draining the lush rain forests and flowing to the sea. The **Layou River,** whose source lies in the Northern Forest Reserve, is the island's longest and largest river, a popular spot for swimming in its refreshing pools or exploring its rapids, waterfalls, and beaches.

Taking a boat trip on the **Indian River**, just south of Portsmouth, is an easy way to experience the natural beauty of the island. Guides paddle visitors in canoes or rowboats (skip the motorboat offers—they're too noisy) from the river's wide mouth through mangrove swamps ringing with exotic bird calls. The rain forest vegetation is so thick it forms a tunnel through which the boats pass.

15

DOMINICAN REPUBLIC

THE DOMINICAN REPUBLIC, or Dominicana as it now calls itself, occupies the eastern two-thirds of Hispaniola, the island it shares with Haiti. It's a land of extraordinary natural diversity, containing the highest and lowest points to be found in all the Caribbean islands. Pico Duarte looms 10,417 feet above sea level and has pine trees and below-freezing temperatures, quite atypical of the Caribbean. Less than 63 miles away, near the Haitian border, salty Enriquillo Lake, in the most arid region of the country, rests 144 feet below sea level. Its hostile environment contains no freshwater, and daytime temperatures frequently exceed 100°F. A burgeoning eco-tourism industry takes visitors into these areas, but most guests prefer to explore the country's coastline, which is edged with lovely sandy beaches.

The capital, Santo Domingo, is a modern city of 2.2 million people. Old Santo Domingo was the first permanent European settlement in the New World, founded by Christopher Columbus's brother Bartolomeo. History lovers can wander the streets and see buildings that were constructed when the old city was the center of Spanish commerce in the New World.

The Dominican Republic has the largest hotel inventory in the Caribbean. Since there can be fierce competition to fill the many rooms built during the country's recent boom, prices tend to be lower than elsewhere on the islands. Many of the resorts in the popular Puerto Plata area on the Atlantic (north) coast northwest of Santo Domingo (which lies on the Caribbean, or south, coast) are well set up for families.

On the southeastern coast in La Romana is luxurious Casa de Campo, truly a vacation village with every kind of sport and leisure activity and its own international airport. At Punta Caña on the far eastern tip of the island is a Club Med with a Mini Club for kids and another convenient airport.

Elements of Spanish culture prevail in this Latin-influenced country, where you'll find late dinners, siestas, and conservative covered-up clothing styles, especially in cities. Tourism brings much-needed income to the country, but crushing poverty is common once you're outside the tourist enclaves.

Baseball, or *beisbol*, is the national sport of the Dominican Republic, and residents are passionate about it. If your family members like the sport, try to attend a game. The season runs from October through January, but practice games are played during much of the rest of the year. Rum and food flow freely, and emotions run high.

TOURIST INFORMATION

In the United States: The Dominican Republic Department of Tourism; 1501 Broadway, Suite 410, New York, NY 10036; 212–575–4966, fax 212–575–5448.

In Canada: The Dominican Republic Department of Tourism, 1454 Crescent Street, Montreal H3G 2B6; 514–499–1918, fax 514–499–1393.

In the Dominican Republic: Dominican Republic Tourist Information Center, 1101 Abraham Lincoln Avenue, Santo Domingo, DR; 800–752–1151. Allow two weeks for materials to arrive.

KNOW BEFORE YOU GO

Arriving and Departing: U.S. and Canadian citizens must have a valid passport or original birth certificate and a tourist card. Visitors pay a departure tax of $10.

Money: The Dominican peso (RD$) is the official currency. Spend your pesos before you leave the country, as it's often very difficult to exchange pesos for dollars.

Language: Spanish is the official language; and while some people in the tourism industry speak English, you're better off knowing a little *Español* before you go.

Staying Healthy: The island has many hospitals with 24-hour emergency rooms.

WHERE TO STAY

CASA DE CAMPO

You name it, Casa de Campo has got it: two 18-hole golf courses, 17 tennis courts, 13 swimming pools, a private airstrip, two polo fields, trap and skeet shooting ranges, horseback riding, deep-sea and river fishing, glorious beaches, and every imaginable water sport. Free mini-buses take guests around the 7,000-acre complex, but you can also rent bikes, golf carts, or scooters. Ask most kids what they like best about the resort, and they mention driving the golf carts. Then comes the tennis, the beach, and the water sports. Sports-loving families who want to get away from it all to a self-contained vacation world give this place the highest marks.

For Kids: The "Kids 'n' Casa" activities program operates every day except Tuesday from 9:00 A.M. to 4:00 P.M. Children between ages five and twelve play baseball, practice for a talent show, enjoy crafts and games, and take bus tours. The program costs $15 per child per day and includes lunch at one of Casa de Campo's restaurants.

Accommodations: One-, two-, and three-bedroom villas were designed by Oscar de la Renta, and these plus casitas and casas suites make up the 600 units on the sprawling property. There are nine restaurants and a variety of beach grills, ice cream vendors, and pizza parlors.

Children under 12 stay free in parents' room. Daily rates, double occupancy: Casitas $125 to $245 depending on time of year; two-

or three-bedroom villa $240 to $650; four-bedroom villa $330 to $800. P.O. Box 140, La Romana, DR; 800–877–3643 or 809–523–3333, fax 809–523–8548.

CLUB MED PUNTA CAÑA

Walk the tightrope, soar through the air on a trapeze, learn to juggle, and then head to the beach to recover under the shade of the palm trees or in the cool saltwater sea. Club Med's popular Circus Workshop is available for adults as well as kids who have always dreamed of being in a circus. The workshop uses the same safety equipment employed by real circuses, and a show is performed by guests and staff each week. Children ages four and up can find out what scuba feels like in the carefully supervised safety of the pool, wearing kid-size tanks and fins. Teens and their parents can sail, windsurf, water-ski, scuba dive, snorkel, kayak, and play tennis, basketball, baseball, or soccer. Rooms are in three-story bungalows that face the long white beaches.

For Kids: Supervised activities run from 9:00 A.M. to 9:00 P.M. The Mini Club has three separate clubhouses: one for Petits (two to three years), one for Minis (four to six years), and another to house the Kids Club (seven to eleven). Activities include waterskiing, sailing, golf, archery, arts and crafts, excursions, boat rides, picnics, and puppet shows. The organized evening program ends when it's time for the big nighttime show. Early optional supervised lunches and dinners feature foods kids enjoy.

Accommodations: Rooms are air-conditioned with two twin beds that can be pushed together; rollaways and cribs can be added, and connecting rooms are available. A room open 24 hours a day is stocked with juices and snacks. Two registered nurses are on site and a pediatrician is on call.

At certain times of year—usually during parts of January, February, March, and April—one child (age two to five) per full paying adult stays free; be sure to ask. Weekly rates, per person: April 29 to December 17, adults $749, children ages two to eleven, $490; December 18 to January 6, adults $1,100 to $1,500, children $650 to $975, depending on precise week; January 7 to February 4, adults $725, children $475; February 5 to April 28, adults

$770 to $1,300, children $500 to $845, with higher prices during February holidays and Easter breaks. Provincia la Altagracia, Apartado Postal 106, DR; 800-CLUB-MED or 809–567–5228, fax 809–565–2558.

FLAMENCO BEACH RESORT, PLAYA DORADA BEACH RESORT, VILLA DORADAS

These three resorts sit side-by-side on a mile of white sand beach, on the "Amber Coast" north of the airport, and guests at any one of them can use the facilities at all three. Flamenco and Playa Dorada are the best choices for families. Flamenco is particularly attractive because it has both a children's pool and an elaborate free-form swimming pool with waterfalls and lapping waves. Between the three hotels, all on the 1-mile beach, is every sport and activity imaginable.

For Kids: Both Flamenco and Playa Dorada offer children's games around the beach and pool for kids ages six and up. Playa Dorada operates full children's summer activity programs both poolside and on the beach, including volleyball, balloon games, water races, and quiet time. Activities are supervised for ages six and up between the hours of 11:00 A.M. and 4:00 P.M.

Accommodations: Playa Dorada can accommodate two adults and two kids in a room with two queen-size beds and a roll-away. Flamenco's rooms have one king-size and two queen-size beds.

Osmar Tours (800–288–4340) offers all-inclusive packages for three nights and four days: winter, $225 to $250 per person; summer, $210, to $230 per person. Children's rates are substantially reduced. Nonpackage all-inclusive daily rates, per person: $90 to $110, with a reduction for children. At Flamenco, children stay free with parents when booking a room only. Daily rates, double occupancy at Flamenco only: $110. Flamenco: Playa Dorada, Puerto Plata, DR; 809–320–5084, fax 809–320–6319. Villas Doradas: P.O. Box 1370, Puerto Plata, DR; 809–320–4720. Playa Dorada, P.O. Box 272, Puerto Plata, DR; 800–423–6902 or 809–586–3988, fax 809–320–1190.

DORADO NACO

This all-suite inclusive resort on a beautiful stretch of beach in the Puerto Plato area has carpeted one- and two-bedroom apartments with full kitchens. There are three clay tennis courts, an 18-hole Robert Trent Jones golf course, horseback riding, bicycle tours, all types of water sports, and fitness classes. Families appreciate the ice cream parlor, small playground, pizzeria, gourmet restaurant, mini-mart, and laundry facilities on site. All meals, nonmotorized water sports, and one-hour daily horseback rides are included in the rates; waterskiing, scuba, and jet skiing cost extra.

Accommodations: One-bedroom suites can accommodate up to four people, and two-bedroom suites can sleep up to six; all living rooms have a sofa bed. Each bedroom has one queen-size or two twin beds. All are air-conditioned and have terraces or patios.

Daily all-inclusive rates, per person: April 18 to December 18, $80. December 19 to April 17, $110. For one-bedroom suite, add $15 per room per night; for two-bedroom suite, add $30 per room per night. Children ages two to twelve, $30 per day. Playa Dorado, Puerto Plata, DR; 800–322–2388 or 809–586–2019, fax 809–586–3608.

PUERTO PLATA BEACH RESORT AND CASINO

Cobblestone pathways connect 23 Victorian-style buildings surrounded by seven acres of colorful tropical gardens. Supervised children's games take place around the pool in the morning and at the beach in the afternoon. The resort's beach is a few steps across the street. An inclusive package offers free water sports and an hour of horseback riding each day. The swimming pool has a shallow children's area at one end; water sports include sailing, windsurfing, and snorkeling, plus free scuba clinics in the pool, horseback riding, bicycling, volleyball, aerobics, disco, and four lighted tennis courts.

For Kids: Poolside activities take place daily from 10:00 to 11:00 A.M. Games take place on the beach each afternoon from 2:00 to 3:00 P.M. Parents can leave children ages five and up with the counselors who conduct the activities.

Accommodations: Suites have tiny kitchens and separate living room and bedroom areas with two double beds. Connecting rooms are available. Standard rooms have one queen-size bed.

Daily all-inclusive rates, per person: April 16 to December 20 $80 to $95, child $40, extra person $60. December 21 to April 15, $90 to $125, child (2–12 years) $45. P.O. Box 600, Avenida Malecon, Puerto Plata, DR; 800–348–5395 or 809–586–4243, fax 809–586–4377.

JACK TAR VILLAGE

Nonstop activities and virtually round-the-clock opportunities to eat and drink are the trademarks of this all-inclusive resort. Encircling the "village" is a challenging Robert Trent Jones golf course, whose greens fees are included in the rates. An activity booklet in each room provides an hour-by-hour listing of the numerous activities for all ages: lawn darts, beach volleyball, ring toss games, bingo tournaments, and merengue dance lessons are just a few. The beach, pool, tennis courts, and all varieties of water sports such as windsurfing, snorkeling, inner-tubing, and boogie boarding are available throughout the day. Special boat and snorkeling excursions cost extra. Guests stay in villa-style two-story units with one to four bedrooms.

For Kids: Children ages three to twelve are occupied in various age-appropriate activities from 9:00 A.M. to 4:30 P.M. most days. They may build sand castles, try sand painting, play dress-up, watch videos, or engage in arts, crafts, games, and funny contests.

Accommodations: All 300 rooms are air-conditioned and have twin, double, or queen-size beds and patios or balconies with outdoor furniture. Housekeeping service is provided twice daily.

Children under six stay free. Daily rates, per person: April 19 to December 20, $130 to $140, kids six to twelve $60; December 21 to January 2, $150 to $160, kids $100. Value rates discount rooms by about 20 percent if you book 30 days in advance during summer season only. P.O. Box 368, Playa Dorada, DR; 809–586–3800 or 800–999–9182, fax 809–320–4161.

WHAT TO SEE AND DO

SANTO DOMINGO

The **Christopher Columbus Lighthouse Monument**, completed in 1992 to commemorate the quintecentennial of Columbus's "discovery" of the New World, is a tall, pyramidlike, cross-shaped building. In its middle is a sarcophagus that supposedly contains the remains of Columbus himself, although several other countries also claim to be his final resting place. Climb the seven stories (there are no elevators) for a breathtaking view, and be sure to stay for the hourly changing of the guard. Avenida España. Open Tuesday through Sunday, 9:00 A.M. to 4:00 P.M.

If the underwater world fascinates your offspring, visit the **Acuario Nacional (National Aquarium)**, which is the largest in the Caribbean. Its tanks hold a vast collection of tropical fish, and its frisky dolphins are popular with visitors of all ages. Avenida de las Americas near the Columbus monument. Open daily, 10:00 A.M. to 6:00 P.M.

Calle las Damas (Ladies Street) is named for the elegant ladies of the court who once lived on the street and promenaded along its length. Its buildings are among the most beautiful examples of sixteenth-century Colonial architecture in the New World. The varied collection in the **Museo de las Casas Reales** (Museum of the Royal Houses) on Calle las Damas is displayed in two early sixteenth-century palaces. The museum houses models of Columbus's three ships—the *Niña*, the *Pinta*, and the *Santa Maria*; a map tracing the route of his four voyages of discovery; old gold coins, coats of armor, gilded furniture, and coaches; a re-created courtroom, pharmacy, and sugar mill; and antique artifacts. Calle las Damas. Open Tuesday through Saturday, 9:00 A.M. to 4:45 P.M., Sunday 10:00 A.M. to 1:00 P.M.; 809–682–4202.

At the **National Zoo and Botanical Gardens**, animals roam in bar-free natural landscapes separated from visitors by a moat. There's a small children's zoo within the grounds and an enormous walk-through bird cage the zoo claims is the largest in the world.

Carriage rides travel through parts of the nearby Botanical Gardens. Avenida de los Próceres. Open daily, 9:00 A.M. to noon and 2:00 to 6:00 P.M.

ELSEWHERE ON THE ISLAND

The re-created fifteenth-century Spanish village of **Altos de Chavón** sits on a cliff above the Chavón River and was created by an Italian set designer. It's about three miles east of the main part of Casa de Campo resort; you can drive in or take a shuttle from the resort. Artists live and work in the balconied buildings along cobblestone streets. The village includes an art school, restaurants, a stone church, an amphitheater, and museums, including one with artifacts of the Taino Indians. Visitors can browse through jewelry and art shops and can take workshops to learn how to make what they see.

16

GRENADA

ICE CREAM IS THE UNOFFICIAL national food of Grenada. You can sample varieties of the creamy frozen confection flavored with whatever exotic tropical fruits are in season: papaya, coconut, banana, lime, mango, even avocado. Rich and aromatic nutmeg ice cream is available year-round, and no wonder, since the fragrant spice is Grenada's number-one export. Even tourism comes in second to nutmeg in Grenada's economy.

Three inhabited islands, Grenada, Carriacou, and Petit Martinique, along with a few tiny, uninhabited islands, make up the nation of Grenada. The largest island, Grenada, is often remembered as the place U.S. troops invaded following an internal coup d'état in 1983, ostensibly to evacuate American students at St. George's Medical School. Small and quiet Carriacou and Petit Martinique, the southernmost inhabited islands in the Grenadines chain, have beautiful beaches and very little tourism. Prices are much lower here than in tonier parts of the Caribbean.

Grenada's tidy farming towns and quaint fishing villages attest to the island's unspoiled character. The island's hillsides are thick with banana, nutmeg, and cocoa crops. Shimmering green rain forests shrouded in mist hide dramatic waterfalls and breathtaking hiking trails. Tourism is concentrated on the island's southwest corner along Grand Anse Beach, a sparkling two-mile crescent of white sand bordered by palm trees and the brilliant turquoise Caribbean Sea, where vendors amble by sunbathers, offering coconut milk straight from the coconut. In the early morning, small boys play cricket by the water's edge.

Grenada's carnival is in August, with parties, dances, parades, steel band and calypso competitions, and a Kiddy Carnival held about a week before the main celebration.

TOURIST INFORMATION

In the United States: Grenada Board of Tourism, Suite 900D, 820 Second Avenue, New York, NY 10017; 800–927–9554 or 212–687–9554.
In Canada: Grenada Board of Tourism, Suite 820, 439 University Avenue, Toronto, Ontario M5G 1Y8; 416–595–1339.
On Grenada: Grenada Board of Tourism, The Carenage, St. George's; 809–440–2279.

KNOW BEFORE YOU GO

Arriving and Departing: U.S. and Canadian citizens need a passport or birth certificate with a photo ID and an onward or return ticket. The departure tax is $10 per person; children under five are exempt.
Money: The Eastern Caribbean Dollar (EC$) is the local currency. You can use U.S. dollars in many shops, hotels, and restaurants, but you'll get a better rate of exchange using EC dollars.
Language: English is spoken throughout Grenada.
Staying Healthy: St. George's Hospital is small (809–440–2051); anyone with a serious medical problem is flown off the island.
Local Food: The word *grog* originated on this island, standing for "Grand rum of Grenada." Maubi, a drink made from tree bark, is said to aid digestion and impart energy. Oil Down is a dish made from breadfruit and salt pork steamed gently in coconut milk covered with callaloo leaves. The ubiquitous lambi, or conch, is popular and plentiful. Christophenes are local vegetables similar to squash.

WHERE TO STAY

BLUE HORIZONS COTTAGE HOTEL

A warm and homey atmosphere brings many of Blue Horizons' international guests back year after year. Its excellent value makes it popular with families who want a housekeeping cottage near a good beach. Grand Anse Beach is just a five-minute walk down the hill, where guests can use the beach chairs and complimentary water sports facilities at the hotel's sister property, the Spice Island Inn. The hotel's highly regarded La Belle Creole Restaurant, one of the best on the island, specializes in imaginatively prepared local cuisine. A swimming pool and small playground are set in 6½ acres of tropical gardens. Car rental services are on the property.

Accommodations: Units have fully equipped kitchenettes, ceiling fans, hair dryers, air-conditioning, TV, radios, and private patios. One-bedroom superior and larger deluxe and two-bedroom units are available.

In winter season, children under twelve stay free; in summer, children under eighteen stay free. Daily rates, double occupancy: winter, one-bedroom unit $100 to $145, two-bedroom unit $230; summer, one-bedroom unit $100 to $110, two-bedroom unit $220. P.O. Box 41, St. George's, Grenada, WI; 800–223–9815 or 809–444–2815, fax 809–444–2815.

THE GRENADA RENAISSANCE RESORT

Twenty acres of shady palm trees and tropical gardens surround the island's largest resort, which is right on Grand Anse Beach and across from the Grand Anse shopping center. Its rooms are typical motel style, but its full-service water sports facility (including a dive shop) and lively evening entertainment give guests plenty of options for filling their days and nights. Dining is at the beachfront open-air restaurant, or indoors in the Greenery.

Accommodations: All rooms have twin or king-size beds, and rates depend on views and air-conditioning. Two-bedroom units are available. All have color TV, radio, balcony or patio, and hair dryer. Cribs are available free of charge.

Children under eighteen stay free in parents' room. Daily rates, double occupancy: winter, one-bedroom units $175 to $350, two-bedroom units $550; summer, one-bedroom units $120 to $300, two-bedroom units $500. Grande Anse Beach, P.O. Box 441, St. George's, Grenada, WI; 800–223–9815 or 809–444–4371, fax 809–444–4800.

COYABA BEACH RESORT

This resort is situated directly on Grande Anse Beach about midway down the 2-mile expanse. All units feature private verandahs and patios with views of the Caribbean Sea or St. George's harbor. A small playground and swimming pool with a popular swim-up bar keep the kids happy when they tire of the beach. The restaurant on the premises serves local and international cuisine. The water sports center, Grand Anse Aquatics Ltd., has PADI certified instructors and conducts scuba and snorkeling trips around Grenada, Carriacou, and Petit Martinique. Windsurfing rental and instruction are available.
Accommodations: Rooms with two double beds can accommodate two adults and two children. All rooms have air-conditioning, balconies and patios, and hair dryers.

For children ages two to twelve sharing parents' room, add $12.50 per child per night in summer, $15 per child per night in winter. Daily rates, double occupancy: winter, $165 (plus kids); summer, $95 (plus kids). P.O. Box 336, St. George's, Grenada, WI; 800–223–9815 or 809–444–4129, fax 809–444–4808.

REX GRENADIAN

One of the newest and largest hotels on the island, this resort is the only one with a program for small children. Its 3-acre lake, one beach for swimming and sunbathing and another for water sports, free-form swimming pool with a waterfall, and busy schedule of activities attract families who like having plenty to do. Many rooms have views across the soft white sands and turquoise waters of Tamarind Bay to St. George's in the distance. Windsurfing, Sunfish sailing, and snorkeling equipment are complimentary; fees are charged for scuba diving, para-sailing, waterskiing, high-performance windsurfing boards, and sports lessons.

For Kids: Supervised activities for four- to twelve-year-olds take place Monday through Friday from either 9:00 A.M. to noon or 2:00 to 4:00 P.M. Planned activities include mask making, beach play, painting, treasure hunts, parties, kite making, movies, and music games. Baby-sitters can be hired for younger children. A children's menu is available for lunch and dinner.

Accommodations: The hotel's 212 rooms and suites have six different styles and sizes. The least expensive rooms have fans; the rest have air-conditioning.

Children under age two eat and stay free; children under age twelve stay free and eat at half price. Daily rates: November 1 to April 15, double room $175 to $280, suites $320 to 360; rest of year, double rooms $115 to $220, suites $240 to $300. Meal plans are available. Point Salines, P.O. Box 893, St. George's, Grenada, WI; 800–255–5859 or 809–444–3333, fax 809–444–1111.

TRUE BLUE INN

Spacious lawns slope down to True Blue Bay, where a small dock reaches out into the azure Caribbean Sea. Guests can use the inn's dinghy to explore nearby coves and offshore reefs. The quiet setting, away from St. George's on a private peninsula, and the availability of full kitchens make this inn a good choice for families. Guests can swim in the freshwater pool or in the blue waters of the bay. The beach is small, so ocean swimming is largely from the platform at the end of the dock, but Grande Anse and Morne Rouge beaches are just a few minutes away. Indigo's restaurant and bar serve breakfast, lunch, and dinner when you tire of cooking. You'll want to rent a car for mobility.

Accommodations: Choose from two-bedroom cottages nestled in tropical gardens or one-bedroom apartments with balconies and hammocks overlooking the sea. All units have ceiling fans, air-conditioning, pullout sofa beds, and daily housekeeping service.

Daily rates: December 16 to April 15, two-bedroom cottages (accommodate up to four people) $165, one-bedroom apartment (double occupancy) $120, add $35 per night for each additional person over age two; April 16 to December 15, two-bedroom cottages $100, one-bedroom apartments $70, add $25 per night for each additional person. P.O. Box 308, St. George's, Grenada, WI; 809–444–2000, fax 809–444–1247.

FLAMBOYANT HOTEL AND COTTAGES

Crab races take place every week at this hotel's Beachside Terrace Restaurant, which serves breakfast, lunch, and dinner. The hotel and cottages, situated on a lush green hillside at the southern edge of the Grand Anse Beach, all have breathtaking panoramic views of the crescent of white sand and the city and harbor of St. George's. A very short path heads directly to the Grand Anse Beach, where guests will find complimentary snorkeling gear, beach towels, and beach chairs. The resort's swimming pool is situated along the path to the beach.

Accommodations: Hotel rooms, one-bedroom suites, and two-bedroom cottages are all air-conditioned with queen-size or twin beds. Suites have fully equipped kitchens, and some have sofa beds. Cottages have two bedrooms and two baths.

Children under age twelve in winter and under eighteen in summer stay free in their parents' rooms. Daily rates, double occupancy: winter, one-bedroom unit $135, two-bedroom unit $215; summer, $95 and $135. Grande Anse Beach, P.O. Box 214, St. George's, Grenada, WI; 800–223–9815 or 809–444–4247, fax 809–444–1234.

WHAT TO SEE AND DO

The **People to People** program brings visitors to the island together with Grenadians who share similar interests for visits and outings. Write to New Trends Tours before you go to request an introduction. Be sure to specify your interests and your children's interests and ages. There is no charge, but it's always most gracious to treat your host to any outing. P.O. Box 797, St. George's, Grenada, WI; 809–444–1236, fax 809–444–4836.

Plan to visit **St. George's**, Grenada's capital city and major port, on Tuesday afternoon to see the loading of the boats with crates and bags of fruits and vegetables bound for Trinidad. **Market day** in St. George's takes place every Saturday morning. Arrive early to see its exotic fruits and vegetables and aromatic spices. Ask permission before shooting any photos. You can buy little baskets of cinnamon, nutmeg, mace, bay leaves, vanilla, and ginger at shops in the market or around town to take home.

Nearby, the **Grenada National Museum** houses archaeological finds, mounted specimens of native fauna, historical memorabilia, and the Empress Josephine Bonaparte's marble bathtub. The most comprehensive exhibit traces the Indian cultures of Grenada. Open weekdays 9:00 A.M. to 1:30 P.M., Saturday 10:00 A.M. to 1:30 P.M.

Fort George, built by the French in 1705, still has centuries-old cannons standing on its ramparts. You can visit the adjacent botanical garden and small zoo with tropical trees and flowers and rare Caribbean birds and animals. Open daily.

Find out how nutmeg goes from the tree to the dusting on cookies, eggnog, and rum punch at the **Nutmeg Processing Station** in the west-coast town of Gouyave, the center of Grenada's nutmeg industry. You'll see old wooden shelling and cracking machinery still at work, sacks of fragrant spices, and nutmeg and mace (the dried fibrous covering of the nutmeg seed, which is removed and used as a spice in its own right) being prepared for export in much the same way Grenadians have prepared them for centuries. Handfuls of nutmeg are passed out as souvenirs at the end of your visit. Open Monday through Friday, 8:00 A.M. to 4:00 P.M., and Saturday 8:00 A.M. to noon.

Just inland, stop in at **Dougaldston Estate** where cloves, cinnamon, mace, nutmeg, and cocoa are sorted and processed. Employees will explain how the spices grow, discuss their uses, and show you the large trays where the spices are set to dry in the sun before being painstakingly separated by hand. Open Monday through Friday 9:00 A.M. to 3:30 P.M., Saturdays 9:00 A.M. to noon; Gouyave, 809–444–8213.

Pack a picnic lunch and take the coast road 8 miles north from St. George's to breathtaking **Concord Falls**. A 2-mile hike will take you to the more dramatic part of the falls, where water cascades 50 feet down to a deep blue pool. After swimming beneath the waterfall, hike along the river through the tropical forest for about an hour to a more remote fall. There's a small changing room at the main falls where you can slip into your swimsuit.

The centerpiece of **Grand Étang National Park** is a large volcanic crater that has become a lake. A number of magnificent waterfalls offer perfect sites for a refreshing swim and a picnic. Annandale Falls is just off Grand Étang Road.

La Sagesse Nature Center on the island's south coast offers hiking trials, an estuary and a salt pond much favored by wild birds, a banana plantation with guided nature walks, an extensive beach, and a cafe for lunch and refreshments.

Saturday is **market day in Grenville**, the largest town on the east coast and locally esteemed as Grenada's breadbasket. This large, colorful market sells fish, spices, fruits, vegetables, bread, pastries, and Grenadian delicacies prepared on the spot.

With visibility often close to 200 feet, **scuba and snorkeling** opportunities are manifold. Grenada's waters are home to the largest shipwreck in the Caribbean, the *Bianca* C., a cruise ship that caught fire and went down in 1961, eventually settling into waters more than 100 feet deep. Turtles, eagle rays, and all kinds of brilliantly colored tropical fish now make it their home.

The **Aquarium Beach Club** (below Point Salines off the airport road) combines dining with such activities as volleyball, snorkeling, and lazing on the golden beach. After enjoying lunch or dinner, rent snorkel gear to explore the reef just offshore. Saturday is volleyball day, and Sunday features a lobster BBQ. Open Tuesday through Sunday; 809–444–1410.

The superb **sailing** between Grenada and the island chain of the Grenadines is best for experienced sailors, although inexperienced sailors can easily rent a crewed boat. **The Moorings**, one of the best charter yacht operators throughout the Caribbean, has facilities at Secret Harbour Hotel.

17

GUADELOUPE

LIKE A LARGE BUTTERFLY floating on a sea of blue, Guadeloupe is really two islands. One wing of the butterfly, Grande-Terre, has tantalizing beaches and a haute scene; as you might guess, it's the center of resort life. The other wing, the rugged and mountainous Basse-Terre, contains a national park and concerns itself with more natural splendors. A seawater channel called the Rivière Saleé separates the two wings, and a drawbridge allows passage between them.

Sophisticated gourmets rank Guadeloupe's cuisine among the best in the Caribbean. The top restaurants and hotels offer elegant meals prepared in the classic French manner, but there are also more than 100 small bistros, beachside cafes, and funky diners where you'll find spicy out-of-this-world Creole cooking.

The island's French influence can be found in more than the cuisine. Shops close for the ritual of a long lunch with wine, as they do all over France; bakeries sell light and flaky French pastries; and itsy-bitsy French bikinis become even smaller when beachgoers remove the tops to ensure the perfect tan.

Windsurfing, or *planche-a-voile*, is excellent on the bays around the island, and several major international competitions are held here. Scuba divers use the French CMAS system rather than PADI or NAUI (see page 34).

TOURIST INFORMATION

In the United States: French West Indies Tourist Board, 444 Madison Avenue, New York, NY 10022; 900–990–0040, fax 212–838–7855.

In Canada: French Government Tourist Office, 1981 McGill College Avenue, Suite 490, Montreal, Quebec H3A 2W9; 514–288–4264, fax 514–844–8901. Or French Government Tourist Office, #700, 30 Patrick Street, Toronto, Ontario M5T 3A3; 416–593–6427, fax 416–979–7587.

On Guadeloupe: Office Départemental du Tourisme de Guadeloupe, 5 Square de la Banque, B.P. 1099, Pointe-à-Pître, Guadeloupe, FWI 97110; 590–82–09–30. The island also has tourist offices in Basse-Terre at the Gendarmerie (590–82–00–05).

KNOW BEFORE YOU GO

Arriving and Departing: A passport or notarized birth certificate with raised seal, or voter registration card with photo ID are required for U.S. and Canadian citizens. You must show an onward or return ticket. There is no departure tax unless you are part of a charter group.

Money: The French franc is the official currency, but U.S. dollars are widely accepted.

Language: French is spoken everywhere, and street signs, shop signs, and menus are in French. If you don't *parlez Français* you'll be better off staying in one of the larger hotels where some staff speak English.

Staying Healthy: Excellent medical facilities and a 24-hour emergency room are available at the Centre Hopitalier de Pointe-à-Pître; 590–82–98–80.

WHERE TO STAY

Like the ones in French hotels in France, the bedrooms and bathrooms in Guadeloupe's hotels are rather small by American standards.

LE MÉRIDIEN ST-FRANÇOIS

This 150-acre resort on St-François beach next to a Robert Trent Jones golf course on Grande-Terre's southern coast is so jam-packed with sports and leisure activities that it has its own TV station to tell you about them. All sorts of sports are offered free of charge: windsurfing, sailing, snorkeling, aerobics, and volleyball. Full and half-day excursions to other islands can be arranged for a fee. There's also a massage and beauty salon, a swimming pool, a Jacuzzi, three restaurants, and evening entertainment such as steel band, jazz music, and dance performances. Rates include breakfast. Both French and English are spoken.

Accommodations: Rooms have one double or two twin beds, and one child can stay in parents' room. Connecting doors are available. All rooms are air-conditioned and have a mini-bar and small sitting area. The resort has 256 rooms and four suites.

One child under age twelve can stay free in parents' rooms. Daily rates, double occupancy: high season, $275, low season, $195. St-François, Guadeloupe, FWI 97118; 800–543–4300 or 590–88–51–00, fax 590–88–40–71.

TROPICAL CLUB HOTEL

This hotel is on Grande-Terre's long northeastern Atlantic coast, which has stronger cooling trade winds than do other areas. Its large beach is protected by a coral reef, yielding safe calm waters. Highlights include water sports, a good pool, and a 50 percent meal discount for children age two to twelve. Families are comfortably accommodated in rooms with a double bed and bunk beds.

Accommodations: Children ages two to twelve stay free in parents' room. All 156 rooms and eight duplex apartments are air-conditioned and have fans, private terraces, a small kitchenette, and table and chairs.

Daily rates, double occupancy: $125 to $190 depending on time of year. Le Moule, Guadeloupe, FWI 97160; 800–322–2223 or 590–93–97–97, fax 590–93–97–00.

RESIDENCE CANELLA BEACH

Adults rave about the highly regarded French cuisine at this resort's La Verandah restaurant, while their offspring report favorably on the beach activities, pool, and children's playground. Built to resemble a Creole village, Canella Beach has studios and duplexes with terrace kitchenettes in three-story buildings on the southern coast of Grande-Terre in the Gosier area. Snorkeling equipment, paddle boats, canoes, and daytime tennis are complimentary; other water sports such as scuba, windsurfing, catamaran trips, jet skiing, and waterskiing cost extra. The resort's restaurants and snack bars have children's menus and low-calorie options.

Accommodations: All 150 rooms have small kitchenettes, air-conditioning, full baths, in-room safe, twin or queen-size beds, living area with sofa bed, TV, radio, and phone. Choose from studios, junior suites that can accommodate up to four, and duplexes that can accommodate five or six people.

Children under twelve stay free in parents' room. Daily rates, double occupancy: January 2 to April 14, studio $143, junior suite $196, apartment $235, duplex $264; April 15 to December 15, studios $104, junior suite $140, apartment $176, duplex $190. Pointe de la Verdure, Gosier, Guadeloupe, FWI 97190; 800–223–9815 or 590–90–44–00, fax 590–90–44–44.

HOTEL MARISSOL

Set in a huge 10-acre park at the edge of the sea on Grande-Terre's southwest coast, this resort has water sports, a holiday children's program, 150 standard hotel rooms and 50 bungalows with two to four rooms each. Folkloric shows take place at least once a week, and there are several restaurants, a disco, and all kinds of "light" sports such as Ping-Pong, pétanque (like bocce ball), volleyball, archery, and board games.

For Kids: The "Ti Pirate" children's program operates daily during French school holidays from 9:30 A.M. to 9:00 P.M. Children ages six to twelve are invited to participate in water sports, games, and arts and crafts for a daily fee of 150 French francs (about $30). Water sports are monitored by certified staff, and kids receive a weekly schedule and welcoming gifts when they register. Each week, children present a show to the hotel's guests. The program is conducted in French.

Accommodations: All rooms are air-conditioned and have a terrace or balcony, mini-bar, radio, and TV. Connecting doors are available. Bungalows have two to four rooms, and a few are situated at the edge of the beach.

Two children under age twelve stay free in parents' rooms and receive a 50 percent discount on meals. Daily rates, double occupancy: December 15 to April 15, $185 to $243; April 16 to December 14, $111 to $128. Rates include a full American breakfast. Bas du Fort, Gosier, Guadeloupe, FWI 97190; 800–221–4542 or 590–90–84–44, fax 590–90–83–32.

WHAT TO SEE AND DO

Guadeloupe Aquarium is one of the best aquariums in the entire Caribbean. Plan to visit early in your vacation so you can learn to identify the indigenous tropical fish, coral species, and sponges before you go snorkeling or diving. Open daily 9 A.M. to 7 P.M. Place Créole in Bas-du-Fort near Gosier. 590–90–92–38.

On Basse-Terre, 70,000 acres of rain forest, a volcano, and dramatic waterfalls make up the **Parc National de la Guadeloupe**, which occupies a generous third of the island without ever touching the coast. Well-marked nature trails that lead through the rain forest begin behind the visitors center on the Route de la Traversée. Favorites include the **Cascade aux Ecrévisses** (Crayfish Falls), a sparkling waterfall and pond perfect for a refreshing dip, and the **Parc Bras David** which has walking tours of varying lengths. The **Zoological Park and Botanical Gardens** displays animals such as iguanas, turtles, and cockatoos. Open daily, 9:00 A.M. to 5:00 P.M. La Traversée, 590–98–83–52. The park's best-known attraction is **La Soufrière**, a volcano near the southern end. La Soufrière's last eruption (in 1976) prompted the evacuation of 70,000 people. You can hike to the top without a guide on any of several trails to see its five-acre center of bubbling lava and strange rock formations. **Carbet Falls,** on a hillside of La

Soufrière, is a dramatic three-level waterfall—the highest in the Caribbean—that you can easily hike to in about 30 minutes. Park headquarters can be reached at 590–80–24–25, fax 590–80–05–46.

Jacques Cousteau spent time in the waters off Guadeloupe and described the area around Pigeon Island as one of the world's ten best snorkeling and scuba spots. The **Cousteau Underwater Park** stretches along Basse-Terre's scenic western coast. The park's glass-bottom boat, *Nautilus*, takes passengers to view the reef and stops for snorkeling and swimming off Pigeon Island. Reservations, 590–98–89–08.

18

JAMAICA

JAMAICA IS HOME to the Caribbean's greatest concentration of all-inclusive resorts, and some of these have been built just for families. Keeping in mind that Mom and Dad's idea of fun may not be quite what the kids had in mind and vice versa, these resorts make it possible for adults to doze in the sun while the kids exhaust themselves with every water sport imaginable. They also feature children's programs, nannies, washers and dryers, and virtually everything necessary for a *"no problem"* family vacation.

Jamaica is the third largest and one of the most scenic of the Caribbean islands. About the size of Connecticut, it was originally called *Xaymaca*, Arawak for "land of wood and water," from which the current word *Jamaica* comes. The 120 rivers that run through the island have thrilling rapids for riding, waterfalls for climbing, and gentle waters for swimming and canoeing. Verdant mountain ranges rich in limestone, marble, porphyry, alabaster, shale, and sandstone cover almost half of the island. The dramatic coastline has some of the world's most beautiful beaches, caves, coves, and reefs.

The first tourists came to Jamaica on banana boats before the turn of the century. Plenty has happened since then, but the allure of the island remains.

TOURIST INFORMATION

In the United States: Jamaica Tourist Board. *Boston:* 21 Merchants Road, Boston, MA 02109; 800–752–2599 or

617–248–5811, fax 617–367–2438. *Chicago area*: 36 South Wabash Avenue, Chicago, IL 60603; 312–346–1546, fax 312–346–1667. *Florida*: 1320 South Dixies Highway, Suite 1100, Coral Gables, FL 33146; 305–665–0557, fax 305–666–1546. *Los Angeles*: 3440 Wilshire Boulevard, Suite 1207, Los Angeles, CA 90010; 213–384–1123, fax 213–384–1780. *New York*: 866 Second Avenue, 20th floor, New York, NY 10017; 212–688–7650, fax 212–759–5012.

In Canada: Jamaica Tourist Board, Suite 616, Eglinton Avenue East, Toronto, Ontario M4P 3A1; 416–482–7850, fax 416–482–1730.

In Jamaica: 2 St. Lucia Avenue, New Kingston 5, Jamaica; 809–929–9200, fax 809–929–9375.

KNOW BEFORE YOU GO

Arriving and Departing: Because airlines offer direct flights from the United States and Canada into both of Jamaica's international airports (Kingston and Montego Bay), you don't have to change planes in Miami or Puerto Rico, as you do for many of the other islands. U.S. and Canadian citizens need a passport or birth certificate or voter registration card with a photo ID. Visitors pay a departure tax of $10.

Money: Jamaica dollars are the legal tender, although U.S. and Canadian dollars are accepted at many tourist-oriented businesses.

Language: English is the official language, but the Jamaican "patois" you will hear has a vocabulary all its own. Lots of words mean great, cool, or A-OK, such as *"irie"* and *"cool runnin's"*; the meaning of others, like *"soon come,"* is easier to decipher.

Staying Healthy: Hospitals and medical centers exist in all major cities in Jamaica, with the biggest and most complete in Kingston.

Precautions: Jamaica no problem? Well, not really. Crime exists in Jamaica, just as it does in any city in the United States or Canada. The difference between the haves (who are often visitors) and the have-nots (who are often local residents) is often extreme and fuels the incidence of crime. Take the same precautions you would at home: be aware of your surroundings, keep your rental car locked, and don't carry valuables. Eager entrepreneurs will approach you on the beach and streets and ask you to buy just about anything, including drugs. A pleasant but firm "No thank you" will discourage them.

Meet the People: If you make arrangements before you go, you can hook up with Jamaican families who have similar interests and spend some of what may turn out to be your most interesting time on the island with them. Contact the Jamaican tourist board or the tourist office in the area where you're staying.

Local Food: The West Indian pimento or allspice is indigenous to Jamaica and constitutes the backbone of Jamaican cooking. Jerk sauces use pimento as well as hot pepper and spices, and jerk chicken and pork are Jamaican specialties featuring meats marinated for hours in a delicious aromatic sauce. Bammie is a toasted flat cassava wafer eaten with fried fish. Ackee, Jamaica's unofficial national vegetable, was originally brought from Africa. You'll find a bottle of Pickapeppa sauce on every cafe table. Matrimony is a fruit salad bound with condensed milk.

MONTEGO BAY

Known affectionately as Mo'Bay, the tourism capital of Jamaica lies adjacent to a body of water Christopher Columbus dubbed "The Gulf of Good Weather." Today it's Jamaica's second largest city and offers the largest number of guest rooms of any resort area on the island. An international airport makes coming and going easy, and its stretch of glittering sandy coastline makes leaving hard.

WHERE TO STAY

HALF MOON GOLF TENNIS AND BEACH CLUB AND HALF MOON VILLAGE VILLAS

Glamorous Half Moon Club has added spacious and luxurious villas to its selection of deluxe accommodations. The main body of the resort houses the hotel, beach water sports center, 18-hole golf course, and riding stables. "Villa Village" is located across a natural wetlands filled with bird life and has its own beach, a croquet court, a putting green, shops, and restaurants. Guests are given the use of a car or golf cart so they can easily travel between the two properties. The resort's equestrian center is one of the best in the Caribbean, and one of its international show jumping events recently hosted Captain Mark Philips (former husband to Princess Anne). Commoners can saddle up one of their horses and ride along the beach or through the Jamaican countryside. Other celebrity guests at the resort have included Eddie Murphy, Shabba Ranks, and Phyllicia Rashad. Sports and amenities of every kind, including glass-bottom boat rides and spa services, are available.

For Kids: The lavishly landscaped grounds that surround the Children's Activity Center have a duck pond, kiddie pool, sandboxes, swings, horseshoes, and a tennis court. Tightly planned daily activities from 10:00 A.M. to noon and from 2:00 to 4:00 P.M. are arranged for three age groups—three to seven, seven to twelve, and twelve to fourteen—and include nature walks, swimming, games, reggae dance lessons, arts and crafts, and ice cream parties. Private nanny service is available for an extra fee.

Accommodations: Twenty-five villas with four to six bedrooms each include a private pool, rental car or golf cart, chef, maid, gardener, and laundry service. The main hotel has seven different styles of rooms. Guests can choose from a number of inclusive plans, all with children's rates.

Daily rates, double occupancy: $240 to $800. Weekly rate, villas: winter, $10,500 to $14,700, depending on number of bedrooms; rest of year, $6,650 to $9,310. All rates include tax and service charge. Children under age two stay free in parents' room. P.O. Box 80, Rose Hall, Montego Bay, Jamaica; 809–953–2211, fax 809–953–2731.

WYNDHAM ROSE HALL BEACH RESORT

Handsomely situated at the water's edge on an old sugarcane plantation, this 400-acre resort has its own golf course and eighteenth-century great house, Rose Hall, whose mistress Annie Palmer is just one of the historical building's claims to fame. She allegedly murdered three husbands, and her ghost is said to haunt the great house. Three interconnected freshwater pools and a lovely sandy beach host the water sports. The picturesque waterfalls on the lushly landscaped golf course were featured in several James Bond movies.

For Kids: Nine- to twelve-year-olds get to tie-dye their own T-shirts, and five- to eight-year-olds have sing-alongs and scavenger hunts at this daily program open between 10:00 A.M. and 4:00 P.M. The schedule changes daily and includes such activities as building sandcastles, competing in a mini-Olympics, taking part in swim races, and playing volleyball.

Accommodations: The resort's 500 standard hotel rooms have two queen-size or one king-size bed and air-conditioning, plus a patio or balcony. One- and two-bedroom suites are available.

From May through September, kids ages twelve and under eat free and stay free in their parents' room. Discounts of up to 50 percent are given on adjoining rooms. Daily rates, double occupancy: $160 to $220, depending on room size and time of year. P.O. Box 999, Rose Hall, Montego Bay, Jamaica; 800–996–3426 or 809–953–2650, fax 809–953–2617.

NEGRIL

At the extreme western end of the island, Negril was a small fishing village until visitors discovered its recreational possibilities a few decades ago. It is now a popular resort locale.

WHERE TO STAY

POINCIANA BEACH HOTEL

This resort bills itself as the place where children can bring their parents for a perfect vacation. Located on a wide swath of Negril's 7 miles of white sand, kids of ages three to twelve can visit the

Kiddie's Club while parents receive a massage, acquire a suntan, or try any number of water sports. The list of attractions goes on and on: two swimming pools; a full water sports program with scuba, snorkeling, windsurfing, sailing, and kayaking; bicycles, table tennis, volleyball, horseshoes, and shuffleboard; a video arcade; and a gym and weight room. The family-friendly atmosphere extends across the street to Anancy Family Fun and Nature Park, which has an 18-hole miniature golf course, go-carts, a nature trail, a boating lake, and a carousel.

For Kids: Camp Anancy children's program operates daily year-round from 10:00 A.M. to 10:00 P.M. Kids also enjoy the resort's playground, complete with sandbox, swings, and jungle gyms. Private baby-sitters are available for day or evening care and can be arranged through the hotel for a small fee.

Accommodations: Hotel rooms have one king or two double beds. Two-room suites with a king-size bed and fold-out couch and fully equipped one- or two-bedroom villas are best for families.

Rates include airport transfers, meals, drinks, and all activities except scuba and massages, which have a separate fee. Family package rates are always available, be sure to ask. Daily rates, per person double occupancy: summer season $165 to $250; winter rates $198 to $325. Norman Manley Boulevard, Negril, Jamaica; 800–468–6728 or 809–957–4256, fax 809–957–4229.

RUNAWAY BAY

The town of Runaway Bay is between Ocho Rios and Falmouth on the north coast.

WHERE TO STAY

FDR RESORT

A Girl Friday trained in childcare, housekeeping, and cooking is assigned to every family at FDR for the duration of their stay. Her job is to make you happy; she'll take the children to the swimming pool, feed the baby, prepare the meal of your choice, or disappear when you require privacy.

The resort's planners have thought of every detail, from the baby gates at the top of the stairways to a stool for children in the bathrooms. Rates include meals, drinks, and excursions. There are two beaches—one protected and shallow and safe for young ones, and the other for teens and adults with deeper water and interesting coral and fish life. Live nightly entertainment will appeal to Mom and Dad or the entire clan.

For Kids: FDR cleverly slips education into its program. Children learn about Jamaica's culture and heritage and learn to speak patois. They collect and learn the names of leaves and shells, and then use them in crafts projects. The "Kiddies Center" has eight computers, educational games, and all kinds of toys, and is open from 9:00 A.M. to 10:00 P.M. for children of ages two to eleven.

Teens have their own supervised daily activities such as bike tours, arts and crafts lessons, trips to nearby Ocho Rios, hikes, and treasure hunts. They can play pinball, pool, and basketball at any time.

Accommodations: Each family has its own villa suite with a kitchen, dining area, spacious living room, and balcony connected to one, two, or three bedrooms.

Rates include all meals, wine, bar drinks, transfers to and from the airport, and use of all sports and entertainment facilities. Weekly rates: $1,720 to $1,820 per person. Children under age sixteen stay free in parents' room. A third adult sharing a one-bedroom suite subtracts 30 percent from the standard rate. Franklin D Resort, Runaway Bay, St. Ann, Jamaica; 800–654–1FDR or 516–223–1786, fax 516–223–4815; in Jamaica: 809–973–3067, fax 809–973–3071.

TRELAWNY BEACH HOTEL

All children under age fifteen stay free in their parents' room at this action-oriented all-inclusive hotel, making for a very reasonably priced vacation. Trelawny is in a secluded setting in the Falmouth area, about half an hour's drive from Montego Bay. Shuttle buses take shoppers and sightseers into Mo'Bay daily, and rafting trips on the Martha Brae River are just a few minutes' away by car. Many people never leave the resort, staying busy with scuba diving, water sports, sunbathing, tennis, a disco, the beaches (including a private nude beach), and entertainment every evening.

For Kids: Daily activities for youngsters of ages two to fourteen take place in the resort's "Fun Center," where a separate day-care section is provided for children less than two years old. Older children are divided by age group—two to five, six to eight, and nine to fourteen—and a schedule of weekly activities is available upon check-in. The center operates daily from 8:00 A.M. to 8:00 P.M. and features a Jamaican-style play jungle and a mini-zoo containing small domestic animals.

Accommodations: Standard and superior rooms are identical except for the mountain or ocean views and have one king-size or two twin beds; one roll-away can be added. Beachfront cottages are slightly bigger, with one king or two doubles, and can accommodate two adults and two children. All have patios or balconies, full baths, and radios.

Free meals and accommodations are offered for children ages fourteen and under. Daily rates per person, double occupancy: December 15 to April 15, standard $149, superior $159, cottage $169; April 16 to December 14, standard $109, superior $119, cottage $129. Inclusive rates cover food and drinks, water sports, horseback riding, tennis, crafts, and events. Falmouth, Trelawny, Jamaica; 800–336–1435 or 809–954–2450, fax 809–954–2173.

OCHO RIOS AREA

Sixty-seven miles east of Montego Bay, Ocho Rios is favored by Jamaicans as a beach escape. Dunn's River Falls is a nearby attraction that your kids will remember long after their tans fade.

WHERE TO STAY

BOSCOBEL BEACH RESORT

Toddlers through teens who like to stay busy with others their own age will find plenty of action at Boscobel, Jamaica's first all-inclusive resort designed and built specifically for families. Parents will find opportunities for rest, recuperation, and family time. Boscobel is popular for family reunions, as it offers fun and relaxation together and apart for every age. All ages are welcome at the resort's Olympic-size swimming pool, while a smaller adults-only pool gives parents a break from the noise and splashing. Toddlers have their own wading pool. A special nursery cares for babies and toddlers, while the Kid's Club offers activities for four- to twelve-year-olds. Teens have a Jump Up Club all their own. If parents want to enjoy a late dinner at the adults-only award-winning restaurant, Allegro, and the kids' centers are closed, they can hire a nannie for a small fee (available 24 hours) and dine without fear of spilt milk. Children under age fourteen stay and eat free in their parents' rooms. Besides a gorgeous white sand beach and clear Caribbean waters, the resort has a mini-zoo, adventure playground, snorkeling, scuba, kayaking, windsurfing, waterskiing, and tennis. Stay in shape at the fitness center, ride bicycles, play tennis, or golf to your heart's content.

For Kids: The Kid's Club is open from 9:00 A.M. until 10:00 P.M. with separate daily activities tailored for ages four to seven and for ages eight to twelve. Children might tie-dye T-shirts, work in the computer lab, learn to play tennis, or take bike excursions. The supervised Teens Jump Up Club, open from 10:00 A.M. to 11:00 P.M., includes computers, Ping-Pong, pool tables, a movie theater, and a jukebox and dance floor. Little ones under age four can find care and comfort in a special nursery open from 9:00 A.M. to 5:00 P.M. Private nannies are available 24 hours a day for a small fee to watch children of any age.

Accommodations: One-bedroom suites and larger junior suites have a king-size bed in the bedroom and a queen-size sofa bed in the living room. Lanai rooms are suitable for older children or for families with one baby.

Boscobel has many different rates, depending on the time of year you visit and the length of your stay. The longer you stay, the less you pay per night. There is a three-night minimum except during Christmas, February holiday week, and Easter, when a seven-night minimum and the highest rates apply. Lowest rates are in September, October, May, and June; highest rates are during winter months and holidays. For a three-night visit, rates per person range from $535 to $850 for smaller accommodations and $605 to $925 for suites. Up to two children (one per parent) sharing parents' room stays, plays, and eats free. Everything is included in the price: meals, snacks, bar drinks, wine, trips and excursions, sports, and tips. P.O. Box 63, Ocho Rios, Jamaica; 800–859–7873 or 809–974–3291, fax 809–975–3270.

PLANTATION INN

This modern version of an elegant plantation is set on a private crescent of warm white sand. It consistently gets high marks for its deluxe rooms and suites, high-class service, and excellent cuisine. At one time, children were not allowed at this tony resort; but that has changed, and guests are now bringing their children, grandchildren, even great-grandchildren. Families traveling with small children are housed on the hotel's lower level, and cribs and baby-sitters are available. A new children's program operates when kids are present. Other options include daily tennis clinics on two courts, windsurfing, snorkeling, glass-bottom boat rides, Sunfish sailboats, croquet, a gym, a sauna, and nightly entertainment, all complimentary. Scuba is extra.

For Kids: Some clever ideas infuse the children's program with fun; kids learn to limbo dance, talk Jamaican, and make a friendship bracelet. They can also take a glass-bottom boat ride and participate in treasure hunts, beach Olympics, and games and stories. The schedule of activities changes daily.

Accommodations: All 63 guest rooms and 15 luxury suites have private balconies, air-conditioning, and ocean views. In addition, there are two villas with private swimming pools.

Children under age twelve stay free in parents' room. Daily rates, double occupancy: March 15 to December 15, $130 to $310; December 16 to March 14, $195 to $485. Two- to four-bedroom deluxe villas, per week: summer, $2,205 to $3,080; winter, $4,375 to $5,110. P.O. Box 2, Ocho Rios, Jamaica; in USA, 800–752–6824 or 800–74–CHARMS; in Canada, 800–567–5327; in Jamaica, 809–974–5601, fax 809–974–5912.

VILLA AND APARTMENT RENTALS

JAVA (Jamaican Association of Villas and Apartments) has been in business for more than 30 years and represents more than 300 villas, cottages, and condominiums. 800-VILLAS6, 809–974–2508 or 312–883–3485, fax 312–883–5140.

WHAT TO SEE AND DO

Anancy Family Fun and Nature Park in Negril was named for Anancy (often spelled Anansi), the mischievous spider character in Jamaican (and African) folktales and children's story books. The park was developed to provide entertainment for the entire family while developing an appreciation for the history, culture, and natural beauty of Jamaica. Visitors can ride a go-cart and then observe cultural exhibits of Jamaican folk arts and crafts, or take a spin on a carousel followed by a walk along a marked nature trail. You'll also find an 18-hole miniature golf course, mini-Jeeps, a boating lake, and a fishing pond where the motto is "you catch it, we cook it." Bait and fishing poles are available for a nominal fee. Across from the Poinciana Beach Hotel; 800–468–6728 or 809–957–4100.

River rafting on the gentle Martha Brae River just east of Falmouth is a popular trip for families, who sit on bamboo rafts steered by experienced pole-wielding raftsmen. You'll cover 3½ miles in about an hour and a half past fern groves, bamboo, bananas, and sugarcane. The river was named for an Arawak Indian who refused to reveal the location of a gold mine to some greedy Spaniards. Instead, she took them to the site of the mine and used magic to change the course of the river, drowning herself and the interlopers. You can book raft trips through most hotels; 809–952–0889.

Rafting on the Rio Grande near Port Antonio, on the island's northeastern coast, carries tourists past people washing clothes, swimming, and bathing in the river. Occasionally musicians serenade from passing rafts in hopes of a tip. Other floating vendors offer cold drinks and souvenirs. Keep a look out to see where the local kids are swimming, and ask your raftsman to stop so you can take a refreshing dip. The trip takes about three hours, longer if you stop to cool off frequently; 809–993–2778.

Walk up **Dunn's River Falls,** a cascading series of broad stone "steps" carved by the swath of cool mountain water that spills to the sea roughly midway between St. Ann's Bay and Ocho Rios. Wear your swimsuit, grab the hand of the person above you and climb the slippery steps. It's best to visit at times or on days when cruise ships' passengers are not present, to avoid crowds. $3 adults, $1 children.

Off-shore **scuba diving** is most common along the west and north coasts of the island. Montego Bay is famous for its wall dives, and Kingston has Port Royal, the sunken city with sunken ships and beautiful reefs.

The Jamaican Tourist Board licenses dive operators. When arranging dive trips, make sure they are licensed by the Jamaica Association of Dive Operators (JADO).

19

MARTINIQUE

LE SOLEIL SHINES BRIGHTLY on the white and gray sand beaches of Martinique's coastlines. The island's leeward side is classically Caribbean, with soft and gentle waves lapping smooth, calm shores. On its windward Atlantic shore, the terrain is more rugged, with rough waters crashing on pretty coved beaches and rough-hewn cliffs. The island holds a surprising variety of attractions, with more than just gorgeous beaches to draw visitors.

Centuries ago the Carib Indians called the island "Madinina," meaning "Isle of Flowers," and hibiscus, frangipani, bougainvillea, poinsettia, orchids, and anthuriums still cover the land. Fields that once grew sugarcane are now rich in guava, mango, papaya, bananas, pineapple, cinnamon, and coffee. In the tropical rain forests, hikers come across giant breadfruit trees and ferns as big as a house.

A mass of intensely hot gas from Mt. Pelée, accompanied by ash and cinders, smothered the Martinican city of St-Pierre in 1902, killing all but one of its inhabitants. Ruins and a small museum in the rebuilt city, now just a fragment of its former glory, offer visitors the chance to see its touching artifacts. A zoological garden shelters 70 animal species, and several oddball museums get high marks from children. The Museum of Seashell Arts displays intricate scenes of life on Martinique made entirely of shells; the Poupées Vegetables Doll Museum exhibits finely crafted and delicate dolls made of wild plants, leaves, flowers, and straw. Your kids will want to embark on a nature treasure hunt and try this craft themselves.

Martinique is West Indian with a French twist. Haute cuisine mixes with island delicacies from the sea and garden, creating a memorable culinary experience almost anywhere you dine. Your sons and daughters might be wide-eyed at the topless sunbathing on most of the beaches, but they are sure to enjoy the mouthwatering baguettes and chocolate brioches they'll find in the local *patisseries*. English is spoken at most hotels, but the official language is French, and it is useful to bring along a French phrase book.

The capital city, Fort-de-France, is backed by lush mountains and crisscrossed by narrow balconied streets. On the south side of the bay, opposite Fort-de-France, are beautiful beaches and the island's greatest concentration of resort hotels.

TOURIST INFORMATION

In the United States: Martinique Development and Promotion Bureau, 444 Madison Avenue, New York, NY 10022; 800–391–4909, fax 212–838–7855.
In Canada: French Government Tourist Office, 1981 McGill College Avenue, Suite 490, Montreal H3A 2W9; 514–288–4264. Dundas Street West, Suite 2405, Toronto, Ontario M5G 1Z3; 800–361–9099 or 416–593–4723.
On Martinique: Along the waterfront in Fort-de-France on Boulevard Alfassa; 596–63–79–60; also at Lamentin Airport.

KNOW BEFORE YOU GO

Arriving and Departing: U.S. and Canadian citizens need a valid or recently expired passport, or original birth certificate or voter registration card accompanied by an official photo ID. You must show an ongoing or return ticket.
Money: The French franc is the official currency, but U.S. and Canadian dollars are accepted almost everywhere.
Language: French is the official language, but Creole, a blend of French and Spanish, is spoken at rapid-fire speed by many locals. English is spoken in major tourist areas.

Staying Healthy: Just outside Fort-de-France in Châteauboeuf, Hopital La Meynard has a 24-hour emergency room, 596–55–20–00. Beware of the manchineel (called *mancenillier* in French) tree with its poison fruits and blistering sap. Most of the trees have red warning signs posted. Atlantic (eastern shore) waters are quite rough and should be avoided except around Cap Chevalier.

WHERE TO STAY

Quite a few family accommodations in Martinique have kitchenettes on outdoor terraces.

LE BACKOUA

One of the most stylish resort hotels on the island, Le Backoua in the Trois-Ilets area south of Fort-de-France is on a beautiful, albeit small, white sand beach. Guest rooms are in four buildings on the hillside or along the beach. Families are most comfortable in the garden-view building, whose rooms connect through communicating doors. A large swimming pool, which seems to spill over one edge into the sea, and the complete water sports center are the center of resort activity during the day. Three restaurants, two bars, and nightly live entertainment draw guests from other hotels. There are two tennis courts, croquet, a golf driving range; scuba and waterskiing are offered at an extra charge.

Accommodations: All 139 rooms have air-conditioning, balconies or terraces, and king-size beds. One child under age twelve is allowed in garden-view rooms on a roll-away bed. Larger families must reserve rooms with connecting doors.

One extra child under age twelve stays free in parents' room. Rates include buffet breakfast and taxes. Daily rates, double occupancy: December 20 to April 30, $250; May 1 to December 16, $150. P.O. Box 589, Fort-de-France, Martinique, FWI; 800–221–4542 or 596–66–02–02, fax 596–66–00–41.

RELAIS CARAIBES

These 16 attractive bungalows have more personality and charm than many other properties on Martinique. They sit on a hill on the south coast of the island, facing Diamond Rock (Rocher du Diamant); the beach is only 200 yards away. A continental breakfast is included in the rates, and the grounds include a small playground, a swimming pool overlooking the sea at the edge of a cliff, a good restaurant serving French Creole cuisine, and tennis courts. Water sports and additional restaurants are nearby.

Accommodations: Each bungalow has a living room area with a sofa bed, a bedroom area, a refrigerator, and bathroom. All are air-conditioned. Superior rooms have one double bed, and one roll-away can be added.

Children under twelve, $26 per day. Daily rates, double occupancy: January to May 31, superior $137, bungalow $213; June 1 to December 14, superior $110, bungalow $213. Pointe de la Chery, Le Diamant, Martinique, FWI 97223; 800–223–9815 or 596–76–44–65, fax 596–76–21–20.

DIAMANT MARINE

Many French families stay at this self-contained apartment complex in units that trail down a hillside to the sea. All rooms feature views of the azure sea and of Diamond Rock. The main hotel building is at the top of the 100-foot hillside, and the climb down to the beach is easy and exciting as little ones anticipate fun in the sea and sand. But the climb back up at the end of a busy day can seem longer than it really is, so bring a few bribes to motivate tired youngsters. A long water slide whisks kids into a lagoon-shaped freshwater swimming pool, and all water sports can be arranged from the resort's water sports center. Other activities include volleyball, Ping-Pong, a game room, and two tennis courts. A shuttle takes guests to the towns of Le Diamant and Fort-de-France. Full American-style buffet breakfasts are included in the rates.

Accommodations: Each of the 150 small apartments is basically a sleeping room with a kitchenette on the terrace. The main room has a sofa sleeper and king-size bed, and the kitchen is outfitted with a refrigerator, a two-burner stove, and all cookware and utensils.

One child under age twelve stays free in parents' room. Daily rates, double occupancy: November 1 to January 4, $163; January 5 to October 31, $144; June, $115. Point de la Chery, Le Diamant, Martinique, FWI; 800–221–4542 or 596–76–46–00, fax 596–76–25–99.

DIAMANT-NOVOTEL

A children's program operates during French school holidays for kids from ages six to twelve, and a year-round evening nursery from 6:00 P.M. to 2:00 A.M. allows adults to linger over a long French-style dinner. Tiny kids have their own paddling pool, while adults and older children swim and splash in the "grown-up" pool. This 5-acre resort on a peninsula overlooking Diamond Rock is filled with palm trees, bougainvillea, and other colorful tropical plants. Several restaurants and bars serve everything from fine Creole cuisine to casual poolside lunchtime snacks and feature evening steel band entertainment. A water sports kiosk offers complimentary pedal boats, sailboats, snorkel gear, windsurfing equipment, canoes, and an introduction to scuba in the pool. A fee is charged for dive trips and waterskiing, Hobie cats, and deep-sea fishing trips. Horseback riding trips begin from the ranch next door. The staff speaks English.

For Kids: Called the "Ti Pirate Child Minder Service," the program operates seven days a week during French school holidays from 9:30 A.M. to 9:00 P.M. with dinner between 6:30 and 7:30 P.M. A fee of 150 French francs (about $30) is charged per child per day. Children age six to twelve are supervised by a qualified staff and receive an activity schedule and welcoming gifts at the beginning of their stay. Sports activities, games, and arts and crafts are planned throughout the week. The kids present a show to the hotel's guests each week. The program is conducted in French.

Accommodations: All 181 rooms (including six suites) overlook the sea, the pool, or gardens and have air-conditioning, double bed, sofa bed, safe, and hair dryer. Connecting rooms are available.

Two children under age sixteen can stay free in parents' room.

Rates include full American breakfast. Daily rates, double occupancy: April 25 to December 20, $128; December 21 to April 24, $195. Pointe de la Chery, Le Diamant, Martinique, FWI 97223; 596–76–42–42, fax 596–76–22–87.

ANSE CARITAN BEACH

Another hotel popular with French families is Anse Caritan Beach in Ste-Anne near the southern tip of the island. Its two-bedroom units and studios all have kitchenettes and are scattered around a central entertainment complex containing a restaurant and bar and complete water sports center with windsurfing, sailing, waterskiing, scuba, paddle boats, and boat rides. There's also a pool, volleyball, billiards, Ping-Pong, and evening entertainment such as dance bands and fashion shows.

Accommodations: All 96 hotel rooms have kitchenettes on the terrace and air-conditioning. Studios hold two people, and two-bedroom units accommodate four.

Daily rates, double occupancy: summer $150, winter $170. Rates include a full American breakfast. 97227 St. Anne, Martinique, FWI; 800–755–9313 or 596–76–74–12, fax 212–254–0654 or 596–76–72–59.

VILLAS

The **Villa Rental Service** run by the Martinique tourist office can arrange vacation home rentals. Most of them are in the southern part of the island near good beaches, and rent by the week or month; 596–63–79–60.

WHAT TO SEE AND DO

St-Pierre on the upper west coast was known as the Paris of the West Indies until 1902, when the Mount Pelée volcano erupted in an avalanche of fiery gas, suffocating ash, and molten rock. Three minutes later, all inhabitants of the town were dead except for one person—a prisoner who was jailed in a thick-walled underground dungeon and survived to become a Barnum & Bailey Circus sideshow attraction. The ruins of his cell and other vulcanized buildings still stand. The **Musée Vulcanologique** portrays the tragedy through old photographs and relics excavated from the site, including a melted tuba, blackened spaghetti, and clocks stopped at 8:00 A.M., the time of the disaster. Open daily, 9:00 A.M. to noon and 3:00 to 5:00 P.M.; 596–78–15–16.

Cyparis Express is a little train that tours the historic town. A rather new **submarine tour** of the Bay of St-Pierre take visitors to see wrecks of ships lost in the volcanic eruption. Reassure your children that the volcano is now dormant. Contact your hotel for details.

South of St-Pierre, **Le Carbet,** a site where Columbus is believed to have stopped in 1502, is home to the **Zoo de Carbet,** also called the Amazona Zoo. You can get up close and personal with animals from the Caribbean, the Amazon, and Africa, including rare birds, caimans, snakes, and wildcats. Open daily, 9:00 A.M. to 6:00 P.M.; 596–78–00–64.

The dolls in **Musée de Poupées Végétales** are so delicately crafted that from a distance they resemble small porcelain figurines. Upon closer inspection you can see the leaf overskirts, bark dresses, and flower hats that turn them into famous French historical figures. Open daily, 7:00 A.M. to 5:00 P.M.; 596–78–53–92. The **Leyritz Plantation** at the northern end of the island, which houses the museum, has a hotel, sugarcane factory, and lovely gardens.

The **Martinique Aquarium** displays marine animals from the surrounding waters and is a smart stop to make before you head out on a snorkeling expedition. Don't worry about the piranhas on display; the only ones you'll see on Martinique are in this aquarium. Open daily, 9:00 A.M. to 7:00 P.M. 3 Boulevard de la Marne, 596–73–02–09.

The **Museum of Seashell Art** in Anse a l'Ane has an extensive shell collection as well as shell artwork depicting scenes of daily life on Martinique. Displays include tiny shell farms worked by shell farmers, complete with cows and chickens; a sugarcane harvest; and a seashell depiction of Napoleon's coronation. Open Wednesday to Monday, 9:00 A.M. to noon and 3:00 to 5:00 P.M.; 596–68–34–97.

20

MONTSERRAT

MONTSERRAT RECALLS THE Caribbean of years ago: friendly, comfortable, and safe. The entire island resembles a small town spread across luxuriant green mountains and fields filled with explosions of flowers, grazing goats, and prolific tropical fruit trees edged by the brilliant blue Caribbean sea. With few white sand beaches to lure big resort development, the island has only two full-service hotels, a few guest houses, and a number of attractive villas. It still has lovely beaches (composed of velvety black volcanic sand), but a quieter life-style pervades.

Mountain bikers like this volcanic island for its physically demanding altitude changes, on- and off-road trails, and breathtaking vistas from anywhere they stop. Two racing events—one in May and one in October—draw cyclists from all over.

In December, carnival is a big homecoming for Montserratians who live abroad, and the island comes alive with calypso competitions, queen shows (similar to a beauty contest, but with a costume competition thrown in), jump-ups, and street fairs. The festivities culminate on New Year's Day with a parade and jump-ups until midnight.

The first European settlers in Montserrat were seventeenth-century Irish colonists from St. Kitts. Today, St. Patrick's Day is celebrated both for the commemoration of St. Patrick and as the day on which the island's slaves staged a revolt. In the village of St. Patrick, a two- to three-day festival takes place with masquerades, jump-ups, street theater, music, and a Freedom Run. Pilgrimage takes place for two weeks in August; it is a bit like carnival with masquerades, jump-ups, and musical performances.

The tidy and compact capital city of Plymouth on the island's southwest coast has many old buildings built of stones that had been used as ballast on sailing ships. At press time, the island's volcano was expected to errupt; contact the tourist office for an update.

TOURIST INFORMATION

In the United States: c/o Joan Medhurst and Associates, 775 Park Avenue, Huntington, NY 11743; 800–642–2002, fax 516–425–0903.
In Canada: c/o New Concepts, 2455 Cawthra Road, Suite 70, Mississauga, Ontario L5A 3PL; 905–803–0131, fax 905–803–0132.
On Montserrat: Department of Tourism, Church Road, P.O. Box 7, Plymouth, Montserrat, WI; 809–491–2230, fax 809–491–7430 (weekdays only).

KNOW BEFORE YOU GO

Arriving and Departing: U.S. and Canadian citizens must show proof of citizenship in the form of a passport or voter's registration card or birth certificate with an official photo. An onward or return ticket is required, and visitors over age twelve must pay a departure tax of $8.
Money: The Eastern Caribbean Dollar (EC$) is the official currency, but U.S. dollars are widely accepted.
Staying Healthy: Glendon Hospital in Plymouth has a 24-hour emergency room. Serious cases are flown to San Juan or Miami.
Language: English is the official language of Montserrat.
Local Food: Most children like the island's roasted fresh coconut chips, called "hospitality chips." Other Montserratian specialties include goat water stew (a rich, meaty dish filled with fresh vegetables) and "mountain chicken" (locally caught frogs legs). The rich soil of Montserrat yields especially good tomatoes, carrots, pineapples, and bananas.
Books, Music and Videos: *The Little Island* by Frané Lessac is a story about a visit two boys pay to Montserrat. Author/artist

Lessac lived on the island for a year and beautifully captures daily scenes. A delightful Reading Rainbow video called My *Little Island* has been made of the story and is available in many public libraries.

WHERE TO STAY

VUE POINTE HOTEL

Run by the friendly Osborne family, Vue Pointe on the island's east coast has hexagonal cottages scattered down a gently sloped green hillside that stops at a curve of black sand beach. All cottages have breathtaking views of Old Road Bluff Bay and the striking turquoise Caribbean Sea. Adjacent to the hotel is a well-priced 18-hole golf course. The hotel's water sports facility on the beach is the most complete on the island. The restaurant, known for its fine cuisine, overlooks the swimming pool and the sea in the distance. With five children of their own, the Osbornes know how to make families comfortable.

The hotel's main building houses an open-air restaurant, terrace and pool, bar, and lounge area. The restaurant hosts a weekly West Indian barbecue with steel band music as well as a weekly cocktail party where children of guests are asked to help, allowing parents to relax and enjoy themselves. A neighbor of the Vue Pointe has several dozen iguanas living on cliffs near his house; and each week, guests are taken to feed (and sometimes even touch) the prehistoric reptiles.

Accommodations: Private, secluded cottages have a queen-size sofabed and two twin beds pushed together to form a king, so various family sleeping configurations can be arranged. All cottages have porches, ceiling fans, several walls of screened windows, and table and chairs. Standard hotel rooms are also available.

Children under twelve stay free in cottages with two adults. Daily rates, double occupancy: cottages, April 15 to December 14, $106, December 15 to April 14, $166; rooms, $90 and $126. Baby-sitting (usually one of the Osbornes' teenage daughters) and room service are available. P.O. Box 65, Olde Towne, Montserrat, WI; 800–235–0709 or 809–491–5210/11, fax 809–491–4813.

MONTSERRAT SPRINGS HOTEL

Perched on a green hill above Emerald Isle Beach, Montserrat Springs has hotel rooms and small apartmentlike suites. Plymouth, the island's capital city, is within walking distance, and the beach is just 500 yards away. A 70-foot-long swimming pool warmed by hot mineral springs sees plenty of action from the younger set. Adults relax around its edges, enjoying the spectacular views of green mountains and blue Caribbean waters. Other features include tennis, a beach bar, a poolside restaurant and bar, and hot and cold baths from a natural mineral spring.

Accommodations: Thirty-four rooms have two double beds; six one- and two-bedroom suites have kitchenettes, big living areas, full kitchens, and washing machines. All have air-conditioning and private balconies.

Daily rates, double occupancy: hotel rooms, April 15 to December 14, $114 to $130; December 15 to April 14, $145 to $165; one-bedroom efficiency suites, April 15 to December 14, $120 to $150 (depending on location), December 15 to April 14, $205 to $215; two-bedroom efficiency suites, April 15 to December 14, $220 to $245, December 15 to April 14, $320 to $335. P.O. Box 259, Plymouth, Montserrat, WI; 800–253–2134 or 809–491–2481, fax 809–491–4070.

SHAMROCK VILLAS

Well-priced one- and two-bedroom apartments rent by the week or more, and are on a hillside in the vicinity of Montserrat Springs Hotel. The beach is a ten-minute walk away. All villas have complete kitchens and ceiling fans, and there is a swimming pool on the premises.

Weekly rates: April 15 to December 14, $350 to $400; December 15 to April 14, $450 to $550. Twice weekly maid service costs extra, about $20. P.O. Box 58, Plymouth, Montserrat, WI; 809–491–2431, fax 809–491–4660

PRIVATE VILLA RENTALS

With accommodations from palatial to simple, Montserrat is known as an island with excellent villa rentals. The best areas for villas are the Richmond Hill, Iselby Hill, and Old Towne areas, all on the west coast north of Plymouth. Many villas have swimming pools, and some are large enough to comfortably accommodate more than one family. Extra services such as daily housekeeping and a cook can easily be arranged. Some villas are not air-conditioned but are well-ventilated by tradewind breezes.

West Indies Real Estate, Ltd. is known for its high-end villa rentals and concierge service, which takes care of anything a guest services desk would handle at a hotel. The staff can arrange water sports, boat trips, golf, baby-sitting, restaurant reservations, and just about anything else you could want. P.O. Box 355, Plymouth, Montserrat, WI; 809–491–8666, fax 809–491–8668.

Neville Bradshaw Agencies Ltd. handles a number of beautiful properties in all price ranges. P.O. Box 270, Plymouth, Montserrat, WI; 809–491–5270, fax 809–491–5069.

WHAT TO SEE AND DO

A visit to **Great Alps Waterfall**, in the southern part of the island, should be planned as a day trip. Pack a picnic lunch, take the 15-minute taxi ride to the beginning of the trail, and then hike to the waterfall through thick rain forests. It takes about 45 minutes to reach the falls—more if you stop and enjoy the scenery. The waterfall plunges 70 feet into a crystal-clear mountain pool. Rainbows color the mist in the noonday sun, and the kids can cool off in the pool for as long as they like.

Mountain biking is popular on Montserrat because of the island's mountainous terrain and the landscape that changes quickly from semi-desert to lush rain forest. Bikers traveling the many roads and trails come across wandering animals, a wide variety of bird life, stone ruins, and breathtaking ocean and island views. **Island bikes** rents 18- and 21-speed mountain bikes by the day or by the week. They deliver to hotels and villas and offer bike parts and a mechanic on duty. P.O. Box 266, Harney Street, Plymouth, Montserrat, WI; 809–491–5552/4696, fax 809–491–8752.

Galway's Plantation, a small picturesque ruin in southern Montserrat that was once a large sugar estate, is now the site of an archaeological excavation. The hillside surrounding the ruined sugar mill is covered in "sensitive plant," which folds its leaves tightly closed when touched. Ask your taxi driver to point it out to you, or look for greenery that spreads like a strawberry plant with smaller, variegated leaves.

Not far from the plantation, **Galway's Soufriere** is a bubbling hot sulfur spring, accessible by a drive and a short hike. Its barren landscape, steaming vents, and oozing sulfur streaks are a vivid reminder that Montserrat is a volcanic island.

21

PUERTO RICO

BORINQUEN, AS THIS ISLAND was first named, was inhabited by several Indian tribes before its "discovery" by Christopher Columbus on his second voyage, in 1493. It was later renamed San Juan and finally Puerto Rico, which means "rich port." Juan Ponce de Leon, who is best known as the seeker of the Fountain of Youth, established a settlement on the island in 1508. His plans for eternal life were thwarted when he died a premature death from a poison-tipped arrow in the jungles of Florida. Spain ceded the island to the United States in 1898 following the Spanish-American War, and Puerto Ricans became U.S. citizens in 1917.

Old San Juan, founded by Ponce de Leon in 1521 on the Atlantic (north) coast of the island, is the oldest capital city under the U.S. flag. It's now a national historic zone with some of the most authentic examples of sixteenth- and seventeenth-century Spanish Colonial architecture in the western hemisphere. Visitors can tour the narrow cobblestone streets and see fanciful wrought-iron balconies, plazas, and sidewalk cafes. The two massive forts that once guarded the city still stand strong and invite exploration. Bustling New San Juan is the island's center of business and commerce.

Less than an hour from San Juan is a lush tropical rain forest and nature reserve known as El Yunque, the only tropical rain forest in the U.S. National Forest System. Numerous hiking trails wind past 240 species of trees, as well as flowers, waterfalls, and birds.

Hundreds of beaches surround the island. The Atlantic side is popular with surfers as its powerful waves make for thrilling rides. The calmer Caribbean side of the island has gentle waves and better swimming for little ones.

Ponce, Puerto Rico's second largest city, is a 90-minute drive southwest of San Juan. It houses an ancient Indian burial ground and the world's most colorful fire station.

TOURIST INFORMATION

In the United States: Puerto Rico Tourism Company. *Los Angeles:* 3575 West Cahuenga Boulevard, Suite 560, Los Angeles, CA 90068; 213–874–5991. *Miami:* 200 S.E. First Street, Suite 700, Miami, FL 33131; 305–381–8915. *New York:* 575 Fifth Avenue, 23rd Floor, New York, NY 10017; 800–223–6530 or 212–599–6262.

In Canada: Puerto Rico Tourism Company, 2 Bloor Street West, Suite 700, Toronto, Ontario M4W 3R1; 416–969–9025.

In Puerto Rico: The Puerto Rico Tourism Company's main office is in a restored former nineteenth-century prison on Paseo la Princesa, Old San Juan, Puerto Rico 00902; 809–721–2400.

KNOW BEFORE YOU GO

Arriving and Departing: Puerto Rico is a commonwealth of the United States, and U.S. citizens can travel freely to and from the island. Canadian citizens need proof of citizenship, and a passport is preferred.

Money: The U.S. dollar is the official currency.

Language: Spanish is the official language of Puerto Rico, but English is widely spoken.

Staying Healthy: San Juan has fourteen private hospitals. All have the same standards as those required on the U.S. mainland. Most physicians are based in San Juan, and most medical specializations are represented.

Caution: Crime is a problem in Puerto Rico, just as it is in many places at home. Avoid deserted beaches, and don't walk alone on a beach at night, even in highly populated areas. Avoid renting an open-air Jeep for touring, and plot your route carefully so you don't get lost in unfamiliar territory.

Local Food: Puerto Rico's cuisine has been influenced by Spanish, Creole, and native Indian cultures. Local vegetables are used frequently. Delicious plaintains are cooked in many different ways, and a variety of beans—especially white beans and *garbanzos* (chick peas)—are common. *Sofrito*, a mix of garlic, onion, sweet pepper, oregano, tomato puree, and coriander, is used as a base for many dishes.

Fritters are fast-food snacks found in roadside stands. These include *empañadillas*, stuffed fried turnovers; *surrullitos*, cheese-stuffed corn sticks; *alcapurias*, stuffed green banana croquettes; and *bacalaitos*, codfish fritters. A Cubano sandwich is made with roast pork, ham, swiss cheese, pickles, and mustard.

Sample the fresh *guarapo* (sugarcane) juice at roadside trucks.

SAN JUAN AREA

WHERE TO STAY

EL SAN JUAN HOTEL AND CASINO

The hand-carved mahogany ceiling and rose marble floor of El San Juan's luxurious lobby exude old-world elegance and distinction. Well located, the hotel is ten minutes from the airport and a short complimentary shuttle bus ride from Old San Juan and El Morro Castle. If you want to explore Old San Juan and your children are too young to appreciate history (or shopping), the hotel has a children's program to keep them occupied. The resort is on a busy strand of beach lined with high-rise hotels, but its secluded tropical gardens surrounding a large swimming pool complex and patio area make you feel worlds away.

For Kids: Afternoon storytime is in the shade of the garden at this full-day program that runs from 10:00 A.M. to 4:00 P.M.

Children ages five to twelve are divided into separate age groups to enjoy water basketball, tennis clinics, treasure hunts on the beach, arts and crafts, Spanish lessons, storytelling, and botanical garden tours. The $28 fee includes lunch and souvenirs. Teenagers learn merengue and salsa dancing at their own Paradise Club.

Accommodations: Most rooms have one king-size or two double beds. Junior suites have a small separate sitting area and a king-size bed; kitchenettes can be added. One- and two-bedroom suites have a full-size Murphy bed in the living room.

Children under age twelve stay free in parents' room. Daily rate, double occupancy: room, December to April, $285 to $325; May to November $220 to $320. Suites and one- and two-bedroom units, December to April, $850 to $1,150; May to November, $595 to $750. (Price for ocean view is higher.) P.O. Box 2872, Avenida Isla Verde, San Juan, PR 00902; 800–468–2818 or 809–791–1000, fax 809–791–6985.

CARIBE HILTON INTERNATIONAL

A boardwalk for strolling is situated along the length of private beach on this deluxe property. Its atrium lobby is decorated with rose marble, waterfalls, and colorful tropical plants; and its lush grounds even include an antique fort. A children's program operates during the summer and over holiday periods, and Old San Juan is a short taxi ride away. The hotel has two pools, six tennis courts lighted for night play, air-conditioned squash and racquetball courts, and all kinds of water sports.

For Kids: Each week, Holiday Camp Coco has a different theme such as "Ecology Awareness," "Peace on Earth," and "Health and Fitness," with games, arts and crafts, parties, water games, and other activities that revolve around the theme. The camp is offered during Presidents Week, Easter, summer, Christmas, and Thanksgiving. A special youth center for teens lets them play games, watch movies, dance, and hang out under supervision during Christmas, Easter, and Thanksgiving holidays.

Accommodations: All 668 rooms have either ocean or lagoon views. Standard rooms have two doubles or one king-size bed, and roll-away beds or cribs can be added. A variety of suites and a full apartment are available.

Children ages sixteen and under stay free in parents' room. Daily rates, double occupancy: winter, standard rooms $320 to $439, suites $495 to $1,200; summer, standard rooms $230 to $366, suites $495 to $635. P.O. Box 1272, San Juan, PR 00902; 800–468–8585 or 809–721–0303, fax 809–722–2910.

WHAT TO SEE AND DO

Free open-air trolleys take you through the narrow streets of **Old San Juan**, past shops filled with folk art from all over the Caribbean, slow-paced sidewalk cafes, department stores, balconied homes, small gardens, and formal squares. Two forts stand at either flank, El Morro and San Cristóbal.

El Morro was constructed by the Spanish from 1540 to 1586 to protect the harbor from invasions, especially from the notorious Sir Francis Drake. Its windswept battlements rise 140 feet above the sea and offer panoramic views of the harbor. Climb through dungeons, towers, and barracks, and visit the small museum, which explains the history of the fortress. Calle Norzagaray. Open daily, 9:00 A.M. to 4:00 P.M.; 809–729–6960.

Casa Blanca was built for Ponce de Leon, who died in the jungles of Florida before he could inhabit it. It now houses the Juan Ponce de Leon Museum and the Taino Indian Ethno-Historic Museum, which re-creates the life and culture of Puerto Rico's first inhabitants. Exhibits include a model Indian village and displays of crop cultivation, hunting, and canoe building. Be sure to look at the sixteenth-century European maps of the world and reproductions of paintings of Columbus and charts of his voyage. 1 Calle San Sebastián. Open Tuesday through Sunday, 9:00 A.M. to noon and 1:00 to 4:30 P.M.; 809–724–4102.

San Cristóbal was an eighteenth-century fortress designed to guard the city from land attack. Even bigger than El Morro, it was known once as the Gibraltar of the West Indies; Open 9:15 A.M. to 5:45 P.M.; 809–724–1974.

Paseo de la Princesa, near the port, is a broad boulevard with flowers, trees, and a playground where the **Children's Theater** has puppet shows, storytelling, and performances every Sunday afternoon.

On Saturdays, prominent Puerto Rican musicians, dance

troupes, and orchestras perform, puppet shows are staged, and local painters and sculptors show their work at **La Cast Tourism Center**, Plaza Darkness across from Pier 1 in San Juan.

BEYOND SAN JUAN

WHERE TO STAY

EL CONQUISTADOR RESORT AND COUNTRY CLUB

Perched atop a cliff in northeast Puerto Rico, overlooking the place where the Atlantic Ocean and the Caribbean Sea merge, El Conquistador is like a city unto itself, with four resort environments including a grand hotel and three distinctive villages, an 18-hole golf course, five swimming pools, and a private island. Water taxis regularly hop the short distance to Palomino Island, a 100-acre private paradise where the children's day camp and water sports center are headquartered. Complimentary snorkeling equipment helps guests explore the coral reefs that lie a few feet from the shore. White sand beaches fringe the island, and nature trails lead to secluded beaches on all sides. Gear for Sunfish sailing, windsurfing (mini-windsurfers are available for kids), and kayaking can be rented on Palomino Island.

The main pool complex features three different freshwater swimming pools totaling two acres of water. A 55-slip marina is the point of departure for deep-sea fishing charters, sailboat, and catamaran trips. El Yunque rain forest is just minutes away.

For Kids: Named after Puerto Rico's indigenous singing tree frog, Camp Coqui offers supervised activities seven days a week from 9:00 A.M. to 3:00 P.M. Each daily session costs $38 per child and includes cultural and educational activities with the fun: marine biology talks are followed by snorkeling excursions; children learn to play taino ball games, native to the Puerto Rican Indians who inhabited the island before the arrival of Europeans and then enjoy private scavenger hunts, arts and crafts, and dance and cooking lessons. Kids of ages three to nine and nine to thirteen have separate activities, and older teens have pool parties, Ping-Pong tournaments, sports "Olympics" and bonfires. All counselors are Red Cross and Lifeguard certified.

Accommodations: Las Casitas Village, designed in the style of Old San Juan, has one-, two-, and three-bedroom villas with full kitchens. La Marna Village has deluxe accommodations overlooking the harbor, with its own park and swimming pool. Las Olas Village is tucked into the cliffside, with a glass funicular traversing the cliff, and the Grand Hotel features everything from standard to super deluxe hotel rooms.

Ask about packages, especially the "Family Holiday" package during the summer. Daily rates, double occupancy: Las Casitas Village one-bedroom suites, spring, summer, and fall $425 to $725, winter $770 to $1,170. One-, two-, and three bedroom casitas, spring, summer, and fall $500 to $1,500, winter $1,170 to $2,290. Grand hotel rooms, spring, summer, and fall $245 to $395, winter, $345 to $445. Fajardo, PR 00738; 800–468–8365 or 809–863–1000, fax 809–863–6500.

HYATT REGENCY CERROMAR BEACH

A river runs through it . . . and twists and turns through pools connected by slippery slides, under waterfalls, past swim-up bars, and finally meanders along to a large pool with a small island. It's the longest freshwater pool in the world, with a current that can carry a swimmer in an inner tube from start to finish in about 15 minutes. And if that's not enough, there's another large separate pool, a kiddie pool, and a three-story spiraling water slide. There's also a white sand beach, but this is the one place in the Caribbean where the pools hold their own against the power of the sand and sea, at least for the kids. Parents can collapse into lounge chairs placed throughout the gardens and patios along the pool, play on two 18-hole golf courses or 14 tennis courts, relax in the spa and health club, bicycle, or ride horseback. The hotel runs a complimentary shuttle bus to the Hyatt Dorado Beach next door, where guests can enjoy the protected beach, restaurants, and other recreational activities. Families can rent in-line skates or bikes and take the path to Hyatt Dorado if they wish.

For Kids: Camp Hyatt for three- to twelve-year-olds is headed by CPR-certified counselors who lead outdoor games, swimming, tennis, and arts and crafts during the day. In the evening, the program features clown and mime shows, movies, talent shows, and video games. Parents of children enrolled in Camp Hyatt can obtain a second hotel room, if available, at a 50 percent discount. The camp operates from 9:00 A.M. to 4:00 P.M. and 6:00 P.M. to 10:00 P.M. and requires registration in advance. Fees per child are $25 for the day program and $15 for the evening.

Accommodations: A modern seven-story building has 504 rooms with king-size or two queen-size beds, air-conditioning, spacious bathrooms, and attractive furnishings. Luxurious suites are available on the top floor, with every amenity. The four restaurants and cafes have children's menus.

Children stay free—in their parents' room. Daily rates, double occupancy: December 22 to April 15, $310 to $445; April 16 to May 31, $215 to $305; June 1 to September 30, $169 to $200; October 1 to December 21, $215 to $305. Dorado, PR 00646; 800–233–1234 or 809–796–1234, fax 809–796–4647.

HYATT DORADO BEACH RESORT AND CASINO

You won't find the spectacular pool complex at this sister property next door to Hyatt Regency Cerromar Beach, but you'll find Hyatt Dorado more intimate and perhaps more elegant. Guests have charging privileges at either resort and full use of all facilities at both establishments, including the pools (Hyatt Dorado has two) and children's programs; shuttles run every 30 minutes between the two. Windsurfing instruction is based here as are other water sports such as deep-sea fishing, jet skiing, para-sailing, water-skiing, kayaking, and canoeing.

Accommodations: Rooms are in two-story buildings scattered throughout 1,000 palm-studded, lavishly landscaped acres. Ground-floor units have patios. All have one king-size or two double beds and views of the pool, golf course, or beach. One-bedroom suites are available.

During high season, American plan (a breakfast and dinner plan) is required. Daily rate, double occupancy: high season, $469 to $585; April to May and October to December 21, $230 to $275; June to September, $160 to $220; suites $830 to $1,785. Children's meal plan, $30 per child age three through fifteen, under age three free. Route 693, Dorado, PR 00646; 800–233–1234 or 809–796–1234, fax 809–796–6065.

PONCE HILTON AND CASINO

This attractive upscale resort on 80 acres of lavishly landscaped grounds on Puerto Rico's south coast has a man-made lagoon and beach and offers a summer children's program with daily activities. It is about ten minutes outside the beautifully restored historical town of Ponce. There's a pool with a waterfall, a children's playground, a golf practice range, four tennis courts lit for night play, bikes for rent, and all water sports.

For Kids: The complimentary youth program is offered during July and August for six- to twelve-year-olds. Kids enjoy crafts, swimming, games, and sports.

Accommodations: Standard rooms have air-conditioning, ceiling fans, balconies, tile floors, mini-bar, coffee maker, and one king-size or two double beds. Suites have one bedroom with a king-size bed, a parlor with a fold-out couch, and a Jacuzzi bath.

Children ages sixteen and under stay free in parents' room. Daily rates, double occupancy: $150 to $190, suites $350 and up. Children have discounts on meals on family programs. P.O. Box 7149, Ponce, PR 00732; 800-HILTONS or 809–259–7777, fax 809–259–7674.

PARADOR VILLA ANTONIO

This intimate and pleasant property is in Rincon on the island's west coast, near Puerto Rico's championship surfing beaches. Board riders in search of the perfect wave stay here, and so do people who like to sail, snorkel, and go deep-sea fishing. Nearby attractions include such surfing beaches as Los Almendros, Black Eagle, and Crash Boat, along with Aguadilla and Wilderness Aguadilla public beach. Other features include a swimming pool, tennis courts, and a children's playground on the property.

Accommodations: All 55 one-bedroom housekeeping apartments have kitchens. Some units sleep three in a double and a twin bed, while others can sleep up to six in a double bed, two twin beds, and additional cots. Up to two children under twelve stay free in their parents' room if no extra beds are needed. Cots $10 per night. Daily rates, double occupancy: $60 to $85, depending on size. P.O. Box 68, Rincon, Puerto Rico 00677. Toll-free information from the United States, 800–443–0266. In Puerto Rico, 809–823–2645; toll-free from outside the San Juan area, 800–981–7575.

VILLA RENTALS

The following businesses can help you arrange to rent a villa, apartment, or home in Puerto Rico:

At Home Abroad, 405 East 56th Street, Suite 6H, New York, NY 10022; 212–421–9165.

Villas International, 71 West 23rd Street, Suite 1042, New York, NY 10010; 800–221–2260 or 212–929–7585.

Hideaways International, P.O. Box 1270, Littleton, MA 01460; 800–843–4433.

WHAT TO SEE AND DO

More than 100 billion gallons of water fall annually on **El Yunque**, a vast 28,000-acre rain forest 35 miles east of San Juan. Dripping with waterfalls and crawling with vines, it shelters more than 20 kinds of wild orchids, 50 varieties of ferns (including giant ferns), and 240 species of trees. The calls of tiny tree frogs lend atmosphere, and many birds, including the rare Puerto Rican parrot, call it home. It's the only tropical rain forest in the U.S. National Forest System, and it is smart to go with a tour group to see the best waterfalls, viewpoints, and swimming holes. Adjacent **Luquillo Beach** is shaded by majestic coconut palms and is a good place to enjoy the sea, sand, and sun, although it is crowded on weekends. If you forget your picnic basket, local *kioskos* (food stands) can supply you with something to eat. The beach has lockers and changing rooms. Many hotels provide tours of El Yunque, or you can arrange tours in the park's Sierra Palm Interpretive Center, on Route 191, km 11.6, which is open daily from 9:30 A.M. to 5:00 P.M. General park information: 809–887–2875 or 809–766–5335.

Two hours from San Juan on the north coast is **Arecibo Observatory**, the world's largest radar-radio telescope, which stretches the length of 13 football fields. Scientists study planets and distant galaxies by gathering radio waves from space and operate SETI, the Search for Extraterrestrial Intelligence. Tours are self-guided, and you can view the telescope from an observation platform. Admission is free. Route 625, Arecibo. Open Tuesday through Friday, 2:00 to 3:00 P.M., Sunday 1:00 to 4:00 P.M.; 809–787–2612.

Río Camuy Cave Park, far to the west of San Juan near Arecibo, is an enormous cave system carved out by the world's third largest underground river. Trams take visitors to the mouth of another cave where a footpath winds through the cave to deeper views. Another tram trip leads to a sinkhole 650 feet wide, with platforms suspended over the Camuy River 400 feet below. Call to make reservations before you go. On Route 129, km 18.9. Open Wednesday through Sunday and holidays, 8:00 A.M. to 4:00 P.M.; 809–765–5555 or 809–893–3100.

Las Cabezas Nature Reserve is about an hour and a half east of San Juan with a restored nineteenth-century Spanish Colonial lighthouse that has breathtaking views of islands as far off as St. Thomas. Boardwalk trails wind through mangrove islands and a bioluminescent lagoon. Ospreys, sea turtles, and an occasional manatee can be seen from the windswept promontories and rocky beach. Route 987. Admission by reservation only on weekdays. Open for tours to the general public on Friday, Saturday, and Sunday at 9:30 and 10:30 A.M. and 1:30 P.M.; 809–722–5882.

Centuries-old **Ponce** has a restored area with trolleys, horse-drawn carriage rides, and many recently restored historic buildings that might remind you of New Orleans or Barcelona. Its beautiful downtown plaza has fountains, park benches, gardens, and sidewalk cafes. Red-and-black-striped **Parque de Bombas Firehouse Museum**, on one side of the plaza, has antique fire trucks, equipment, and memorabilia.

Just outside town is the oldest known Indian burial site in the area, **Tibes Indian Ceremonial Park**, where you can explore seven ceremonial ball courts, two dance grounds, and a re-created Taino Indian village. Route 503, km 2.7. A museum on the premises displays Indian ceremonial objects, jewelry, and pottery. Open Tuesday through Sunday, 8:00 A.M. to 4:00 P.M.; 809–840–2255.

Mayagüez, Puerto Rico's third largest city, has the **Mayagüez Zoo**, showing off 45 acres of reptiles, birds, and mammals, plus a lake and a children's playground. Route 108 at Barrio Miradero. Open Tuesday through Sunday, 9:00 A.M. to 4:30 P.M.; 809–834–8110.

The sea comes alive with dazzling sparks of life on moonless nights at **Phosphorescent Bay**, near La Parguera, south of San Germán at the end of Route 304. Boats leave for the bay about every half hour from just past dusk until 10:30 P.M. The millions of microscopic dinoflagellates light up when they are disturbed by movement. Boat crews dump buckets of sea water on the deck so you can see the "fireflies of the sea" up close; $4 to $8 per person.

Puerto Rico's **baseball** season runs from October through April, and stadiums are in San Juan, Ponce, Santurce, Caguas, Arecibo, and Mayagüez. The tourist office can give you a schedule of games, or contact Professional Baseball of Puerto Rico at 809–765–6285.

22

ST. BARTHÉLEMY

ST. BARTS IS FASHIONABLY French, with its haute cuisine, French bakeries, sidewalk cafes, and monokinis. Yet it also maintains a strong element of "Caribbean casual" across its 8 square miles of low green mountains, its sparkling coral sand beaches, and its quaint red-tile-roofed capital port city. The island's understated glamour is reflected in its stylish continental visitors and its *très chic* prices.

Columbus "discovered" this island in 1493 and named it for his brother Bartolomeo, but the Carib Indians living on the island called it Ouanalao, meaning "Land of the Hummingbirds." Now nicknamed St. Barts, its first successful European settlers were colonists from Brittany and Normandy. Later, the island became a popular port-of-call for pirates, privateers, and buccaneers who provided defense and protection for the inhabitants in exchange for provisions. Residents were more than happy to have the pirates spend their quickly gained fortunes in the island's shops and taverns. St. Barts' most famous pirate was Captain Montbars (also known as Montbars the Exterminator), a Frenchman who is thought to have buried his treasure on the island.

The buccaneers dubbed the capital "Carenage," as it was here that the careening (scraping of barnacles from the hulls) of their ships took place. Later its name was changed to Gustavia.

St. Barts is an easy island to explore by car, and you should plan to rent one whether you stay in a hotel or in a villa. Be sure to book the car when you make your hotel reservations, as cars can get scarce during high season.

TOURIST INFORMATION

In the United States: French West Indies Tourist Board, 444 Madison Avenue, New York, NY 10022; 900–990–0040, fax 212–838–7855.
In Canada: French Government Tourist Office, 1981 McGill College Avenue, Suite 490, Montreal, Quebec H3A 2W9; 800–361–9099 or 514–288–4264, fax 416–979–7587.
On St. Barts: Office du Tourisme on the Quai Général de Gaulle across from the Capitainerie in Gustavia; 590–27–87–27, fax 590–27–74–47. Mailing address: St. Barts Tourist Office, B.P. 113, Gustavia, 97098 Cedex, St. Barthélemy, FWI.

KNOW BEFORE YOU GO

Arriving and Departing: U.S. and Canadian citizens need proof of citizenship in the form of a valid or recently expired passport or a voter registration card or notarized birth certificate, both accompanied by official photo IDs.
Money: The official monetary unit is the French franc, but many stores and restaurants accept U.S. dollars.
Language: The official language of St. Barts is French, although many hotel and restaurant staff speak a little English.
Staying Healthy: The island's small hospital is Gustavia Clinic at the intersection of rue Sadi-Carnot and rue Jean Bart; 590–27–60–35.

WHERE TO STAY

GUANAHANI

This posh 80-room resort, the island's largest, is situated on the northeast coast between two rather different beaches—one protected and calm, and the other with rolling ocean waves. Its 7 acres of gardens and West Indian–style cottages with gingerbread trim spill down a hillcrest of Grand Cul de Sac Beach. A magnificent freshwater swimming pool and Jacuzzi overlook the exclusive beach, and many rooms have their own private pools. Coral reefs just offshore invite excellent snorkeling. There are two restaurants; one serves casual breakfast and lunch by the pool, and the other serves French cuisine. Two night-lit tennis courts, a full water sports facility, boutiques, and room service are all available. **Accommodations:** One- and two-bedroom suites and deluxe rooms can be combined in a variety of ways for families. All have ceiling fans, air-conditioning, mini-bars, and a terrace or patio. Suites consist of a living room and bedroom, and have private pools or Jacuzzis.

Children under age five stay free in parents' room. Daily rates, double occupancy: deluxe rooms, December 23 to January 2, $495 to $610, January 2 to April 30, $390 to $515, May 1 to October 29, $205 to $295, October 30 to December 22, $385 to $515; suites, December 23 to March 30, $800 to $885, April to December 22, $440 to $810. P.O. Box 609, Grand Cul de Sac, 97098 St. Barts, FWI; 800–223–6800 or 590–27–66–60, fax 590–27–70–70.

HOTEL BAIE DES FLAMANDS

Families return year after year to this 24-room hotel on a beautiful quiet beach on the northwest coast at Anse des Flamands. Ground-floor units have terrace kitchenettes, allowing the kids to run out the door, grab a snack from the refrigerator and head right to the beach a few steps away. The hotel also has a very good restaurant that offers French and West Indian cuisine. Other features include a TV/library room, saltwater swimming pool, baby-sitting on request, and a rental car desk. One of the oldest hotels on the island, it's rather motellike in appearance, but it is spotlessly clean and well-kept.
Accommodations: Superior rooms are on the beach level with kitchenettes, while moderate rooms offer more privacy on the upper floor and balconies. All units have two double beds and are air-conditioned.

Children under age five stay free. Daily rates, double occupancy: December 23 to March 15, $240 to $300; March 16 to December

22, $175 to $275. A continental breakfast is included during the summer period. Free airport transfers. Closed in September. Rates include a car, and the seventh night is free. Extra person pays $50 per night. P.O. Box 68, Anse des Flamands, 97133 St. Barts, FWI; 590–27–63–61, fax 590–27–83–44.

FILAO BEACH

Breakfast is served on your private terrace or by the pool at this Relais et Chateau hotel on the bustling St. Tropez–style St-Jean beach, one of St. Barts' most popular sandy strands. The breakfast, American-style during the winter and continental during the off-season, is included in your rates. A pool, complete water sports center and boat charter, good service, and casual French scene keep many guests coming back year after year.

Accommodations: The hotel's 30 small rooms are in two-unit bungalows and vary in price according to their proximity to the beach. All have air-conditioning, a refrigerator, one double or two twin beds, and a small sitting area.

Children ages three and under stay free in parents' room; third person pays $50 to $60 per night. Daily rate, double occupancy: April 1 to December 16, $206 to $325; February 1 to March 30, $350 to $585. P.O. Box 167, St-Jean, 97133 St. Barts, FWI; 590–27–64–84, fax 590–27–62–24.

EMERAUDE PLAGE

Right next door to Filao Beach hotel amid the chic bistros and sidewalk cafes of the lively beach at St-Jean, this bungalow-style hotel has several spacious family-style units with kitchenettes, and a beachside villa for rent. It's situated around a green lawn and tropical gardens bordered by white sands—just step out of your bungalow and you're on the beach. Kids under thirteen stay free in parents' room.

Accommodations: The 21 bungalows, three two-bedroom suites, and a two-bedroom villa all have air-conditioning and ceiling fans. Bungalows have a kitchenette that opens onto a terrace.

Daily rates: bungalows, December 15 to April 14, $185 to $345 (depending on view and size), April 15 to December 14, $135 to $215; 2-bedroom bungalow, $400 and $235; 2-bedroom villa, $565 and $390. Baie de St-Jean, 97133 St Barts, FWI; 590–27–64–78, fax 590–27–83–08

EL SERENO BEACH HOTEL AND VILLAS

Twenty-four apartmentlike units are arranged around an attractive garden courtyard on Grand Cul de Sac Beach. An offshore reef makes the ocean waters shallow and offers ideal swimming for small children. Hammocks are strategically placed throughout the palm-shaded tropical gardens. The hotel has a swimming pool, a water sports center on the beach, and an excellent restaurant on the premises.

Accommodations: One-bedroom suites are well set up for families, each with a living room, bedroom, kitchenette, and spacious terrace. Private rooms are also available. All units are air-conditioned and include a small refrigerator.

Kids under age four stay free in parents' room. January 7 to April 14, $265 to $295 (depending on view); April 15 to December 18, $155 to $185. Higher over Christmas. P.O. Box 19, Grand Cul de Sac, 97133 St. Barts, FWI; 590–27–64–85, fax 590–27–83–98.

VILLA RENTALS

Many people rent villas when they visit St. Barts. **St. Barth Properties, Inc.** handles 60 simple to ultra-deluxe private villas scattered throughout the hills of St. Barts. The staff greets guests at the airport, escorts them to their villa, and is their on-island contact should there be any problems. 18 Depot Street, Franklin, MA 02038; 800–421–3396 or 508–528–7727, fax 508–528–7789.

SIBARTH is managed in the United States and Canada by WIMCO (800–932–3222); it is the rental agency for 200 villas and apartments throughout the island. The staff meets you at the airport and escorts you to your villa.

WHAT TO SEE AND DO

St. Barts' capital **Gustavia** has the charm of a small port city. A steady stream of dinghies and small boats enters and leaves the harbor. Pleasant walkways and plenty of sidewalk cafes invite visitors to stop, snack, and watch the action. The **Musée de St. Barthélemy** showcases the island's history through photographs, documents, costumes, and other exhibits. Open Monday through Thursday, 8:00 A.M. to noon and 1:30 to 5:30 P.M., and Saturday 8:00 A.M. to noon. No phone.

All of St. Barts' beaches are lovely, but a few are worthy of special mention. Secluded **Anse du Gouverneur Beach** on the island's southern coast is reputed to have buried treasure somewhere under its glistening sands. From it, in clear weather, you can see the islands of Saba, St. Eustatius, and St. Kitts. **Anse du Grand Galet** near Gustavia is known as shell beach, and you can spend happy hours sifting for natural treasures from the sea.

In the town of **Corossol** northwest of Gustavia, visit the **Ingénu Magras Inter-Oceans Museum**, a remarkable collection of 7,000 seashells. Open daily 10:00 A.M. to 5:00 P.M.; 590–27–62–97. Residents of the town are known for the exquisite woven hats, bags, and mobiles they offer for sale. Some of the older women still wear the traditional white sunbonnets called *quichenottes* ("kiss-me-not" hats).

The Aquascope is a semi-submersible glass-bottom boat based at Marine Service in Gustavia. Journeys through coral formations, schools of tropical fish, and the wreck of the yacht *Non Stop* last about an hour; 590–27–70–34. Another semi-submersible vessel offering excursions is the **Aquarius**, based at La Maison de la Mer; 590–27–81–00.

Scuba diving is known as "plongée" in the French-speaking part of the Caribbean. The most popular dive spots are around the islet of Pain de Sucre, because of its sheer drop off, cave, coral, and sponges. Les Petits Saintes—several small islets off the western edge of Gustavia harbor—are home to sea turtles.

23

ST. KITTS AND NEVIS

ST. KITTS AND NEVIS have more monkeys than people. The French brought African green or vervet monkeys centuries ago as food tasters, and now these hardy creatures make themselves comfortable in the islands' rain forests. Another imported animal that still thrives, the mongoose, was brought from India to rid sugarcane fields of rats. Unfortunately, the rats slept during the day and mongoose slept at the night, so the rats remained and the mongoose flourished at the expense of nonpest native species. Sugarcane is still grown on St. Kitts, the larger of the two islands, while tourism has replaced cane as the leading source of revenue on Nevis.

Columbus sighted St. Kitts in 1493 and named it St. Christopher after the patron saint of travelers. Its nickname, St. Kitts, stuck, and its British colonizers in 1623 changed its name permanently. Don't miss the chance to explore Brimstone Hill Fortress, a gigantic fort the British strategically placed at the crest of a hill overlooking the island and sea. It took over 100 years to construct.

Most hotels in St. Kitts are concentrated in the Frigate Bay area on the Caribbean side of the southeastern shore, but a newly constructed road that leads to the beach-plentiful southeastern peninsula has opened the door for more development. The Atlantic side of the island is too rough for swimming, so if you stay in one of the many resorts on that side, you'll need a car (or hotel shuttle) to get to safe swimming beaches.

Nevis was named by Columbus during his second voyage to the New World upon seeing its mountain peak topped with snowy white clouds. (*Nieves* is the Spanish word for snow.) Greener and less developed than St. Kitts, it is known for its gracious plantation inns and as the birthplace of Alexander Hamilton, born in Charlestown in 1755. Hamilton left the island at age seventeen to continue his education, and ultimately died in a duel with Aaron Burr. His former home now contains the Museum of Nevis History. Two special Nevisian resorts have much to offer families: the posh Four Seasons and nature-rich Golden Rock Inn.

Charlestown, the capital city, is a lively little town. The island's Culturama is held every August with calypso shows, parades, bands, and local food for sale.

There are no direct flights from the United States (you'll need to fly to San Juan or St. Thomas and take a short hop from there) and most cruise ships don't dock here, so these islands offer quiet vacations. By law, no building can be taller than a palm tree, and the pride and good manners of the friendly people are a pleasure to encounter.

TOURIST INFORMATION

In the United States: *New York:* St. Kitts and Nevis Tourist Board, 414 East 75th Street, New York, NY 10021; 800–582–6208 or 212–535–1234, fax 212–879–4789. *Chicago:* South Presidents' Plaza II, Suite 800, 8700 West Brynmawr, Chicago, IL 60631; 312–714–5015, fax 312–714–4910.
In Canada: St. Kitts and Nevis Tourist Office, 11 Yorkville Avenue, Suite 508, Toronto, Ontario M4W 1L3; 416–921–7717.
On St. Kitts: Tourist Board, Pelican Mall, Bay Road, Basseterre, St. Kitts, WI; 809–465–2620.
On Nevis: Tourism Office, Main Street, Charlestown, Nevis, WI; 809–469–5521, fax 809–465–8794.

KNOW BEFORE YOU GO

Arriving and Departing: U.S. and Canadian citizens need to show passports, or voter registration cards or original birth certificates with an official photo ID. All visitors must have a return or onward ticket. A 45-minute ferry service between Basseterre on St. Kitts and Charlestown on Nevis runs regularly. Departure times can vary, so check with the tourist office before you leave. A departure tax of $10 is charged at the airport.

Money: The Eastern Caribbean dollar (EC$) is the official currency, but U.S. dollars are widely accepted.

Language: English is spoken throughout the two islands.

Staying Healthy: Joseph N. France Hospital in Basseterre, St. Kitts (809–465–2551) and Alexandria Hospital in Charlestown, Nevis (809–469–5473) both have 24-hour emergency rooms.

ST. KITTS

WHERE TO STAY

OCEAN TERRACE INN

Manicured tropical garden terraces spill down a lush green hillside overlooking the Basseterre harbor. The landscaped gardens have antique cannons, caged parrots, a rock grotto, bench swings, and several swimming pools. Comfortable suites with kitchens and efficiency apartments are most suitable for families.

The OTI, as the locals call it, is a ten-minute walk from downtown Basseterre. The resort's two swimming pools (and most rooms) have views of the harbor and of the sea beyond. A daily shuttle goes to Turtle Beach, one of St. Kitts' most beautiful beaches on the southeastern peninsula, where the hotel has a water sports center (with complimentary snorkeling equipment) and a restaurant/grill; guests have signing privileges at both.

Accommodations: One-bedroom suites have full kitchens, spacious dining areas, two queen-size beds in the bedroom, and a living room with a fold-out couch. A second bedroom can be added. Efficiency apartments have small kitchens and are across the street from the rest of the complex, overlooking fisherman's wharf. Other rooms in the hotel have connecting doors.

Daily rates, double occupancy: summer, hotel rooms $101 to $164 (depending on size), one-bedroom suites $177, two-bedroom suites $235, efficiency apartments $138; winter, hotel rooms $116 to $225, one-bedroom suites $242, two-bedroom suites $346, efficiency apartments $165. Extra person pays $45 per night. P.O. Box 65, Basseterre, St. Kitts, WI; 800–223–5695, 800–524–0512 or 809–465–2754, fax 809–465–1057.

JACK TAR VILLAGE

All you can eat and drink is rolled into one budget price at the St. Kitts version of the Jack Tar Village. Many activities, including beach contests, bike riding, and pedal boating, are free, while others such as horseback riding and motorized water sports are available for a small fee. The resort is across the street from the Atlantic Ocean, with an attractive beach on the ocean, but the water is too rough for swimming. A shuttle runs frequently to a calm beach on the Caribbean side of the island, just five minutes away. Guests can also use cruiser bikes to ride to the Caribbean beach. The resort has two swimming pools (called the noisy pool and the quiet pool), fishing and pedal boating in the saltwater lagoon, and all kinds of wacky contests.

For Kids: Daily activities for three- to twelve-year-olds take place in a separate little one-room house. A full-time staff person is there whether any kids drop in or not. Its loose schedule changes according to the interests of the children, but might include movies, games, art, and stories.

Accommodations: Simple hotel-type rooms have either one king-size or two double beds, and most have connecting doors for families. Upstairs rooms have decks. The food is plentiful but uninspired.

Children under age five stay free. Children ages five and over pay $80 per day from January to April, $100 per day during the Christmas holidays, and $60 per day the rest of the year. Daily rates, double occupancy: January through April, $155; Christmas holidays, $170; and rest of the year, $120. P.O. Box 406, Frigate Bay, St. Kitts, WI; 800–999–9182 or 809–465–8651, fax 809–465–1031.

SUN 'N SAND BEACH VILLAGE

An ice cream parlor, a well-stocked mini-market, a bank, and a gift shop are a few steps away from this resort's simple studio and two-bedroom cottages. A continental breakfast is included in the rates. At the back of the resort is the Atlantic beach—great for building sand castles, but a bit rough for swimming on most days. A freshwater pool with a slide is in the middle of the rather plain grounds.

Accommodations: Two-bedroom cottages and studio apartments aren't fancy but are very serviceable. The mini-market has all the supplies you'll need; other condominium and apartment renters in the area come here to stock up, too.

Daily rates: two-bedroom cottages (accommodate up to four people) April 16 to December 20, $130 per night; December 21 to December 31, two-bedroom units $275; and January 1 through April 15, two-bedroom units $200 to $250, studios $120 to $150. Extra person in room pays $20 per day. Baby cribs are $5 per day. Seventh night is always free. Frigate Bay, P.O. Box 341, Basseterre, St. Kitts, WI; 800–223–6510 or 809–465–8037, fax 809–465–6745.

SEALOFTS ON THE BEACH CONDOMINIUMS

Reasonably priced very basic two- or three-bedroom condos are a good place to headquarter to explore the island. The water off the Atlantic beach in back is a bit rough for swimming, but a Caribbean beach is less than a three-minute drive away, and the swimming pool is refreshing. It's located in the Frigate Bay area within walking distance of grocery stores, restaurants, and banks.

Accommodations: Condominiums have living rooms, a full kitchen, washer and dryer, private deck and patio, and bedrooms with queen-size and twin beds. Two-bedroom units comfortably accommodate four people, and three-bedroom units house six.

Rates vary depending on the view; ocean views are the most expensive, golf course views are the least expensive, and pool views are in between. Winter rates: two-bedroom condo $125 to $155 per day, $850 to $1,100 per week; three-bedroom $260 per day, $1,800 per week. Summer rates: two-bedroom $90 to $115 per day, $625 to $800 per week; three-bedroom $195 per day, $1,350 per week. P.O. Box 139, St. Kitts, WI; 809–465–8004, fax 809–465–8454.

WHAT TO SEE AND DO

Brimstone Hill Fortress sprawls across a strategic hillside 800 feet above the Caribbean Sea. Its massive walls were built of igneous rock by thousands of slaves over the course of a century. One of the best-preserved fortresses of its type in the Caribbean, it was once so intimidating that ship captains changed course rather than come within range of its powerful cannons. A tour of this fort fuels a child's imagination: stand in the damp, dark rooms of the officers' quarters; marvel at the immensity of each block of volcanic stone and the tremendous effort and skill required to cut and place them; straddle any of the many cannons and imagine crowds of militia getting blasted by volleyball-size iron balls. Green grassy areas and stone stairways separate areas of the fort, allowing for plenty of uninhibited exercise. On the Main Road northwest of Basseterre. Open daily 9:30 A.M. to 5:30 P.M. No phone. Adults $5, children $2.50.

Signs off the Main Road near Old Road Town direct you to Romney Manor, which houses **Caribelle Batik,** where artisans hand-print fabric by the ancient Indonesian method. Visitors can watch the artisans work; questions are welcomed. The manor is set in a large tropical garden. Open Monday through Friday from 8:30 A.M. to 4:00 P.M.; 809–465–6253, fax 809–465–3629.

Young stamp collectors should stop in at the **St. Kitts Philatelic Bureau** (open weekdays, 8:00 A.M. to 4:00 P.M.) on the second floor of the Social Security building on Bay Street in capital city, Basseterre; 809–465–2521. A colorful weekend **produce market** also takes place on Bay Street.

The **Sugar Factory** tour shows kids how sugar is made during the cutting season, from February through July. Call the Department of Tourism at 809–465–4040 for details. The factory is between the airport and Basseterre.

NEVIS

≈≈≈

WHERE TO STAY

FOUR SEASONS

It's hard to find an elegant luxury resort with first-class cuisine and exceptional service that welcomes children, but the Four Seasons does it all. The resort stretches along a white sand beach lapped by gentle ocean waves. Two pools, a separate lap pool, and a spectacular Robert Trent Jones 18-hole golf course that travels up the side of a volcano are almost as big a draw as the beach. Loads of recreational activities and the friendly, welcoming Nevisians who staff the luxury resort make it a superior destination.

Guests can swing rackets on four clay or six hardtack tennis courts, play golf, get a massage, play croquet on a perfectly manicured croquet court, or work out in the Four Seasons' well-equipped exercise room. Children's beach toys are available at the water sports center, as are all kinds of boats and adult water toys. This place is serious about pampering its guests. As you lounge on a beach chair, members of the staff regularly stop by, offering chilled face towels, ice water, and chilled Evian face misters.

For Kids: The well-planned program for children ages three to ten operates from a cheerful room filled with all kinds of enticing toys. Different local foods, folktales, music, plants, and wildlife are highlighted each morning with stories, outdoor exploration, and art and cooking projects. Croquet, tennis, and outdoor games take place during the early morning and late afternoon to avoid the intense midday tropical sun. Breakfast and lunch are provided through room service. Parents can bring kids under age three to play with the many toys, but they must remain with their children. Baby-sitters are available any time for younger children; all of the Four Seasons' baby-sitters have attended the hotel's three-week baby-sitting seminars. Staff in the children's program have been trained by the hotel as well. Baby supplies are available in case parents forget the Pampers or the playpen.

Accommodations: Spacious and elegant standard rooms have two queen-size or one king-size bed (a roll-away can be easily added). Suites are larger and have varied configurations. Many rooms have connecting doors for families, and all have air-conditioning, ceiling fans, and window screens. Complimentary washer and dryer are located in all buildings, each of which houses 12 of the rooms, called "cottages." Upstairs rooms have large screened porches with lounge chairs, while bottom-floor rooms have patios.

Four Seasons room rates vary depending on the season, type of room, and view. Daily rates, double occupancy: June 1 to October 31, standard room $174 or $225, suite $350 to $2,700; November 1 to December 20, standard room $300 or $350, suite $650 to $2,700; January through March, standard room $500 or $550, suite $950 to $3,300; April through May, standard room $325 or $375, suite $700 to $2,950. Children can order from the children's menu or order half-portions from the adult menu, for half-price. Staff will do a full bag of children's laundry for $1.50. Full meal plan is available. P.O. Box 565, Charlestown, Nevis, WI; 800–332–3442 or 809–469–1111 (in Canada, 800–268–6288), fax 809–469–1112.

GOLDEN ROCK HOTEL

Wild African green monkeys frequently play in the gardens of this unusual inland plantation inn, where families can stay in a restored two-story sugar mill made of hand-carved lava stones. Take the Golden Rock Nature Trail into the rain forest behind the hotel to see more of the local monkeys, or peek from behind the monkey blind for a view of the frolicking primates. Golden Rock is located in Gingerland, the lushest part of Nevis, where gardens flourish and ginger was once grown for export. Naturalist programs such as guided hikes, slide shows, and cultural talks are a trademark of Golden Rock and are tailored to guests' interests and ages. If you're staying elsewhere on Nevis, arrange to come for lunch so your children can hike the nature trail and explore the monkey-filled grounds.

The hotel has its own beach restaurant and water sports center with towels and lounge chairs at beautiful Pinney's Beach; a free shuttle runs daily. West Indian storytelling, slide shows on native flora and fauna, and other cultural programs take place throughout the week. A games room has bumper pool, board games, books, and chess. The hotel's large spring-fed swimming pool is a good place to cool off after a hike.

Accommodations: Twelve cottages overlook the Caribbean Sea; most have two bedrooms that connect through the deck, one with a king-size bed, one with two twin beds; each has a bathroom. The largest cottage has three bedrooms. The sugar mill has a king-size bed, a double bed, and two twin beds on two levels, with full bathrooms on both floors. Cribs are available free of charge. An excellent restaurant serves breakfast, lunch, and dinner.

Daily rates, double occupancy: April 15 to December 19, $110; December 20 to April 14, $185. Breakfast or dinner and breakfast can be included in the rates. Food charge for kids ages thirteen and under is 50 percent off with breakfast and dinner. Sugar mill for a family of four: April 15 to December 19, $195 to $285; December 20 to April 14, $435. P.O. Box 493, Gingerland, Nevis, WI; 809–469–3346, fax 809–469–2113.

OUALIE BEACH CLUB

Situated on a beautiful white sand beach in a sheltered bay with calm, shallow water, Oualie Beach Club has one of the island's most complete water sports centers, with Sunfish sailing, snorkeling, fishing excursions, and yacht charters. Its dive shop, the only one on the island, has a NAUI-certified instructor. Twenty-two rooms in pastel gingerbread cottages all have ocean views. Saturday nights feature a Caribbean string band and a carnival masquerade troupe dancing to traditional drumming rhythms.

Accommodations: All rooms have screened verandahs and ceiling fans. Studios have full kitchens and connecting bedrooms for families. The children's menu is simple, healthful, and sensible. The resort also handles villa rentals above the bay.

Daily rates, double occupancy: summer, double room $90, one-bedroom studio, $170, two-bedroom studio $230; winter, double room $130, one-bedroom studio $240, two-bedroom studio $320. Oualie Beach, Nevis, WI; 800–682–5431 or 809–469–9745, fax 809–469–9176.

24

ST. LUCIA

A *DRIVE-THROUGH VOLCANO*? You *can* view the bubbling, belching, stinky, steaming seven-acre crater through a car
window if you want, but you'll feel the heat and smell the sharp
sulfur fumes if you explore the rocky moonscape of dormant Mt.
Soufrière on foot. More evidence of St. Lucia's volcanic past can
be seen in the twin peaks, known as the Pitons, that dominate
the landscape and rise abruptly from the sea for almost a half
mile. Behind them, a national rain forest covers 19,000 acres of
mountains and valleys. Many consider this island one of the most
beautiful in the Caribbean chain, combining acres of emerald
green hillsides and banana plantations with near-perfect beaches.

St. Lucia didn't escape the island battles that took place
throughout the Caribbean; in the eighteenth century alone, it
changed hands 14 times between the French and British. The
British finally won out, but St. Lucia still has a strong French
influence, particularly in the dialect spoken by its people.

The island has become a center for yacht charters, especially
at the beautiful anchorage town of Marigot Bay on the west coast
where the Moorings' fleet is headquartered. St. Lucia's location
in the southern Caribbean between Martinique and St. Vincent
means that many islands are within easy sailing distance.

Carnival takes place in February before Lent, with calypso
competitions, costume contests, jump-ups, and parades.

TOURIST INFORMATION

In the United States: St. Lucia Tourist Board, 820 Second Avenue, Ninth Floor, New York, NY 10017; 800–456–3984 or 212–867–2950, fax 212–370–7867.
In Canada: St. Lucia Tourist Board, 4975 Dundas Street West, Suite 457, Etobicoke "D" Islington, Ontario M9A 4X4; 800–456–3984 or 416–236–0939, fax 416–236–0937.
On St. Lucia: St. Lucia Tourist Board at Pointe Seraphine complex on Castries Harbor, St. Lucia, WI; 809–452–4094.

KNOW BEFORE YOU GO

Arriving and Departing: U.S. and Canadian citizens must present a valid passport and an onward or return ticket. Departure tax is $11 per person.
Money: St. Lucia's official currency is the Eastern Caribbean dollar (EC$) but U.S. dollars are readily accepted.
Language: English is the official language of St. Lucia.
Staying Healthy: St. Jude's Hospital in Vieux Fort at the southern tip of the island (809–454–6041) and Victoria Hospital in Castries on the northwest coast (809–452–2421) both have 24-hour emergency rooms. The rainfall responsible for St. Lucia's lush appearance is also responsible for bumper mosquito crops; bring mosquito repellent and use it generously. Avoid contact with manchineel trees, whose applelike fruits and shiny green leaves are extremely poisonous.

WHERE TO STAY

WINDJAMMER LANDING

Patterned after a whitewashed, red-tile-roofed Mediterranean village, Windjammer Landing offers private villas (many with their own plunge pools), the concierge services of a hotel, and a full-scale daily children's program. The spacious villas are tucked away with seclusion in mind within Windjammer's 55 acres of scented gardens, waterfalls, footpaths, and foliage. Five different restaurants offer everything from local Caribbean dishes to wood-oven pizza to international cuisine.

All guests enjoy complimentary water sports including waterskiing, windsurfing, snorkeling, and banana boat rides. In addition there's tennis, a children's playground, two large pools, a children's pool, and a beautiful crescent of white sand beach. Scuba and fishing charters cost extra.

For Kids: The complimentary program for four-to twelve-year-olds is open year-round from 10:00 A.M. to 4:00 P.M. Kids can drop in and out as they wish, and participate in beach Olympics, treasure hunts, nature walks, art classes, pedal-boat rides, calypso and limbo lessons, and more.

Accommodations: One- to four-bedroom three-story villas have ceiling fans, air-conditioning, living and dining rooms, full kitchens, and plunge pools. Some villas have sofabeds on request, but most accommodate two people in each bedroom. If a family does not want an entire villa, the villas can be divided into superior and deluxe rooms, both of which have private baths, mini-refrigerators, coffee makers, and small sitting areas.

Up to two children under age twelve stay free in their parents' villa; children ages four and under stay free in deluxe and superior rooms. "All in the Family Plan" package offers eight days and seven nights in a villa with 11 meals, five days of nanny services, water sports, and airport transfers for $2,100 to $4,000 per family. Daily rates, double occupancy: superior or deluxe rooms $140 to $275 (depending on size and time of year), villas $205 to $560 (depending on size and time of year). Baby-sitting by the hour, $7 per child, $10 for two kids. P.O. Box 1504, Labrelotte Bay, Castries, St. Lucia, WI; 800–743–9609 or 809–452–0913, fax 809–452–0907.

WYNDHAM MORGAN BAY RESORT

Waterskiing clinics, tennis lessons with oversize rackets, and a grill next to the beach that serves hamburgers, hot dogs, and ice cream all day long are a few of the activities this 240-room all-inclusive beachfront resort has in place to attract families. All water sports, meals, and drinks are included in one price, and a children's program operates during the summer months.

Activity options include day and night tennis, windsurfing, Sunfish and catamaran sailing, snorkeling, pedal boating, badminton, croquet, a fitness room, steam room, whirlpool, and nightly entertainment.

For Kids: In the summer, the resort has a complimentary drop-in program for ages four to seven and ages eight to twelve. The schedule (from 10:00 A.M. to 4:00 P.M.) includes arts and crafts, sandcastle building, scavenger and shell hunts, nature walks, volleyball, pool games, swim races, and dance lessons.

Accommodations: Clusters of three-story buildings contain rooms with views of the garden area or beach. The best rooms for families have two double beds. All rooms have marble bathrooms, air-conditioning, and balconies.

Rates include all meals, drinks, taxes, gratuities, water sports, and activities except scuba diving and deep-sea fishing. Daily rates, per person double occupancy: $170 to $245, depending on room size and time of year. "Kids on Us" program from May to September allows children under age twelve to eat and stay free in their parents' room. Rest of year, children ages three to twelve pay $50 to $70 per night. P.O. Box 2216, Gros Islet, St. Lucia, WI; 809-450-2511, fax 809-450-1050.

CLUB ST. LUCIA

This all-inclusive resort with nonstop fun keeps adults and children busy day and night. Evening entertainment for the entire family might be Pirate Night, Caribbean Night, or a guest talent show. Two swimming pools, (including one three-section pool with a wading area, water-volleyball court and special deep area) satisfy water enthusiasts of all ages. Plus, there's a beautiful beach, tennis, bicycles, Sunfish sailing, waterskiing, canoeing, windsurfing, snorkeling, and various games.

For Kids: The complimentary Children's Club has its own playroom for four- to twelve-year-olds. It is open Monday through Saturday from 9:30 A.M. to 12:30 P.M. and 2:00 P.M. to 5:00 P.M. Activities include cartoons, face painting, cooking classes, games, and field trips. Special evening activities are organized just for teens.

Accommodations: One-bedroom family suites have living rooms with sofabed, air-conditioning, and patio. Most standard rooms have one king-size bed and can accommodate an extra twin. Six different restaurants serve menu selections; others have buffet-style presentations.

Kids under age sixteen are free in parents' rooms. One child can stay free with two adults in standard rooms; two kids can stay in larger rooms. Rates include all meals, drinks, taxes, gratuities, and water sports, but not airport transfers. Daily rates, double occupancy: April 17 to December 23, $254 to $320, December 24 to April 16, $308 to $386. Be sure to ask about special packages that include airfare for children. P.O. Box 915, Smugglers Village, Castries, St. Lucia, WI; 800–223–9815 or 809–452–0552, fax 809–450–0281.

JALOUSIE PLANTATION

Lounge by the pool with dramatic green Pitons soaring on either side of you and a velvety gray volcanic sand beach just a few steps away. Jalousie's complete spa lets you pamper yourself with a massage and seaweed wrap, facial, or other luxurious treatment. Most cottage-style accommodations include a plunge pool and verandah set in a tropical garden. Inclusive rates cover meals and drinks at four different restaurants, waterskiing, catamaran trips, windsurfing, and two massages per week. Other facilities and equipment include complimentary Sunfish and catamaran sailing, kayaking, night-lit tennis (with a pro shop and instructors), air-conditioned squash courts, and workouts at the fitness center. Scuba diving, deep-sea fishing, horseback rides, and most spa treatments cost extra.

For Kids: The complimentary children's program operates daily year-round from 10:00 A.M. to 5:00 P.M. Kids ages four to twelve are entertained with nature walks, crafts, aerobics, water sports, and island tours. A small fee is charged for the island tours.

Accommodations: One-bedroom cottages and suites have air-conditioning, ceiling fans, queen-size beds, mini-bars, and coffee makers. The resort's banana and soursop trees are used to produce organic juices for guests, and the hydroponic garden grows other fruits, vegetables, herbs, and spices used in meals.

Virtually everything is included, even taxes and service charges. Children under age five stay free in parents' room. Children ages five to fifteen add $125 per night; sixteen and over are classified as adults and cost $175 per night. Daily rates, double occupancy: winter $350 to $800; spring and fall, $325 to $450; and summer $290 to $400. P.O. Box 251, Soufrière, St. Lucia, WI; 800–392–2007 or 809–459–7666, fax 809–459–7667.

CLUB MED ST. LUCIA

Go-carts for young Indie 500 wannabes, an intensive English riding program for the horse-loving set, and a full circus workshop for all ages make this Club Med an action-packed vacation choice for just about any family. Pre-schoolers to grandparents can participate in the circus workshop, learning trapeze skills, juggling, acrobatics, vaulting, clowning, and walking the tightrope. A supervised children's program for two- to eleven-year-olds offers parents the time to perfect their windsurfing skills or relax uninterrupted on the beach.

Other activities include scuba lessons in the pool, snorkeling, golf, tennis, archery, picnics, football, softball, swimming (the beach, on the Atlantic side, is a bit rough), special excursions, and aerobics. Adults can take two and a half hours of riding instruction daily, including dressage, jumping, and trail rides.

For Kids: Operating from an activities center within the vacation village, kids can drop by anytime from 9:00 A.M. to 9:00 P.M. for activities such as waterskiing, sailing, golf, archery, arts and crafts, boat rides, pony rides, go-carting, excursions, and puppet shows. Youngsters are divided by age into three separate groups: Petit Club for two- to five-year-olds, Mini Club for four- to six-year-olds, and Kids Club for seven- to eleven-year-olds.

Accommodations: All rooms are air-conditioned and have two double beds plus a bathroom with shower. Some have connecting doors. Families of five or more must take two rooms. Early supervised lunches and dinners are offered for youngsters.

All-inclusive rates cover everything but drinks. Kids ages two to five stay free (one per full-paying parent) for certain weeks of the year, usually from mid-November to mid-December and during certain weeks of January through March. The full horseback riding program, golf, scuba trips, and special excursions cost extra. Weekly rates: November 1 to April 22, adults (ages 12 and over) $850 to $1,500, children $520 to $1,000; closed April 23 through October 31. Special air packages are available. Vieux Fort, St. Lucia, WI; 800-CLUBMED or 809–455–6001, fax 809–452–0958.

HARMONY MARINA SUITES

Renuit Beach is a short walk away from this two-story family-owned apartment hotel whose affordable rates, good location, and one-bedroom apartments have always attracted vacationing families. The ground-level poolside apartments are quietest and most convenient, allowing little ones and their escorts to step out the door, cross the lawn, and head straight to the pool. Complimentary water sports include windsurfing and canoeing, and other water sports are easily arranged. There's a restaurant, bar, small market/deli, and car rental on the property. Rodney Bay Marina and other restaurants are nearby.

Accommodations: Four one-bedroom suites have kitchenettes and sofa sleepers. Eighteen one-bedroom suites have refrigerators, coffee makers, and wet bars but no other kitchen appliances. All have twin or king beds, air-conditioning, and balcony or terraces.

Daily rates, one bedroom luxury suites with kitchenettes: April 15 to December 14, $125; December 15 to April 14, $215. P.O. Box 155, Castries, St. Lucia, WI; 800–223–6510 or 809–452–8756, fax 809–452–8677.

VILLA RENTALS

Tropical Villas can help you arrange to rent a villa on St. Lucia. From the United States: 800–387–2715, 800–367–2720, or 800–387–2726. In Canada: 800–265–6070 or 800–387–1201 (Ontario, Quebec). P.O. Box 189, Castries, St. Lucia, WI; 809–450–8240, fax 809–450–8089.

WHAT TO SEE AND DO

The town of **Soufrière**, south of Castries, was named after the nearby volcano, **La Soufrière**, which has been dubbed the world's only drive-in volcano. Most of the island's mangoes, breadfruit, tomatoes, limes, and oranges are grown in this lush and fertile region. **Soufrière Estate** has a small zoo and botanical gardens with an operational waterwheel. Next to the estate are the **Diamond Falls Botanical Gardens and Mineral Baths** which were built during the time of Louis XVI and restored in the 1960s. For a small fee, you can tour the grounds and gardens and enjoy a steaming bath fed by an underground stream of water from nearby sulfur springs. **Morne Coubaril Estates** in Soufrière recreates an eighteenth-century family cocoa plantation. There's a sugar mill, a cocoa house (where a demonstration of cocoa processing takes place), a recreated slave village, and farm animals such as goats and pigs. Open daily 9:00 A.M. to 5:00 P.M.; 809–459–7340.

Union Nature Trail in the northern part of the island near Rodney Bay has an easy-to-walk nature trail good for children and visitors who want to acquaint themselves with the animals and woodland landscape of the island. The trail takes 45 minutes to complete and meanders past Caribbean pine, cashew, cinnamon, calabash, and mahogany trees. A nature center has a medicinal herb garden and a miniature zoo with agouti, parrots, iguanas, and boa constrictors.

Pigeon Island, on the northwest coast, was once frequented by pirates. Later a causeway was built to connect the island to the mainland. The notorious French buccaneer Jambe de Bois (the name means "wooden leg") used to hide out on this 40-acre island, now a national park, featuring the ruins of a British fort, picnic spots, long stretches of sandy beaches, and tranquil waters for swimming. The Pigeon Island Interpretive Centre houses a small display on the history of St. Lucia. Open 9:00 A.M. to 5:00 P.M. daily. A pub beneath the center serves snacks, and a restaurant nearby serves lunch only.

25

ST. MARTIN/ ST. MAARTEN

TWO NATIONS, FRANCE AND the Netherlands, share this island of 37 square miles. Both sides have seen a building boom in recent years, and most of the beaches are hemmed in with condos and hotels.

French-speaking St. Martin is known for its French atmosphere, excellent restaurants, and slightly more reasonable prices. Dutch St. Maarten is known for its casinos, shopping, and high-rise resort hotels. While overbuilding has caused both sides to lose much of their green island charm, you can get good deals if you work the package angle, especially during the off-season, when many places are nearly empty. You'll probably need to rent a car as taxis are expensive.

TOURIST INFORMATION

In the United States: Dutch side, St. Maarten Tourist Office, 275 Seventh Avenue, New York, NY 10001; 212–989–0000. French side, French West Indies Tourist Board through France-on-Call (900–990–0040; 50 cents per minute), 444 Madison Avenue, New York, NY 10022.

In Canada: Dutch side, St. Maarten Tourist Office, 243 Ellerslie Avenue, Willowdale, Toronto, Ontario M2N 1Y5. French side, call the French West Indies Tourist Bureau through France-on-Call (900–990–0040) or write to the French Government Tourist

Office, 1981 McGill College Avenue, Suite 490, Montreal, Quebec H3A 2W9; 514–288–4264 or 1 Dundas Street West, Suite 2405, Toronto, Ontario M5G 1Z3; 800–361–9099 or 416–593–4723.

On St. Maarten: Tourist Information Bureau, Cyrus Wathey Square, Philipsburg, 599–52–23–37.

On St. Martin: Tourist Information Office on the Marigot Pier, 97150 Marigot, 590–87–57–21.

KNOW BEFORE YOU GO

Arriving and Departing: U.S. citizens need a valid or recently expired passport or original birth certificate or voter registration card. Canadian citizens need a valid passport.

Money: St. Maarten's currency is the Netherlands Antilles florin or guilder (NAfl). On French St. Martin, the French franc is legal tender. U.S. dollars are widely accepted on both sides of the island.

Language: Dutch is the official language of St. Maarten, and French is the official language of St. Martin; but most people who work in the hotels and tourist attractions speak English.

Staying Healthy: St. Rose Hospital, Front Street, Philipsburg, St. Maarten, is fully equipped; 599–5–22300. Another hospital is in Marigot, St. Martin; 599–87–50–07.

FRENCH ST. MARTIN

WHERE TO STAY

LA BELLE CRÉOLE

Modeled after a Mediterranean fishing village on the French Riviera, the resort's villas are linked by cobblestone streets, sidewalks, and courtyards, all of which surround a central plaza. Many of the 138 spacious rooms and 18 one-bedroom suites connect, and some are wheelchair accessible and are set up for disabled guests. Features include three beaches, a water sports center, and a large free-form pool. The tennis program is one of the best on the island.

Accommodations: Rooms have one king-size or two double beds, air-conditioning, private balconies, mini-bars, and TVs.

Children up to age twelve stay free in parents' room. Daily rates, double occupancy: winter, $315 to $455; summer, $205 to $280. Rates include a continental breakfast. P.O. Box 118, Marigot, St. Martin, FWI 97150; 800–223–6510 or 590–87–58–66, fax 590–87–56–66.

LE MERIDIEN L'HABITATION

On a very private beach, this luxury property sprawls across 150 acres of prime St. Martin real estate. Rates include snorkeling, squash, racquetball, volleyball, pedal boats, and canoes. Waterskiing, jet skis, scuba, riding, and tennis lessons are extra. A sports and entertainment complex nearby is accessible by minibus. Along with 314 rooms and 82 suites, there are two freshwater pools, a 100-slip marina, aerobics classes, a disco, four bars, four restaurants, six lighted tennis courts, and miniature golf.

Accommodations: Deluxe terrace rooms are on second and third floors and have two queen-size beds, air-conditioning, and refrigerators. One-bedroom apartments have fully equipped kitchen, bedroom with king-size bed, and a sleeper sofa. Marina suites offer views of the boats going in and out.

Kids under age twelve stay free in parents' room. Daily rates, double occupancy: winter, $260 to $340; summer, $150 to $210. P.O. Box 581, Marcel Cove, St. Martin, FWI 97150; 800–543–4300, 590–87–33–33, or 590–87–78–80, fax 590–87–30–38.

GRANDE CASE BEACH CLUB

At the water's edge on a beautiful crescent of Grande Case Beach, this condominium complex offers plenty of water sports within easy reach. On solid ground, try your hand at *pétanque*, the French equivalent of bocce ball. Rates include continental breakfast. Grocery stores and restaurants are within walking distance. Car rentals, an exercise room, tennis, water sports, baby-sitting on request, and a small library are on site.

Accommodations: Choose from 75 airy studio, one-bedroom, and two-bedroom units, all with rattan furnishings, private patios, daily housekeeping service, kitchens, and air-conditioning. There are 40 studios and 33 one- and two-bedroom apartments.

Children under age twelve stay free in one-bedroom units. Daily single- or double-occupancy: mid-April to mid-October, studio $95 to $110, one-bedroom $110 to $130, two-bedroom $200 to $215. Mid-October to mid-April, studio $125 to $150, one-bedroom $160 to $175, two bedroom $275 to $300. P.O. Box 339, Grande Case, St. Martin 97150; 800–223–1588, 212–661–4540, or 590–87–51–87.

CONDO AND VILLA RENTALS

Several establishments handle villa rentals on both sides of the island.

WIMCO, P.O. Box 1461, Newport, RI; 401–849–8012, fax 401–847–6290.

Villas of Distinction, P.O. Box 55, Armonk, NY 10504; 800–289–0900, fax 914–273–3387.

WHAT TO SEE AND DO

Fun City is an entertainment center with limbo dancers, folkloric dancers, and steel drum players. Two shows take place daily, at 11:00 A.M. and 2:00 P.M. For information, call the Caribbean Entertainment Center in Philipsburg at 599–5–22261.

Live Eagle Spectacular, in Maho Bay on the road to Pointe Pirouette, has falcons, eagles, and other birds of prey. Shows daily at 10:30 A.M., 2:30 P.M., and 4:00 P.M.

Turtle Pier Bar on Simpson Bay has live sea turtles, a natural aquarium, fish, ducks, and geese, along with well-priced barbecue lunches and dinners. On Airport Road, St. Maarten.

Calm waters, shallow reefs, and visibility of up to 200 feet make for excellent **snorkeling and diving**. The best snorkeling on the Dutch side is below Fort Amsterdam off Little Bay Beach, the west end of Maho Bay, Pelican Key, and the rocks off Dawn Beach and Oyster Pond. On the French side the area around Orient Bay, Green Key, Ilet Pinel, and Flat Island has been classified as a nature reserve.

26

~~~~~~~~~~~~~~~~~~~~~~~~~~~~~~~~

ST. VINCENT AND
THE GRENADINES

THIRTY IDYLLIC ISLANDS AND cays make up St. Vincent and the Grenadines, a fully independent country within the British Commonwealth. Fertile St. Vincent, larger than all the Grenadines put together, handles the bulk of the tourist trade. Its green volcanic mountain slopes are covered with banana, breadfruit, lime, and nutmeg trees, and its valleys are lined with blooming flowers, coconut palms, and arrowroot leading to beautiful black or white sand beaches.

Bequia (pronounced Beck-way), just nine miles south of St. Vincent, is the second largest of the islands. Best known of the smaller islands is Mustique, for its chic homes-away-from-home of Princess Margaret, David Bowie and Iman, and Mick Jagger and Jerry Hall. All of the Grenadines have kind and welcoming people and splendid beaches.

This island chain is the place to be if you want a quiet vacation with few planned activities other than the ones you and your family create and enjoy for yourselves. The sailing crowd has long enjoyed the area's quiet bays, easy island anchorages, secluded sandy coves, and magnificent snorkeling and diving opportunities. Prices are lower here than at more glamorous island destinations. Tourism is gaining a prominent place in the economy, but bananas—or "green gold," as they're often called—supply St. Vincent with half of its foreign exchange earnings.

TOURIST INFORMATION

In the United States: 801 Second Avenue, Twenty-first Floor, New York, NY 10017; 800–729–1726 or 212–687–4981, fax 212–949–5946. Or, 6505 Cove Creek Place, Dallas, TX 75240; 800–235–3029 or 214–239–6451, fax 214–239–1002.
In Canada: 32 Park Road, Toronto, Ontario M4W 2N4; 416–924–5796, fax 416–924–5844.
On St. Vincent: on Bay Street, P.O. Box 834, Kingstown, St. Vincent, WI; 809–457–1502, fax 809–456–2610.

KNOW BEFORE YOU GO

Arrivals and Departures: U.S. and Canadian citizens need a passport, a birth certificate, or a voter registration card and a photo ID to visit, plus a return or onward ticket. Departure tax is $12.

Most visitors from the United States and Canada fly into Barbados and then fly LIAT (Leeward Islands Air Transport) or Mustique Airways into St. Vincent and the Grenadines. When leaving St. Vincent, you must pay a departure tax of about $12. Daily ferry service is available to Bequia; and three days a week, mail boats and freight-carrying schooners can take you to Canouan, Mayreau, and Union islands. Mustique, Canouan, and Union islands all have airstrips that allow small planes to land.
Money: The larger resorts accept U.S. currency, but the Eastern Caribbean dollar is used in most other places.
Language: English is the official language of St. Vincent and the Grenadines.
Staying Healthy: Kingstown General Hospital in St. Vincent has emergency care as well as general medical services; 809–456–1185.

ST. VINCENT

~~~~~~~~

WHERE TO STAY

YOUNG ISLAND

At this small, private island resort just 200 yards off the southern shore of St. Vincent, guests have 35 acres of fruit trees, flowers, ferns, turtle ponds, and beaches to explore. Hammocks hang under thatched roofs, and the island's swim-up bar is in the ocean instead of the pool; Coconut Bar is attached to a small dock and serves drinks in coconut shells, giving lingerers the nourishment they need for the short swim or walk back to shore. On Friday night guests can attend a cocktail party on a small rocky island behind Young Island. There's also a swimming pool, windsurfing, glass-bottom boat rides, and snorkeling gear to borrow. Ferries to the mainland are complimentary and run 24 hours on demand. **Accommodations:** All guests are housed in cottages with a refrigerator, king-size or twin beds, a ceiling fan, and a private patio. Four of the cottages have an alcove that can hold extra beds to accommodate families of three or four.

Room rates include breakfast and dinner, and the daily rate for children under age twelve sharing their parents' room is $40 per child (for meals). Rates depend on size of rooms and precise time of year. Daily rates, double occupancy: April 15 to December 18, $275 to $495; December 19 to April 14, $430 to $590. Discounts and other bonuses such as airport pickup and boat trips are offered for seven- and ten-night stays. P.O. Box 211, Young Island, St. Vincent, WI; 800–223–1108 or 809–458–4826, fax 809–457–4567.

GRAND VIEW BEACH HOTEL

This old cotton plantation great house on 8 acres of tropical gardens in southern St. Vincent has been turned into a gracious hotel run by the Sardine family. Its secluded beach has spectacular snorkeling, and the terrace next to the free-form swimming pool offers staggeringly beautiful views of Young Island and the Grenadines beyond. Bonuses include tennis and squash, aerobics classes, a small gym, and a water sports center.

Accommodations: All rooms have both air-conditioning and ceiling fans and can accommodate up to four people.

Doubles start at $210 per night and include complimentary breakfast daily. Each child between ages two and twelve sharing a room with parents pays $30 per day. Children under age two stay free. Daily rates, double occupancy: high season, $210 to $270; low season, $130 to $190. Meal plan, $25 per adult, $18 per child. P.O. Box 173, Villa Point, St. Vincent, WI; 800–223–6510 (in the United States), 800–424–5500 (in Canada) or 809–458–4811, fax 809–457–4174.

INDIAN BAY BEACH HOTEL AND APARTMENTS

Located right on Indian Bay Beach, this very reasonably priced 14-unit hotel/apartment combination has one- and two-bedroom units, some with equipped kitchenettes, and daily housekeeping service. Its beachfront restaurant serves Caribbean and international cuisine, and fresh seafood is a specialty. The hotel's own beach can keep you busy for hours. Water sports such as snorkeling, scuba, and sailing are nearby. This is a great headquarters for enjoying the beach, but you'll want to rent a car if you plan to participate in any water sports or explore the island.

Accommodations: Units have two twin or double beds. Some have kitchenettes, while others have mini-bars and refrigerators. All are air-conditioned, and some rooms also have fans.

Daily rates: one-bedroom unit $70, two-bedroom unit, $85. Roll-aways are available for $10. P.O. Box 538, Kingstown, St. Vincent, WI; 800–74-CHARMS or 809–458–4001, fax 809–457–4777.

WHAT TO SEE AND DO

Your hotel or the tourist office can help you arrange a boat trip to the **Falls of Baleine** near the northern tip of the island; and getting there is half the fun as you skim along the blue Caribbean Sea, glimpsing the lush green island scenery. Be prepared to hop off the boat into shallow water and wade to shore. The falls are a ten- to fifteen-minute hike from the shoreline. Bring water shoes or sneakers, since you'll be walking through the stream to get to the falls. Swim and splash in the pool at the foot of the falls.

In addition to being the oldest such gardens in the Western Hemisphere, **St. Vincent's Botanical Gardens**' claim to fame is a breadfruit tree grown from the original plant brought by Captain Bligh of the *H.M.S Bounty* in 1793. St. Vincent's endangered endemic parrot, *Amazona guildingii*, is represented at a small aviary here. In Kingstown, 809–457–1003. Open weekdays 7:00 A.M. to 4:00 P.M., Saturdays 7:00 to 11:00 A.M., and Sundays 7:00 A.M. to 6:00 P.M.

BEQUIA

WHERE TO STAY

FAIRMONT APARTMENTS

Comfortable apartments overlook Admiralty Bay on the island's west coast and are just a few minutes' walk from restaurants, shopping, and the ferry service to St. Vincent. Each apartment features a large porch, a kitchen, living and dining rooms, and housekeeping service.

Accommodations: Studio apartments, one- and two-bedroom apartments, and a two-bedroom house with its own swimming pool are available.

Weekly rates: December 1 to April 30, one-bedroom apartment $450, two-bedroom apartment $500, house $700; May 1 through November 30, one-bedroom apartment $300, two-bedroom apartment $350, house $575. Daily rate for one-bedroom units is $100 all year. Belmont, Bequia, St. Vincent, WI; 809–457–1121 or 809–458–4037 (after working hours), fax 809–456–2333.

THE FRANGIPANI

Once a family home, the Frangipani was converted into an inn two decades ago and is now owned by the prime minister of St. Vincent. Yachting enthusiasts gather here to stretch their sea legs while enjoying a meal and perhaps some evening entertainment. Thursday night steel band jump-ups at the beachfront bar are not to be missed, and folksingers and string bands perform throughout the week. The St. Vincent ferry stop is a several minute walk away.

Accommodations: The inn has five simple rooms with shared bathrooms and cold water only, but the garden units and two-bedroom dwellings are larger, have hot and cold running water, a small refrigerator, and are better suited for families.

Daily rates, double occupancy: inn rooms $45 and garden units $95. P.O. Box 1, Admiralty Bay, Bequia, St. Vincent, WI; 809–458–3255, fax 809–458–3824.

PLANTATION HOUSE HOTEL

Cottages and guest rooms overlook the beach or are tucked into palm-shaded gardens on 11-acre Plantation House. Two beachfront cabanas have three bedrooms each, and cottages nestled into the gardens have one or two bedrooms. Five air-conditioned double rooms are in the main house; other rooms are cooled by tradewind breezes. A small swimming pool, an Italian restaurant and verandah bar, a beach bar, tennis, scuba diving, and waterskiing are on-site.

Accommodations: Cottages and cabanas have ceiling fans and refrigerators. Deluxe accommodations in the main house have air-conditioning.

Cottage prices range from $190 to $290, depending on the type of accommodations and the time of year. The price includes a full English breakfast. P.O. Box 16, Admiralty Bay, Bequia, St. Vincent, WI; 800–223–9832 or 809–458–3425.

MUSTIQUE

WHERE TO STAY

More than 40 luxury villas, one hotel, and a small guest house are the sum total of posh Mustique's tourist accommodations. You'll need to reserve villas up to a year in advance through **House Rentals Department, Mustique Co.**, Ltd., P.O. Box 349, Mustique, St. Vincent, WI; 809–458–4621, fax 809–456–4565, or **WIMCO**, P.O. Box 1461, Newport, RI 02840; 800–932–3222 or 401–849–8012, fax 401–847–6290. Most rentals cost about $3,000 to $15,000 per week, depending on the season and the amenities, size, and service you require. Mick and David's houses are not for rent, but you can reserve Princess Margaret's pad for a week in the summer for about $3,600.

27

TRINIDAD AND
TOBAGO

MUSICAL TRINIDAD SPAWNED the steel drum band and calypso, both of which now flourish throughout the Caribbean and beyond. Just seven miles off the Venezuelan coast, Trinidad is a geographical extension of South America, as is Tobago, 20 miles further out. Residents of both melting pot islands trace their roots to every corner of the globe—Africa, India, China, and Great Britain.

The two sister islands, one bustling and commercial and the other quiet and shy by comparison, became independent from Britain in 1962 and have a fully democratic government. Originally sugar producers, the two-island nation now makes its living from oil and gas, petrochemical industries, manufacturing, and tourism. The national capital is Port of Spain in Trinidad.

Tobago has the world's oldest preserved rain forest, protected by law since 1776, and is home to 433 species of birds, and hundreds of types of butterflies. Enormous leatherback turtles nest on beaches in April and May on the northwestern coast from Great Courland Bay to Turtle Beach. Tobago may have served as the fictional island in Daniel Defoe's Robinson Crusoe. Many people visit Trinidad for the action during Carnival time or for one of the many other celebrations, and visit Tobago to enjoy the tranquility and spectacular beaches.

Trinidad's carnival is the biggest, liveliest street party in the Caribbean. Preparations begin early in the new year with Calypso "tents" (now concert spaces) scattered throughout the city hosting rehearsals and performances. Judges visit the tents, and select the best Calypso artists to compete in the semi-finals. Steel pan musicians rehearse their numbers in Port of Spain's pan yards; you can visit them and listen as long as you like. Mas camps (mas means masquerade) throughout the city allow visitors to come in and order a costume if they like what they see. Pick up your costume before carnival and dance through the streets with other revelers who look just like you. Costumes are artistic and technical wonders, made of balsa wood, gauze, carved foam, shimmering fabrics, sequins, and everything else you can think of. Tourist publications list names and addresses of calypso, steel band, and mas tents.

Celebrations occur throughout the two islands, but the best bash is in Port of Spain. Plan to arrive at least several days before the main parade and party, so you can participate in the events that lead up to Monday and Tuesday's extravaganzas. A children's carnival takes place on Saturday morning, when toddlers to teen-agers come out in costumes as elaborate and beautiful as their adult counterparts.

TOURIST INFORMATION

In the United States and Canada: Call the consumer hotline at 800–595–1TNT.
In Trinidad: Tourism and Industrial Development Co., 10-14 Philipps Street, Port of Spain, Trinidad, WI; 809–623–1932, fax 809–623–3848.

KNOW BEFORE YOU GO

Arriving and Departing: U.S. and Canadian citizens need a valid passport for visits of less than two months. Longer visits require a visa. There is a ferry service between Trinidad and Tobago six days a week. An airport departure tax of $TT75 (about $14 US) must be paid in local currency.
Money: The Trinidadian dollar (TT$) is the official currency.

Language: The official language of Trinidad and Tobago is English.

Staying Healthy: Trinidad and Tobago are only 11 degrees north of the equator, so slather on the sunscreen. June through December is the rainy season, when insect repellent is vital.

TRINIDAD

WHERE TO STAY

The **Bed and Breakfast Association** (809–637–9329) can arrange a stay in a Trinidadian home. Often visitors can arrange for babysitting with their host families.

Many hotels increase their prices during carnival time. The rates published here do not include carnival dates.

TRINIDAD HILTON

An Olympic-size pool cools down hot kids after they've explored Port of Spain, wandered through the zoo, or danced in the streets at Carnival. The hotel is above the city near Savannah Park and is especially well suited to business travelers, but families wanting to stay in town find it convenient, too. Rooms are spacious and although more than three people may not stay in one room, connecting doors are available. There's lawn tennis, Ping-Pong, and buffets with entertainment by the pool. Shopping districts are nearby.

Accommodations: Rooms have king-size, queen-size, or twin beds. All 394 rooms have balconies, a small sitting area, air-conditioning, TV, and radios.

The "Family Plan" allows kids to stay free in their parents' room. Daily rate, double occupancy: $149 to $200 depending on view and amenities; junior suite $275 to $395. P.O. Box 442, Lady Young Road, Port of Spain, Trinidad, WI; 800–445–8667 or 809–624–3211, fax 809–624–4485.

HOLIDAY INN

Situated near the port and within walking distance of the National Stadium in Port of Spain which hosts the pre-carnival Dimanche Gras, this Holiday Inn has a revolving rooftop restaurant offering glittering city views. Its large pool is an important commodity for reviving weary children; it also has paddle tennis, shuffleboard, and an exercise room. Live entertainment performs regularly, and baby-sitting can be arranged.

Accommodations: Standard rooms contain two double beds. Several three-room suites are available with a living room, a bedroom with king-size bed, and another bedroom with two queen beds; all rooms are air-conditioned.

Children ages nineteen and under stay free in their parents' room. Daily rates, double occupancy: standard room $95, roll-away $10, three-room suite $500. Wrightson Road, Port of Spain, Trinidad, WI; 800–465–4329 or 809–625–3361, fax 809–625–4166.

HOTEL NORMANDIE

Located a short walk from the Savannah and Hilton Hotel, this establishment has comfortable rooms with sleeping lofts suitable for families, as well as more traditional hotel accommodations. A small swimming pool is bordered by patios and tropical gardens; most rooms face the pool. La Fantasie Restaurant serves what they call "nouvelle Creole" cuisine, but its homemade ice cream is what your kids will savor. Room service is available until 11:00 P.M. The hotel is near a lively shopping area of crafts and clothing shops.

Accommodations: Standard rooms have one double or two twin beds; superior rooms have two double or queen-size beds. Loft bedrooms have a queen-size bed and double futon. All rooms are air-conditioned and have cable TV.

Kids under twelve stay free in their parents' room. Daily rates, double occupancy (except during Carnival, when rates increase): standard room $86, superior $104, loft bedrooms $116. 10 Nook Avenue, St. Ann's Village, Port of Spain, Trinidad, WI; phone and fax 809–624–1181.

KAPOK HOTEL

The zoo and botanical gardens of Savannah Park are very close to this attractive hotel. Families with one child can stay in a comfortable hotel room or studio with a kitchenette, while larger families should try the one-bedroom suite, also with a small kitchenette. Self-service Laundromat facilities, a pool flanked by caged monkeys and birds, and a good location makes this a popular choice for families. There are several restaurants and casual cafes, small shops, a car rental, and currency exchange on the premises. **Accommodations:** Standard rooms and studios can accommodate three people only; studios have small kitchenettes. Two roll-away beds can be added to a one-bedroom suite for a larger family. Connecting rooms are available, and all 71 rooms, including six suites and nine studios, are air-conditioned with ceiling fans, satellite TV, and data ports.

One child under twelve stays free in parents' room; two children under twelve, add $13 per night. Daily rates, double occupancy: standard rooms and studios $83; suites $140. 16–18 Cotton Hill, St. Clair, Port of Spain, Trinidad, WI; 800–344–1212 or 809–622–6441; fax 809–622–9677.

WHAT TO SEE AND DO

Queen's Park Savannah in Port of Spain is a sprawling public park with lily ponds, playing fields, enormous trees, and manicured lawns. On its western edge sits a group of mansions called **The Magnificent Seven.** Built in 1904 by wealthy plantation owners, each tried to outdo the other with their showy architecture and opulence. Just north of the Savannah are the **Emperor Valley Zoo** and the **Botanical Gardens.** The zoo features animals and birds of the Caribbean region in addition to animals from all over the world. If you don't get a chance to see the scarlet ibis in the Caroni Bird Sanctuary (see below), you can see it here or get a close-up look at a massive anaconda or python. Open daily 9:00 A.M. to 6:00 P.M. Small admission fee; 809–622–3530.

Caroni Bird Sanctuary, about a 30-minute drive from Port of Spain, is part large swamp and part lagoon with mangrove islands in the middle and waterways winding through it. Boats explore the swamp in the early morning and late afternoon, taking guests to see the thousands of brilliant scarlet ibis who leave at sunrise and arrive again at sunset to roost in the small islets in the middle of the sanctuary. Boats leave the roadside dock at 4:30 A.M. and 4:00 P.M., and reservations are essential (most hotels will make the arrangements for you). Keep a sharp eye out for other animals, too, such as the anteaters who can be spotted encircling a branch where they've coiled up to sleep. A good dose of insect repellent will help keep voracious mosquitoes at bay and a sweater will ward off any late evening chills. Tours of Caroni can be arranged through Winston Nanant (809–645–1305) or David Ramsahai (809–663–4767).

TOBAGO

WHERE TO STAY

GRAFTON BEACH RESORT

A beautiful powdery sand beach, good dining options, a pool with a swim-up bar, and luxury apartments attract guests from all over the globe. Golfers can play on a nearby course, bird watchers can visit adjacent Grafton Bird Sanctuary, and beachcombers can park themselves on a lounge chair and never move. There are also air-conditioned squash courts, tennis, a gym with a sauna, canoes, sailboats, and windsurfers included in the rates. Local steel and calypso bands and folkloric shows are staged nightly. A dive shop, games room, and shopping arcade are on the premises. **Accommodations:** All 114 rooms have air-conditioning, minibars, marble bathrooms, TVs, and balconies with ocean views. Standard rooms have two double beds; superior rooms are larger and closer to the sea. Two suites have a sitting room with a dining area and balcony and a bedroom with a private bath.

Daily rates, double occupancy: December 16 to April 5, standard room $225, superior $252, suite $600. April 6 to December 15, standard room $161, superior $225, suite $550. Children under five are free, ages five to twelve pay $20 per night. Black Rock, Tobago, WI; 800–223–6510 or 809–639–0191, fax 809–639–0030.

REX TURTLE BEACH

Lumbering leatherback sea turtles lay their eggs from March to August and tiny hatchlings scramble to the sea just a few steps from the guest rooms in this two- and three-story full-service resort hotel. Children under two receive free accommodations and meals, while two- to twelve-year-olds stay free in their parents room and receive a 50 percent discount on meals. Two restaurants, one casual and the other more elegant, offer international, local, and vegetarian cuisine. The full compliment of water sports and activities such as windsurfing, Sunfish sailing, snorkeling, water-skiing, beach volleyball, shuffleboard, and table tennis are on the premises. Evening entertainment keeps the fun rolling into the wee hours with steel band performances, live bands, and dancing to folk drums.

For Kids: The Children's Club operates weekdays from 9:00 A.M. to 4:00 P.M. with a short break at lunch time. Kids ages four to twelve are invited to participate in supervised games and activities within the hotel grounds. Baby-sitting services can be arranged.

Accommodations: Superior rooms have various bed configurations, and can house a maximum of two adults and two children. All 125 rooms have balconies or terraces with a view of the ocean and air-conditioning.

Daily rates, double occupancy: November 1 to mid-April, $160; mid-April to October 31, $120. Meal plans are available. P.O. Box 201, Cortland Bay, Scarborough, Tobago, WI; 809–639–2851, fax 809–639–1495.

PLANTATION BEACH VILLAS

Spacious fully equipped luxury villas are situated on a hillside sloping down to Stonehaven Beach facing the Caribbean Sea. Each of the six villas can sleep up to six people. The front desk has games and puzzles to borrow and can arrange rental cars, baby-sitting, and cooks. Daily maid service is part of the package, and a starter kit of food is in the kitchen when you arrive. There's a pool and the beach is just a few steps away from your villa.

Accommodations: Each villa has three double bedrooms (each with a full bath), a living room, verandah, and modern kitchen with a dishwasher and a microwave. All bedrooms have air-conditioning and ceiling fans. Washers and dryers are in each villa, and baby cribs and roll-aways are available.

Daily rates: December 16 to April 15, $400 to $465 (depending on number of people); April 16 to December 15, $270 to $335. Baby-sitting starts at $5 per hour. Stonehaven Bay Road, Black Rock, Tobago, WI; phone and fax, 809–639–0455.

WHAT TO SEE AND DO

Every Saturday, ornithologist and nature guide David Rooks takes visitors on a 2½ hour **tour of the rain forest** to explore its plant, animal, and bird life. He will also design customized tours to accommodate your family's interests and ages, such as a walk to a waterfall and swimming hole with bird-watching along the way. Rain forest tours are $45 per person over age eleven; children up to age six are free of charge, and ages seven to ten years are half price. Prices for other trips vary. Phone and fax, 809–639–4276.

28

U.S. VIRGIN ISLANDS

THE THREE SIBLINGS THAT make up the U.S. Virgin Islands have distinctly different personalities. St. Thomas is a bustling vacation hub with world-renowned duty-free shopping and a wide selection of resorts, hotels, restaurants, and activities. Quieter St. Croix, once a large producer of sugarcane, now has attractive resorts scattered along the shore and the ruins of long-abandoned sugar mills and rum distilleries scattered across rolling hills and valleys. Beautiful back-to-nature St. John, protected by its status as a National Park, has pristine beaches of legendary beauty and a cover of lush jungle in its interior.

Columbus came across these islands on his second trip to the New World in 1493; and the English, French, Spanish, Knights of Malta, and Danes ruled over them at different times. The United States purchased the islands in 1917 for $25 million in gold from Denmark to protect U.S. interests in the Panama Canal. Despite the American flag, driving is on the left side of the road.

TOURIST INFORMATION

In the United States Call 800-USVI-INFO or contact the office of tourism nearest you.

Atlanta: 225 Peachtree Street NE, Suite 760, Atlanta, GA 30303; 404–688–0906, fax 404–525–1102.

Chicago: 500 North Michigan Avenue, Suite 2030, Chicago, IL 60611; 312–670–8784, fax 312–670–8788.

Los Angeles: 3460 Wilshire Boulevard, Suite 412, Los Angeles, CA 90010; 213–739–0138, fax 213–739–2005.

Miami: 2655 Le Jeune Road, Suite 907, Coral Gables, FL 33134; 305–442–7200, fax 305–445–9044.

New York City: 1270 Avenue of the Americas, Suite 2108, New York, NY 10020; 212–332–2222, fax 212–332–2223.

Washington, DC: 900 17th Street NW, Suite 500, Washington, DC 20006; 202–293–3707, fax 202–785–2542.

In Canada: 33 Niagara Street, Toronto, Ontario M5V 1C2; 800–465–8784 or 416–362–8784, fax 416–362–9841.

On St. Thomas: P.O. Box 6400, Charlotte Amalie, USVI 00804; 809–774–8784, fax 809–774–4390.

On St. Croix: P.O. Box 4538, Christiansted, USVI 00822; 809–773–0495, fax 809–778–9259. Or Frederiksted Custom House Building, Strand Street, Frederiksted, USVI 00840; 809–772–0357.

On St. John: P.O. Box 200, Cruz Bay, USVI 00830; 809–776–6450.

KNOW BEFORE YOU GO

Arriving and Departing: St. Thomas has the larger airport, St. Croix has a smaller one, and St. John has none. A ferry runs regularly from Charlotte Amalie and Red Hook on St. Thomas to Cruz Bay on St. John. A new and long-awaited ferry service makes daily round trips between Christiansted on St. Croix and Charlotte Amalie on St. Thomas.

Language: English is the official language of the U.S. Virgin Islands.

Staying Healthy: Qualified doctors practice on all three islands. The St. Thomas Hospital (809–776–8311) in Charlotte Amalie is open 24 hours a day. St. Croix has two hospitals: St. Juan Luis Hospital in Christiansted (6 Diammond Bay; 809–778–6311), and Frederiksted Health Center in Frederiksted (809–772–1992). St. John has the Morris F. De Castro Clinic in Cruz Bay (809–776–6400).

Mosquitoes and no-see-ums come out in force in the evening; be sure to bring insect repellent and use it generously.

Local Food: Local dishes you're likely to come across include conch fritters; "fungi," a cornmeal and okra mixture usually served with fish; "kalaloo," a dish based on a spinachlike leafy green; fried plantains; and "bullfoot soup," made from what it says.

ST. THOMAS

St. Thomas is the number one cruise port in the West Indies and has been nicknamed the Manhattan of the Caribbean for its hustle, bustle, and traffic jams. The island was known more as a trading port than as a plantation island in the seventeenth century, and its main city, Charlotte Amalie (founded in 1672) was originally called Tappus by the Danes after the tap houses frequented by pirates and buccaneers.

Most of the hotels and condominiums are on the flatter and quieter eastern end, where beautiful white sand beaches can stretch for miles. Steep green mountains provide breathtaking viewpoints throughout the island; it's 13 miles long and less than 4 miles wide.

WHERE TO STAY

SAPPHIRE BEACH RESORT AND MARINA

Situated along a sparkling white ribbon of sand with calm protected aquamarine waters on the island's east coast, Sapphire offers family comfort in a casual setting with all the amenities of a luxury resort. Suites and villas have full kitchens and private balconies in several buildings along the beach and marina. If you'd rather not cook, the resort's Seagrape restaurant allows children to eat free with their parents. Seventy percent of Sapphire's business is families, so your children's exuberance will blend in rather than disturb.

Complimentary activities include free introductory scuba diving course for ages twelve and up, snorkel gear, Sunfish sailing, windsurfing, tennis, and an adventure playground. A professional volleyball player is on hand to play with anyone who wants to, and special weekend tournaments are held on the beach. Evening entertainment might include steel band music or a performance by Madame Voodoo, who walks on glass and leads the limbo contest (and always wins!). The quarter-acre swimming pool and wading pool overlook the ocean near the marina.

For Kids: Indoor and outdoor activities are well balanced at this high-quality daily drop-in program for three- to twelve-year-olds. Kids can drop in for an hour or two to swim and work on arts and crafts, or they can arrive at 8:00 A.M. and stay until the program ends at 6:00 P.M. Lunch and snacks are part of the complimentary program.

A special "Mini-Gems" program for babies and toddlers operates from a separate facility during Thanksgiving, Christmas, February holidays, and Easter break. Teen activities such as parasailing, scuba, and a sunset sail take place at special vacation times for an extra fee. A supervised evening program from 6:30 to 10:30 P.M. costs $10 per child and includes dinner.

Accommodations: Luxurious beachfront suites accommodate up to four people, and two-story villas with private balconies have room for families of up to six people. All have full kitchens, spacious living rooms, air-conditioning, ceiling fans, and daily housekeeping service, and adjoin other units through the deck. Laundry facilities are on the property. An inexpensive shopping shuttle takes guests to a nearby supermarket to stock up on necessities.

Children under age thirteen stay, eat, and play free when accompanied by parents. Daily rates: December 21 to April 14, suites (up to four people) $295 to $350, villas (up to six people) $355 to $405; April 15 to December 20, suites $190 to $245, villas $235 to $285. P.O. Box 8088, St. Thomas, USVI 00801; 800–524–2090 or 809–775–6100, fax 809–777–3555.

POINT PLEASANT

Bringing along the kids actually lowers the rate for Point Pleasant's comfortable villa-style suites. Adults receive a discount of $25 per child off their daily rate when traveling with up to two kids.

This, plus the complimentary use of a car for four hours each day and your own kitchen, make Point Pleasant a good value for families.

The resort spills down a steep tropical garden hillside that stops at the edge of the Caribbean Sea. Guests can follow a nature trail tucked under the trees or take a shuttle bus from their rooms to the beach and pool. The award-winning Agave Terrace restaurant allows children to eat free while their parents enjoy a gourmet meal and a spectacular view of St. John and the British Virgin Islands in the distance.

The resort's own beach is tiny, but Point Pleasant also owns half the beach chairs at Stouffer Resort's Pineapple Beach next door. Most guests take the short trail to the neighboring beach to enjoy its white sands and gentle waters. A water sports desk can arrange excursions, and guests have free use of windsurfing gear, snorkel equipment, and sailboats. The resort's two pools are small.

Accommodations: Villa suites come in four sizes, from studios to two-bedroom units. All have full kitchens and decks or patios with ocean views. Superior suites and deluxe suites both have one bedroom and can sleep up to four people. Two-bedroom suites can accommodate six.

Kids up to age 21 stay free with their parents, who receive a daily $25 room discount and $25 food coupon for up to two kids. Daily rates, double occupancy: mid-December to March 31, one-bedroom suites $295 to $380, two-bedroom suites $545; April, one-bedroom suites $265 to $310, two-bedroom suites $460; rest of year, one-bedroom suites $215 to $280, two-bedroom suites $375. Four hours' free car rental available daily. Estate Smith Bay, St. Thomas, USVI 00802; 800–524–2300 or 809–775–7200, fax 809–776–5694.

STOUFFER GRAND BEACH RESORT

Tucked unobtrusively among 34 acres of tropical flowers, ferns, and trees, Stouffer's has been carefully landscaped so you don't see a lot of hotel. It's a full-service 297-room resort with several restaurants, poolside grill and bar, water sports center on the beach, and car rental. An enormous free-form pool with a wading area is almost as popular as the 1,000-foot-long white sand beach.

A complete water sports center and dive shop rents sailboats, windsurfing equipment, and kayaks and arranges sailing trips, scuba, fishing expeditions, and para-sailing right off the dock. Six tennis courts are available for day or night play.

For Kids: Stouffer's Kids Club is a daily year-round program for ages four to twelve. Activities begin in the Kid's Club Room and move to the beach, pool, and grounds throughout the session. Wednesday has the only full-day program; other days have morning, afternoon, or evening sessions. You must sign up 24 hours in advance, and there are no drop-ins. This licensed day-care program offers iguana hunts, carnival games, nature walks, a trip to Coral World, movies, and more.

Accommodations: Standard rooms have two queen-size beds, and superior and deluxe rooms offer more space. Two-story townhouses and one- and two-bedroom suites are popular with families.

The Family Value Package, which runs from April through mid-December, includes six days and five nights. Kids under age eighteen stay free when sharing a room with their parents. Half-price discounts are available on a second room for children traveling with their parents. P.O. Box 8267, Smith Bay Road, St. Thomas, USVI 00801; 800–233–4935 or 809–775–1510, fax 809–775–2185.

SUGAR BAY PLANTATION RESORT

Children under age nineteen stay free in their parents' room in this enormous white edifice that dominates 31 acres on the island's east end. Most of the action takes place off one side of the building, where the swimming pool, bird lagoon, and beach sit. The sprawling pool complex is a magnet for kids, who never seem to tire of its waterfalls, volleyball net, and hidden corners. Much of this hotel's business is from conventions, but it's a good value if your family is small enough to stay in one room. Kids age twelve and under eat free from the children's menu during summer months in the elegant plantation-style dining room. The water sports center can arrange windsurfing and kayak rentals, and the resort has tennis courts and a fitness center. Complimentary movies are offered four times a week, with two selections suitable for children.

For Kids: Headquartered in a converted hotel room, the children's program operates year-round from 9:15 A.M. to 4:00 P.M. ($35 per child) and 6:00 to 10:00 P.M. ($20 per child, includes dinner), as long as you reserve in advance. In the morning kids enjoy games, shell crafts, palm weaving, iguana hunts, story hour, and videos. Afternoons are more active with tae kwon do, swimming lessons, and volleyball. The program accommodates each child's interests and abilities.

Accommodations: Rooms are spacious and have one king-size or two queen-size beds. Price differences are based solely on view. All rooms have a small refrigerator and storage cupboards, handy for late-night snacks.

Daily rates, double occupancy: December 22 to April 16, $289 to $400, April 17 to December 21, $193 to $310. Be sure to ask about the family packages offered throughout the off-season. Estate Smith Bay, St. Thomas, USVI 00802; 800-HOLIDAY or 809–777–7100, fax 809–772–7200.

BOLONGO RESORTS

Three different properties make up this family-owned and -operated business: Bolongo Club Everything, Limetree, and Elyssian. All guests can use the facilities at the other resorts, and complimentary shuttles run back and forth throughout the day and evening. Each resort is known for something different.

Upscale Elyssian has elegant rooms and suites that can accommodate large families. Bolongo has a catamaran dock and simple apartmentlike villas with one, two, or three bedrooms. Limetree has honeymooners, night life, and the most active water sports beach due to its calm harbor.

All properties have beautiful sandy beaches with snorkel gear, kayaks, windsurfing equipment swimming pools, restaurants, nightclubs, and yacht trips.

For Kids: Bolongo's carousel-like playroom is the headquarters for the children's program, "Kids Korner," for ages three to twelve. It operates on a complimentary drop-in basis on Monday, Wednesday, and Friday, but advance arrangements can often be made for the other days. Kids help determine the program, which might include beach bingo, cartoon hour, sand-castle building, and hermit crab races. Older kids can participate in volleyball, basketball, tennis lessons, snorkeling, sailing, and water aerobics. A new video game center has the latest in arcade machines.

Accommodations: Elyssian has a flexible room configuration, allowing families to have two bedrooms and a third bedroom loft flanking the living/dining and kitchen areas. It's a new property, nicely furnished and well maintained.

Bolongo has individually owned villa/apartments, many of which are older and beginning to show a bit of wear, but remain quite serviceable. Standard hotel rooms are also available; Limetree can accommodate families in simple rooms with a queen-size bed and folding couch. Elyssian: Rates include continental breakfast. Children under twelve, $15 per day. December 23 to April 15, rooms $225 to $275, studio suites $235 to $285, one-bedroom suites $375 to $425, two-bedroom suites $515 to $690. April 16 to December 22, rooms $175 to $205, studio suites $180 to $210, one-bedroom suites $245 to $275, two-bedroom suites $365 to $475. Limetree and Bolongo: Daily rates are substantially reduced the longer you stay.

Children under twelve stay free and eat free with parents in the villas. All nonmotorized water sports are included. Bolongo Bay Beach Resort, 7150 Estate Bolongo, St. Thomas, USVI 00802; 800–524–4746 or 809–775–1800.

WHAT TO SEE AND DO

Charlotte Amalie has a dizzying number of shops, most catering to the cruise ship trade. Its duty-free shops sell jewelry, watches, designer clothes, and many other things younger kids couldn't care less about. If you take them to just one store, let it be **Dockside Bookshop** in the Havensight Mall (809–776–4937), right next to the cruise ship dock. It has an excellent children's books section, with two shelves devoted to picture and story books about the Caribbean.

Kids too young to strap on a dive tank can descend through translucent Caribbean waters to a depth of 150 feet on an **Atlantis Submarine** ride. The battery-powered nonpolluting sub cruises past sponge gardens, flashy tropical fish, and sunken ships on its hour-long underwater journey. A boat picks up passengers at a dock and takes them out to an area rich with coral gardens, where the sub is anchored. After everyone boards the submarine, it begins its journey down. Cards identifying different marine plants and animals are placed by every window. Adults, $65 per person; kids four (the minimum age permitted) to twelve, $25; teens thirteen to eighteen, $35. Building IV, Havensight Mall; 800–253–0493 or 809–776–5650.

Get a bird's-eye view of the town and harbor of Charlotte Amalie on **Paradise Point Tramway.** Similar to a gondola at a ski lift, the 3½-minute tram ride takes you to the top of 697-foot Paradise peak, where you can stop at the restaurant for a bite to eat and a breathtaking view. Leaves from the Havensight mall area.

Blackbeard's Castle sits at the top of the city's **99 steps**, a staircase street built in the 1700s. Climb the steps and stop for lunch. The kids can swim in the pool after they eat, while Mom and Dad sip a cool drink and enjoy the panoramic vista of the town and harbor. The castle tower was built in 1679 and was thought to have been used by the notorious pirate Edward Teach. Today it is a lovely guest house and restaurant.

Drake's Seat, above Charlotte Amalie, is the mountain lookout from which Sir Francis Drake kept an eye on his fleet, and watched for enemy ships. Come here in late afternoon or at dusk to avoid the crowds.

Go nose to nose with fish, seahorses, giant rays, and sea turtles at **Coral World**, a marine complex that features an underwater observatory 20 feet below sea level. Windows look out at the fish, rays, turtles, and other sea creatures going about their daily business. Saltwater tanks throughout the rest of the property contain excellent examples of the variety of sea life you'll view snorkeling around the islands. It's a good place to learn to identify the native coral and fish before heading out in fins and mask to see it on your own. In addition to the marine exhibits, there is a funny bird show, touch pond, tropical nature trail, sea turtle pool, and exotic bird habitat. Open daily, 9:00 A.M. to 6:00 P.M.

Adults, $16; children ages three to twelve, $10. 6450 Coki Point, St. Thomas, USVI; 809–775–1555, fax 809–775–9510.

After visiting Coral World, use one of the lockers there to store your belongings and head next door to beautiful **Coki Beach**, known for its superior snorkeling and transparent waters. Showers are available.

Magen's Bay on the northeast coast is one of the most beautiful long strands of beach in the Caribbean. A popular snorkeling spot, it has lifeguards, equipment rental, changing rooms, restaurants, and bars.

ST. CROIX

Once one of the most productive sugar producers of the West Indies, St. Croix at one time had more than 150 sugar plantations in operation. The crumbling stone remnants of the sugar mills can still be seen throughout the island. Sea turtles nest on many of the island's beaches, and areas have been protected to safeguard their eggs.

St. Croix's two quaint towns located at opposite ends of the island have a distinctly Danish flavor. Historic Christiansted has been the commercial center of the island for hundreds of years. Its eighteenth-century fort, built to protect the harbor, has been repeatedly damaged by hurricanes. In 1989, Hurricane Hugo's 200-mile-an-hour winds actually lifted boats out of the water and threw them against the fort's rock walls. At the other end of the island, Frederiksted's Fort Frederik was the site where the slaves from the Danish West Indies were freed in 1848. Buck Island, offshore, is a national monument with an underwater trail clearly marked for snorkelers and scuba divers.

WHERE TO STAY

THE BUCCANEER

This gracious plantation-style luxury resort has old world charm and new world amenities and service. Set on 240 acres of rolling hills edged with broad palm-shaded beaches, the Buccaneer offers guests an 18-hole golf course, eight tournament tennis courts, a health spa, and all kinds of water sports. The original walls, built in 1733, were six to eight feet thick to withstand hurricanes; you can still see some of the exposed bricks made of crushed seashells and molasses.

There are three palm-shaded beaches, two pools, and three restaurants. In addition to handling all kinds of snorkel and small boat rentals, the water sports desk can arrange scuba diving and boat trips, most of which depart from and return to the Buccaneer's private dock. A two-mile jogging and nature trail, two pools, spacious grounds, and changing daily activities keep your vacation action-packed.

Sea turtles nest on the Buccaneer's beaches, and families can help patrol the beaches each morning when the turtles are laying their eggs. The Buccaneer was recently recognized for its contributions to sea turtle research, and the students they sponsor give slides shows and lectures on sea turtle preservation throughout the summer and fall.

For Kids: The game room has a large Ping-Pong table, and kids can check out games and baseball bats and balls at the front desk any time of year. The complimentary children's program operates from April 1 to September 15 and over Christmas and Easter holidays. Children ages five to twelve are entertained from 10:00 A.M. until 2:00 P.M. daily with activities including local crafts such as making calabash maracas from the gourds of calabash trees, beach time, hair braiding and beading, games, and swimming. Younger children may participate if they are accompanied by their parents. A published schedule makes it easy for kids to drop into an activity they like, or stay for the entire day. The children's menu has pizza, hamburgers, hot dogs, and fresh fruit salad and vegetable choices.

Accommodations: Six different types of accommodations are available, all with air-conditioning, small refrigerators, private balconies, and terraces. Small families can fit into a standard, superior, or ocean view room, with two queen-size beds (or one king) and views of golf course or ocean. Deluxe ocean view suites and cottage suites have two rooms, one with a king-size bed and the other with two twin daybeds. A lavish menu-ordered breakfast is included in the room rate.

Be sure to inquire about the seven-day family packages that offer a comfortable two-room suite and full breakfast. The Eco-Package features nature walks and opportunities to view the Sea Turtle Research Project.

Daily rates: winter, single rooms $195 to $350 (depending on size, location, and view), two-room suites $305 to $400, three-room suites $500; summer, single rooms $160 to $240, two-bedroom suites $215 to $315, three-bedroom suites $325. P.O. Box 218, Christiansted, St. Croix, USVI 00821–0218; 800–223–1108 or 809–773–2100, fax 809–773–0010.

CHENAY BAY BEACH RESORT

These family-oriented bungalows have fully equipped kitchenettes and private patios. Guests can use the resort's picnic area and barbecue, and can ask the staff to arrange rental cars, boat trips, and just about anything else. Just a ten-minute drive from Christiansted, Chenay's 30 acres of property make for a very private and secluded vacation. The large wide beach has very shallow water and is a particularly safe swimming spot for toddlers and young swimmers. Older kids may want to take lessons from the Lisa Neuburger Windsurfing School on the property. Guests can take a shuttle into Christiansted, or a grocery shuttle. Other amenities include a swimming pool, two tennis courts, complimentary snorkeling equipment, ocean kayaks, and floating mats. The beach bar and restaurants serve breakfast, lunch, and dinner. **Accommodations:** Fifty one-bedroom cottages are outfitted as efficiency apartments with ocean or garden views, and all have air-conditioning.

Kids under age eighteen stay free in parents' room; third person in room over age eighteen pays $25 per night. Daily rates: winter, $170 to $220 (depending on view and proximity to ocean); summer, $135 to $175. P.O. Box 24600, Christiansted, St. Croix, USVI 00820; 800–548–4457 or 809–773–2918, fax 809–773–2918.

WHAT TO SEE AND DO

Building codes were used in **Christiansted** as early as 1747 to spare the town from fire. Consequently, the town looks much as it did in its heyday as a port in the eighteenth and nineteenth centuries. Many of the original buildings, made of thick coral brick or ballast bricks from sailing ships, still stand. **Old Scalehouse** was built in 1856 to house the huge scale used to weigh merchandise coming into the harbor. Bright yellow **Fort Christiansvaern** (its color is typical of those used by the Danes) dates back to 1749. You can tour its dungeons and scramble about on its ramparts and old cannons. Open daily, 8:00 A.M. to 5:00 P.M.; 809–773–1460.

Christian "Shan" Hendricks Market, built in 1735 as a slave market, now sells market goods and produce. Company street. Open Wednesdays and Saturdays, 8:00 A.M. to 5:00 P.M.

Buck Island Reef National Monument is an 850-acre island and reef system with waters perfect for exploring marine life. At a depth of 12 feet, with visibility of over 100 feet, visitors can snorkel the spectacular marked underwater trail and experience a virtual rainbow of fish, sponges, and coral in a marine garden. The underwater snorkeling trail takes less than an hour, and there are many other areas to explore as well. If you don't want to get wet, you can inspect the reef from a glass-bottom boat. On Buck Island, 2 miles off St. Croix's north shore, visitors will find powdery sand beaches, hiking trails, and an observation tower. We saw the remains of turtle eggs left behind by tiny hatchlings that had scrambled to the safety of the sea the night before. Ninety species of fish and several species of coral inhabit these waters. Mile Mark Charters has several trips a day and a good supply of snorkeling equipment in all sizes; 809–773–2628.

Estate Whim Plantation Museum is a restored sugarcane plantation that includes a windmill and a cookhouse, and offers a look at life on a sugarcane plantation in the 1800s. Look closely at its building materials of native rock and coral with mortar made of seashells and sugar molasses. Open Tuesday through Saturday, 10:00 A.M. to 4:00 P.M. P.O. Box 2855, Frederiksted, St. Croix, USVI; 809–772–0598.

Christopher Columbus and his crew came ashore looking for

fresh water at **Salt River** and tangled with the local Carib Indian population. His landing spot has been commemorated with a marker, and the area has been designated a National Park. Its significance goes beyond Columbus, however, as Indian burial grounds and artifacts from three different native cultures have been discovered here. You'll also find the island's largest mangrove forests, 27 species of threatened or endangered plants and animals, and a huge submarine canyon with superb scuba diving. The **St. Croix Environmental Association** (6 Company Street, Christiansted, St. Croix, USVI 00822; 809–773–1989) offers guided hikes of the area for adults and children over the age of six.

Sandy Point National Wildlife Refuge, at the southwestern end of the island, offers protection to the endangered leatherback turtle. The massive sea reptiles nest here from March through June, while environmentalists work year-round to track the female turtles, save nests, and conduct research to help regenerate the population of leatherbacks.

Hundreds of species pass through the tanks of **St. Croix Aquarium** each year. Owner Lonnie Kaczmarsky's aquarium recycles the sea life that it has on display, setting specimens free and catching fresh examples. Visit before scuba diving or snorkeling to learn about the sea life of the area, or catch a lecture on the effect snorkelers and divers can have on the environment. Open Wednesday through Sunday, 11:00 A.M. to 4:00 P.M. Located on the Frederiksted waterfront, 3A Strand Street; 809–772–1345.

Take a **horseback ride** through rain forests, past hidden Danish ruins, along the beach, and across hilltops with panoramic vistas of the Caribbean Sea at Paul and Jill's Equestrian Stables. Make reservations a day in advance. Reining, trotting, and cantering lessons are included for beginners. No children under age eight. Sprat Hall, Route 58; 809–772–2880/2627.

ST. JOHN

St. John is guaranteed to remain Caribbean postcard-perfect. Its spectacular fine white sand beaches bordered by brilliant turquoise waters and emerald green hillsides thick with flowers are protected from any kind of development by its status as a U.S. National Park. Laurence Rockefeller donated most of the island to the National Park Service in 1956. You'll find two world-class full-service resorts, villas tucked into tropical hillsides, and two unusual campgrounds. The rest of the island is full of unspoiled beaches, hiking trails through the woods, and a couple of small towns. Just a 20-minute ferry ride from St. Thomas, St. John is a world away in slow-paced casual living. Many families rent a villa (and a car) to explore the unspoiled beauty of the island. Cruz Bay is the biggest city, although compared to Charlotte Amalie it's a small town.

WHERE TO STAY

HYATT REGENCY

A quarter-acre pool complex with islands and a waterfall is the centerpiece of this glamorous 34-acre resort. If you can drag the kids out of the pool, a fine white sand beach is just steps away. The relaxed elegance for parents and guaranteed fun for kids make this Hyatt an unbeatable destination for all family members. There are all kinds of water sports, a daily children's program, and six lighted tennis courts. Sailing, scuba diving, and deep-sea fishing excursions can be arranged.

For Kids: "Camp Hyatt" operates daily year-round with both full-day and evening sessions. Daytime activities from 9:00 A.M. to 4:00 P.M. feature swimming and snorkeling lessons, beach games, photography, cooking, and sandcastle building and cost $35 per child, which includes lunch. Evening sessions offer dinner, movies, and quiet games from 6:00 to 10:00 P.M. for $25 per child.

Accommodations: Hotel rooms have one king-size or two queen-size beds; one-bedroom suites and two-bedroom townhouses have a pull-out sofa bed in the living room. All rooms have air-conditioning and a refrigerator.

Hyatt's room rates start at $315 per night, double occupancy. Children under age twelve stay free in their parents' room. Hyatt's "Family Program" gives families who pay the full rate for one room a second room for the children at half-price. In addition discounts are offered throughout the year, especially for off-season visits and stays of longer than four or five nights. P.O. Box 8310, Great Cruz Bay, St. John, USVI 00831; 800–233–1234, 800–693–8000, or 809–776–7171, fax 809–779–4985.

CANEEL BAY RESORT

Follow the sun from beach to beach—seven in all—as it warms posh Caneel Bay's 170-acre private peninsula that is completely surrounded by national parkland. Laurence Rockefeller purchased the land when it was a sugarcane plantation in 1952, and began turning the junglelike environs into a discreet and elegant tropical vacation wonderland where guest cottages are concealed among jacarandas, tropical orchids, palm trees, and bougainvillea. Its service and delicious restaurants are legendary, and jackets are requested for men after 6:00 P.M. during the winter.

Children's games and videos can be checked out, and lessons in sailing, scuba, and tennis can be arranged. The full complement of water sports and day trips, eleven all-weather tennis courts, swimming pool, and weekly undersea slide shows are available. Nature trails spread out into the primitive natural beauty of the Virgin Islands National Park.

For Kids: Caneel Bay was adding a children's program at press time.

Accommodations: All rooms and cottages have views of one or more of the seven beaches and gardens. Up to three people can stay in a room, and rates are determined by room size and location. There are no telephones or TVs.

One child up to age sixteen can stay free in parents' room. A second bedroom for children accompanying their parents is half-price from May 1 to September 30. Daily rates, double occupancy: spring and fall, $275 to $525; summer, $225 to $450; winter, $335 to $695. P.O. Box 720, Cruz Bay, St. John, 00831–0720; 800–928–8889 or 809–776–6111, fax 809–693–8280.

CINNAMON BAY CAMPGROUND

Situated on the island's northern coast, on its longest stretch of white sand beach, Cinnamon Bay has cottages, completely outfitted tents, and bare campsites for those like to pack and carry their own gear. The campground has many of the extras that you'd find at a full-service resort, such as a complete water sports center, a snack bar, a restaurant (with good food and reasonable prices), and superb snorkeling. A roped-off swimming area extends to a tiny island a few hundred yards offshore so that snorkelers can avoid any interference from boats. Huge hermit crabs scale the palm trees and scuttle across paths, providing endless entertainment for children.

The water sports center has windsurfing equipment, sea kayaks, sailboats, and snorkeling gear for rent. An attractively priced boat tour allows you to tailor a day trip to your interests. Park rangers lead daily tours of the Virgin Islands National Park, and guests have access to public phones, safe deposit boxes and lockers, a general store, and a gift shop. The island's only snuba center operates from here for adults and children ages eight and up.

Accommodations: The 15-by-15-foot screened cottages have four twin beds, electric lights, and an outdoor terrace. Two extra cots can be added for a family of six, and linens are changed twice weekly. All units have a ceiling fan, picnic table, charcoal grill, propane gas stove, ice chest, water container, and cooking and eating utensils. The 10-by-14-foot canvas tents are on a solid floor and have cots, picnic tables, charcoal grills, propane gas stove, ice chest, water container, gas lantern, and cooking and eating utensils. Bare sites have a picnic table and charcoal grill. All are near central bathhouses. Taxi buses run frequently from Cinnamon Bay to other parts of the island.

Daily rates, double occupancy: December 15 through April 30, cottages $90 to $98, tents $70; rest of year, cottages $60 to $65, tents $46. Extra person, $12 per day. Bare sites $15 per day year-round, $5 per extra person. Children under age three free of charge. P.O. Box 720, Cruz Bay, St. John, USVI 00831–0720; 800–539–9998 or 809–776–6330.

MAHO BAY CAMPGROUND

Simple screened tent cabins are tucked onto a hillside high above the beach and connected with Swiss Family Robinson–style wooden walkways. There are 105 tent cottage sites on 14 acres;

some offer spectacular Caribbean views, while others are hidden in the trees. A restaurant serves breakfast and dinner and has views of the sparkling aquamarine bay below. You won't need a car if your kids are good hikers, because nearby beaches offer wonderful snorkeling areas. A shuttle stops here several times a day and goes into town. The campground is not recommended for children under age four.

The activities desk will help you plan sailing, scuba diving, snorkeling, windsurfing, island boat tours, Sunfish sailing, rafting, and sea kayaking at a reasonable cost. Snorkeling equipment, beach chairs, and rubber rafts can be rented. Weekly slide shows describe the local flora and fauna.

Accommodations: Each tent cottage in Maho has an ice chest and pantry shelves and can comfortably sleep four to five people. Their translucent fabric screen and wood construction breathes with the trade winds. All housekeeping equipment is supplied (sheets, towels, pots, pans, dishes, and so on), and every unit has a propane stove, an ice cooler, and an electric fan. The store sells blocks of ice, basic groceries, and sundries. Communal bathhouses have hot and cold water and flush toilets. No laundry facilities are available.

Daily rates, double occupancy: May 1 through December 14, $65; December 15 through April 30 (seven-night minimum), $95. In summer, children under age sixteen are $10 each per night; over age sixteen, $12 per night. In winter, extra person is $15 per night.

MAHO BAYS' GREEN ACCOMMODATIONS

Ecology-minded travelers can stay in the more upscale "green" properties that offer the comforts of a traditional resort but are powered by the ubiquitous St. John sunshine. The dwellings are constructed of recycled materials: lumber made from discarded plastics, recycled clay tile floors, recycled steel nails. **Harmony** is located above the tent cabins of Maho Bay, and **Estate Concordia** is 25 minutes away, near the southeastern tip of St. John, on Salt Pond Bay where the island's best snorkeling, shelling, and hiking are found.

Harmony has two sizes of studios that sleep three to four people, all with kitchens, full baths, and decks. Estate Concordia units sleep three to five people and offer full kitchens and more luxurious furnishings.

Harmony: Daily rates, double occupancy: May 1 to December 14, $95 to $135; high season, $160 to $180. Add $25 per night per extra person, regardless of age.

Concordia: Rates, double occupancy: $190 per night, $1330 per week (minimum one week stay). Extra person pays $25 per night

VILLAS AND CONDOS

Renting your own home by the week or month is one of the most popular ways to vacation on St. John. You can rent first-class luxury homes with private pools and cooks or simple cottages with only the basics; but all are just minutes from a magnificent white sand beach. The following business offer all types of villas:

Catered To, P.O. Box 704, Cruz Bay, St. John, USVI 00831; 800–462–6641 or 809–776–6641, fax 809–693–8191.

Private Homes for Private Vacations, phone or fax 809–776–6876.

St. John Villa and Condo Rentals, 800–338–0987.

WHAT TO SEE AND DO

Virgin Islands National Park has well-mapped nature trails criss-crossing through it and some of the most beautiful unspoiled beaches in the world. The **Visitor Center** in Cruz Bay (809–776–6201) offers all kinds of nature talks and guided tours such as snorkel trips, bird walks, guided hikes to see petroglyphs and an old sugar mill, and seashore walks. Rangers set up evening programs at Maho Bay Campground, Cinnamon Bay Campground, and Caneel Bay Resort.

The perfect first snorkeling experience for kids is the self-guided 225-yard underwater trail at **Trunk Bay**. Large underwater signs clearly identify species of coral and other items of interest. There are changing rooms, equipment rentals, snack bar, showers, and a lifeguard. More serious diving is done about 2 miles out. Check the cruise ship listings and pick a day when the fewest ships are docking, as many passengers come here to snorkel. **Annaberg Plantation**, a ruined plantation great house, has cultural demonstrations such as basket weaving and bread making.

INDEX

〜〜〜〜〜